DISCARD

HOMO SAPIENS
from man to demigod

HOMO SAPIENS
from man to demigod

BERNHARD RENSCH
translated by C. A. M. Sym

Columbia University Press

NEW YORK   1972

First published as
Homo Sapiens: Vom Tier zum Halbgott
by Vandenhoeck & Ruprecht, Göttingen.
This English translation published in 1972
by Columbia University Press, New York,
and by Methuen & Co Ltd., London
© *1972 Methuen & Co Ltd.*
Printed in Great Britain

Library of Congress Cataloging in Publication Data
Rensch, Bernhard, 1900–
Homo Sapiens.
Translation of Homo Sapiens: Vom Tier zum Halbgott.
Bibliography: p. 203
1. Human evolution. 2. Man. 3. Civilization–
History. I. Title.
GN281.R413   573.2   72-80482
ISBN 0-231-03683-3

To Sir Julian Huxley
to whom in the problems of man's unique
phylogenetic position, we owe so great a debt

Contents

Contents

Preface

Man's unique place among living organisms is mainly determined by his particular physical development. It seems miraculous that one of the innumerable branches of the phylogenetic tree should have produced a species which differs absolutely from all other creatures by his mental abilities, his culture and his control over all other living beings. We are beginning to comprehend this development which has also determined our social and ethical customs and our philosophical problems.

The present book, which is based on the author's publications in this field over the last thirteen years, attempts to survey in an intelligible manner the multifarious problems involved. Beginning with the palaeontological discoveries on which ideas for human ancestry are based the author tries to discuss our mental evolution and those biological aspects of our cultural development which are partly governed by the same laws as our bodily evolution. He also ventures a glimpse at our possible future and its attendant dangers. The philosophical questions involved are only briefly touched upon.

My grateful thanks are due to Miss Sym for her sympathetic understanding of my German text.

Munster (Westphalia)
April 1972
Bernhard Rensch

CHAPTER ONE

The problem of man

What are we, we humans? How did we come to be on this planet? Where is our history leading us? Man has been asking these questions ever since he has become aware of himself, created a culture and grown up within a framework of stable tradition. The answers have varied enormously at different epochs and with different peoples. Those with an animistic faith see man as similar in kind to the animals, even as directly derived from animals species. To Hindus and Buddhists he is an incarnation of the eternal principle of life, which journeys through various stages (perhaps including animal ones) until at last it merges in the brahman, the universal soul, or the Nirvana. Jews and Christians believe man to have been created by the finger of God and formed in his image. Today, those with a scientific training recognize that he is descended from animal ancestors and that his unique cerebral development has made him the first, and only, creature with creative power and a sense of values. Most Christian theologians have recently accepted this view in a more liberal interpretation of the Book of Genesis.

But how was it that *Homo sapiens* emerged from among the millions of other species? How did he achieve his unique position among the higher animals, which he resembles so much in physique? What direction will his future evolution take? What may be regarded as the 'meaning' of his existence? These are questions for which no real basis of discussion existed before the present century; and today some of them are still without a definite answer.

Our own age is one that particularly calls for reflection on these elementary problems of existence. Undoubtedly man's cultural development has today reached an important turning-point.

I

Homo sapiens

Within the last decades he has immeasurably expanded and deepened his knowledge of the structure of the universe, of matter, molecules, atoms, elementary particles and radiation, as well as his knowledge about the nature of life and the development of mental processes. All this has formed the basis for expanding technical skills, which have already made drastic alterations in our way of life, and will continue to do so. Atomic energy is being harnessed and is beginning to affect our lives profoundly; our electronic computers can solve technical and theoretical problems of a complexity greater than anything tackled by mathematicians before. Space research has opened up entirely new prospects. The separate achievements of leading nations are fusing into a universal culture; and this culture is expanding at an immense pace, now that all sections of their populations are able to rise to higher social levels – and especially as the backward countries are making spectacular strides towards a more advanced civilization.

We can now offer at least a partial answer to these questions of man's origin, biological uniqueness and possible future development; and they involve such important considerations and open up possibilities of such consequence that it is the duty of every cultured individual to have some measure of aquaintance with them. The essentials of man's phylogeny are vouched for by a wealth of material, and the literature on the subject is immense. So too is the number of publications on the problem of man's separate existence – though these vary enormously according to whether their authors are biologists, historians, philosophers or theologians. An abundance of Utopian novels, stories and plays, deal with future possibilities, while specific problems, mostly biological, sociological and economic, now begin to receive rather more scientific treatment.

The present work makes no attempt to enumerate and assess this huge mass of writings. Its aim is rather to see the whole complex of questions from a coherent point of view, with special consideration of findings which may help to throw some new light. Observations will be based as far as possible on factual material drawn especially from the fields of palaeontology, comparative psychology and cultural history.

The first task will be to determine how and why any progressive phylogenetic development of living organisms took place on this planet, and what in particular led to the emergence of man in his present form. We shall consider how the human mind emerged from earlier animal stages. With the rise and progress of cultures we shall have to sketch the outlines of man's strange and unique position, touching on certain imperfections and various dangers in the path of his future evolution. We shall see that although it springs from an entirely different root the rise of man's culture has been subject to similar laws and constraints to those that have governed the evolution of other living organisms. The fact of these far-reaching parallels has largely escaped notice so far, and indeed many historians deny that there is any system of laws underlying the course of historical events. In my view, however, it is most important to recognize these constraints; we shall then be able to attempt a cautious forecast of the future development of man's specifically human characteristics, as well as to outline a clear-cut aim – namely, a rather more purposive progressive development of man's special features and a more consistent direction of his cultural future. Naturally enough, this can only be expressed with some caution; but in view of the vast theoretical and practical importance of the problems, it must be attempted. For the steady advance of science teaches us not only the constant need for a critical outlook; it also sanctions unshakeable optimism about such aims as are attainable.

The ensuing chapters will be concerned with biological, psychological and cultural facts. But, as we have said, we shall always lay particular stress on the data that are capable of proof rather than on more or less arresting phrases. By so doing we hope to escape the criticism expressed by the astute late-eighteenth-century cynic G. C. Lichtenberg: 'If we think of Nature as our teacher and poor mankind as her hearers, we tend to arrive at a strange idea of the human race. Here we sit together in a *Collegio*, with all the faculties necessary to understand and appreciate what is said; but we are constantly listening more to the chatter of our companions than the words of our instructress.'

CHAPTER TWO

Man's physical evolution

A. *The stream of life*

On the evidence of the many subfossil and fossil remains of human skeletons it is safe to say that *Homo sapiens*, man as we know him today, came into being towards the end of the Pleistocene epoch, in all probability no more than 100,000 years ago. The line of his ancestry quite clearly leads back to apes. The late Phiocene and early Pleistocene South African Australopithecines, standing midway between animals and man, make this abundantly plain. At first these Australopithecines were taken to be highly advanced anthropoid apes ('super-chimpanzees')', but after the discovery of more fossil material they were ranked as 'still' belonging to the Hominidae, though this has meant considerably extending the characteristics of that family. In 1953 G. H. R. von Koenigswald [118] expressed the uncertainties of classification when he described the Australopithecines as an 'animal manifestation of man', which had not yet advanced beyond the animal stage. At present anthropologists are more and more inclined to consider these types as a basic branch of the human family tree.

It is certain that man is descended from the Old World (Catarrhine) monkeys, which in turn derive from early Tertiary lemurs (*Tarsioidea*). The line of ancestry can be traced further back through the insectivores and primitive mammals to mammal-like reptiles (the *Theriodontidae* of Upper Triassic), to primitive reptiles (the Cotylosaurs of the Carboniferous), to Amphibia (early Devonian) and to the earliest jawless fish (the Agnatha of the Ordovician). On all these phylogenetic levels anatomical and physiological characteristics arose that represented an advantage (see below). They were retained and

4

improved during phylogeny, right up to the emergence of present-day man. In order to understand man as a biological phenomenon, we must examine in turn the main structural advances at each stage in his animal ancestry.

This involves going still further back. The phylogenetic tree just outlined, which is based in general upon fossil material, begins with the earliest of all fish, the jawless Agnatha. It is impossible to say exactly from what earlier animal stages these most primitive vertebrates derive. Such creatures, having in all probability no bony skeleton, could hardly leave fossilized traces. Studies in comparative anatomy, however, and in comparative embryology, show that the ancestors of the vertebrates were probably similar in structure to the existing 'lancelets' (*Branchiostoma* – headless and limbless invertebrates). We cannot be positive, but it is likely that these Acrania are in turn descended from certain groups of worm-like Hemichordata. We may further assume that all the higher animal groups derive primarily from protozoa. These single-celled organisms already have many features which are retained in multicellular animals, including the mammals and man himself (proteins and nucleic acids forming the most important building blocks, cell nuclei containing chromosomes, mitosis as the precise mechanism of nuclear division, cytoplasm, mitochondria, and so on).

We must also give at least brief consideration to the question of the genesis of life itself, because man still retains some characteristics that originated at this stage, which are of importance in typically 'human' problems. The exact nature of life has not yet been fully explained, but we already know a good deal about it. Intensive study of many structures and processes typical of living organisms have at least established that we no longer need to trace life back to mysterious 'biogenetic molecules' absent in inanimate matter, or to the influence of vital forces (what H. Driesch termed 'entelechies') that defy analysis. On the contrary, living organisms are composed of the self-same molecules and atoms that are found in inanimate substances. The living substance, in all its activities, is continually taking in and excreting those molecules and atoms. Every vital function (not taking the phenomenon of consciousness

5

into account here) derives originally from physico-chemical processes. It is thus possible to state the problem of life in terms of the following questions: (1) How could a system of organic molecules, capable of identical reduplication, develop and remain more or less constant over a long period? (2) How can one explain the further evolution of this living substance into more complex organisms? (3) How can more complex organisms, made up of many diverse substances, continue to take in and excrete inanimate matter and yet remain constant with regard to their individual cycle of development (as for instance from the ovum to the adult individual) in spite of the law of entropy?

It is not yet possible to give a complete answer to all the problems raised here; but an extremely varied stock of facts in the spheres of biochemistry, physiology, genetics and evolution enables us to give a positive reply to many important points, and a very probable one to others [8, 26, 30, 40, 44, 46, 61, 72, 84, 98, 99, 121, 146, 148, 151, 164, 169, 181, 196, 199, 205, 242].

The first beginnings of life inaugurated processes that were to affect every organism up to man himself. Most recently it has seemed increasingly probable that life came gradually into being. The vital factor in this evolution was the development of proteins, allowing very complicated and manifold chemical processes, and of special nucleic acids, substances capable of identical reduplication forming the basis for reproduction, heredity, and long-term stability of the organism – in other words for the continuance of life. The development of these and other complicated organic compounds seems to be possible, because it is possible to prove that they could have originated under prebiological conditions, after the solid surface of the earth had been formed (cf. section D of this chapter).

It is this same process of reduplication that has produced every new generation of living organisms and their prestages. From the earliest stage the principle has held good that life springs from life. The axiom, *omne vivum e vivo*, established in the seventeenth century and confirmed by Pasteur's classic experiments in 1862 [170], has invariably proved to be true. Among animals and plants, among protozoa and multicellular organisms, no completely new individual has ever sprung into being; each has always developed out of the germ cells or out of somatic cells of previous generations, or protozoa have divided into two or more units. In other words, life flows on in a continuous stream, an uninterrupted chain of self-dividing cells. Among multicellular organisms, including man, the succeeding generations form a chain of individual life cycles linked together by the continuity of the germ cells or other 'totipotent' cells. In most cases the ovum is at first fertilized by a sperm; then, by cell division and the subsequent differentiation of certain groups of cells to form tissues and organs, the adult individual gradually emerges. One group of cells, the germ cells, is always set aside within each individual. Since their future development is unimpaired by specialization, they remain 'totipotent'. This succession of immature and mature germ cells emerging one from the other, this 'germ tract', constitutes the real unbroken thread of life. The individuals, growing and adult, strung along its length, form specialized cell complexes whose structures and physiological processes help to ensure its continuance (Fig. 1). Our chief concern, of course, is with these 'outgrowths', these actual individuals, whether plants, animals or humans [181, 196].

Fig. 1 The germ tract, the continuous chain of immature and mature sex cells, linking the generations in an unbroken thread of life. Dots indicate germ cells in the embryo and adult.

B

Homo sapiens

Each individual normally produces several offspring. Therefore the stream of life regularly divides and branches out. Some branches, however, undergo alterations by mutations and new gene combinations, and the most favourable to the relevant environment are perpetuated, while unfavourable ones are eliminated. Yet however diverse the forms that gradually emerge in this way may be – new races, species, genera, families and classes – the categories are all branches of the same single ancestral tree. It is of prime importance for us to grasp this point if we are to come to an understanding of ourselves as human beings. All that is and was alive is a unity in that it is homogeneous in its origin and its continued growth; it branches out down the ages like a tree whose sole growing points at any given time are the countless living organisms representing the tips of its outermost twigs. This means that all organisms are genuinely related to one another, for they share common ancestors with whom they are linked in substance through an unbroken tract.

As individuals transmit life by the identical reduplication of nucleic acid threads, and hence of the germ cells, in each succeeding generation more and more individuals come into being. A dividing unicellular organism increases in number by geometrical progression: from 2 to 4, 8, 16, 32 and so on. This rapidly leads to a number of individuals which outruns the space and food available. Many are bound to perish. Competition occurs, and natural selection more or less eliminates the less favourable variants. At all levels of life, even the lowest, this undue increase has always led to the danger of overpopulation. So, the human race, threatened by the same danger, is suffering an affliction as old as life itself.

B. *Factors and laws determining the phylogeny of animals and man*

It is probable that the identical reduplication of the nucleic acids, and the proteins they synthesize, represents the first decisive stage in the emergence of life. We have already noted that in the prestages of organisms these factors have led to a high degree of stability, though mutation keeps it from being

8

complete. Later, as mutation and natural selection involved greater and greater complexity, leading to real organisms, it was vital that the structure of the whole life cycle (from the germ cell to the adult) should remain stable over long periods. If each generation had differed essentially from the one before, life could not have survived, because the conditions under which subsistence and reproduction were possible for a particular organism were always limited. Heredity, then, is a necessary factor in the development of life.

In recent years the chemical structure of the substances that determine heredity has been analysed by ingenious methods. Some astonishing findings have been made. These researches revealed a system of filamentous molecules, sometimes as much as several centimetres long, spiralled and in places sharply coiled, known as deoxyribonucleic acids (DNA). These are double helices of alternating phosphate and sugar groups (Deoxyribose) interconnected by four different bases held together by hydrogen bonds and matched in pairs, adenine with thymine and cytosine with guanine. These pairs occur in a constantly varied order along the molecular thread, and this variety gives rise to differing *loci* ('genes') at which the development of specific characteristics originates. A recent view is that the 'genes', whose existence had already been deduced purely from their genetic effects, constitute morphological entities or 'operons', which are groups of sub-units in the nucleic acid thread.

These molecules are capable of identical duplication. The double helix splits into two, each part taking up what it lacks from the available cellular material. The surprising point is that the molecules that transmit hereditary characteristics in both animals and man are always made up of the same elements. It is only the differing sequence and number of the paired bases that determines a particular course of development, whether the result is to be an amoeba, an earthworm, a beetle or a man. By the basic structure of the hereditary substance that governs his specific nature man is bound up in the totality of living organisms.

All animals and plants have become adapted to their special

9

habitats in the same way – by mutation, by spreading of mutants (gene flow), by sexual processes that have brought about re-arrangements of the hereditary factors, and by natural selection. Size of populations and variations of the gene stock (gene drift) influenced the speed of evolution. With the exception of sexually determined rearrangements, the same is true of the viruses, rudimentary forms resembling organisms in many characteristics. Since the three processes mentioned above have also dominated the emergence of man, we must now briefly characterize their meaning.

By mutation we mean a random change in hereditary structure, normally occasioned by the 'spontaneous' alteration of a basic hereditary factor, a 'gene' ('locus'), or of the gene arrangement. Gene mutation is brought about by a change in the arrangement of base pairs in the DNA molecules; the change occurs rarely, but once made it persists in all subsequent self-replications. We do not yet fully know the causes of such spontaneous 'hereditary defects'. They may include disturbances in the chemical environment of the DNA thread during reduplication, the influence of ionizing radiations (e.g. ultraviolet or X-rays), a rise in temperature as reduplication is taking place, or other factors. By such influences, for instance, tautonymous restoring of the bases in the DNA molecules is possible. Mutations may also occur if parts of two chromosomes become exchanged, if a part of a chromosome becomes attached to another chromosome, if a part turns over through 180°, or if a small piece at the end of a chromosome is lost. In all these cases the alteration in the hereditary characteristics is brought about purely by new combinations of existing basic elements. These types of mutation may occur in any gene or chromosome and so they may change any characteristic determined by hereditary factors.

Mutations are 'random', i.e. successive mutations do not follow any consistent line. Although they are very rare, their occurrence among the thousands or millions of individuals in an animal species is regular enough to allow the estimation of mutation rates for specific genes (0·001 – 0·0002 per cent in the case of the common fruitfly, *Drosophila melanogaster*). Mutations are normally disadvantageous, since they change a long-established and harmonious organic system which is adapted in many ways to its own special circumstances. Most mutations modify only one 'locus'. Since in almost all animals the chromosome set in the body cells is double (diploid), it follows that in the majority of cases the mutational alterations do not show themselves; the unaffected locus on the homologous chromosome (i.e. the unaffected allele) is often sufficient to ensure normal development. These disadvantageous mutants become noticeable, however, if both alleles (from the mother's and the father's side) are modified, in other words when the characteristic is in the homozygous condition (as happens in inbreeding). H. F. Muller's genetic analyses of marriages among close relatives show that every individual has on average at least ten highly detrimental hereditary characteristics in his genetic stock [156, 157]. He is unaware of them, however, because their genes are recessive. It is only when close relatives intermarry that the probability of homozygosis increases. When it happens, the hereditary defect, transmitted by both alleles, becomes apparent. Observation of this fact probably underlies the common ethical or religious code which forbids marriage between siblings or between parents and children.

There are also a few dominant mutations whose detrimental effects are evident even in a heterozygous condition, i.e. in every individual involved.

Individuals affected by harmful mutations normally prove to be either inviable or else unable, in the long run, to compete with their normal counterparts. But there are always a few mutants that the organism is able to tolerate and some others that confer some positive advantage. However, a further complication has to be considered: if they become associated with different gene combinations within a population, mutated genes may acquire a different selective value. But in most cases competition and the battle for survival normally lead to natural selection of all or the most suitable of the hereditary combinations within the population.

All organisms produce a much larger number of progeny than is essential for the continuance of their species at its normal

level. By far the greater number perish before they naturally
decline through old age. The probability is that, on average,
unfit or weaker individuals or populations perish in greater
numbers than the rest. Selection may operate through the
environment, for instance by winter minima (on mutants
unable to withstand it) or drought conditions. Living enemies,
too, may destroy mutants lacking protective characteristics or
the skill to escape. Again, selection may operate through patho-
genic agents (preferentially attacking mutants with inadequate
powers of resistance) or – most of all – through competition for
food, for habitat, or for a reproductive partner. Every living
organism, at every stage in its individual life cycle, is almost
constantly subject to these processes of selection. They ensure
that the unprofitable variants produced by mutation or recombination tend to perish, while those few mutants and recom-
binants whose structure or function shows some advantage
survive and multiply more rapidly.

In this way every organism has undergone changes in
structure and mode of life, which, though very slow, have
persisted for millions of years. This is how new species have
come into being. This kind of evolution has never ceased,
because habitats, and therefore selective conditions, have been
subject to gradual and continual alterations. These have included
the uplift, erosion and levelling of mountain ranges, the separation of land masses, changes in climate, and the appearance of
new enemies or competitors, etc. Organisms, under pressure
of continual overpopulation, have also sought to extend into
fresh marginal regions, where they have frequently come into
contact with new selective conditions.

The evolution of species has been studied and clarified in
many different organisms and analysed by many different
methods – by cytological, genetical and ecological investigations, selection experiments, and palaeontological statements.
We know that its tempo has been affected by the size and the
fluctuations of populations. On the whole, smaller populations
have shown more rapid phylogenetic evolution. This would
explain why *Homo sapiens*, originally living in relatively small
groupings, in small reproductive communities, has come to

differ so remarkably within (geologically speaking) a short period. Europeans, Eskimos, Papuans, Congolese, Pygmies, Hottentots and other races became morphologically as diverse as are the species in an animal genus.

In the animal kingdom, selective processes operate more intensively and count for more than mutation rates. Another important factor has been the isolation of developing races and species. Living apart from one another, they often became sexually and genetically estranged; as for instance when the instinctive patterns leading to mating changed, or mutant genes when crossed with the parent form produced inviable or enfeebled stock (hybrid sterility). Geographical isolation was one most frequent cause of the splitting off of new animal races. This is the kind of isolation to which the human races also owe their origin (relatively pure races still existing among sub-races and tribes in the Malay Archipelago, in New Guinea, in the Amazon Basin, etc.). But a good deal of migration and intermingling has later blurred the distinctions.

Given the random nature of mutation, geographical separation into races has led to all kinds of diversity of characteristics. For instance, the colour patterns in many races of tropical birds and butterflies differ, although this has no obvious connection with selective environmental factors. In man, too, the various races show random differences, for instance in the convolutions of the ear, the shape of the nose and lips, and the proportions of the face. These characteristics seem to have nothing to do with selection.

However, in most cases natural selection is what has mainly determined the lines along which most animal and human characteristics have developed and altered. Because the conditions of the environment, notably climate, have often led to some specific trend in selection, we can frequently state certain evolutionary rules. In temperate and cooler zones both birds and animals, being warm-blooded, are subject to a climatic selection affecting among other characteristics their size and colouring. Whereas the volume of a body increases by three dimensions, the surface area does so by the square; a larger body therefore has a relatively smaller surface area than a smaller one of similar shape. Since the amount of heat a body dissipates is proportional to its surface area, a large body loses relatively less heat than a small one. For warm-blooded creatures it is therefore an advantage to be rather larger in cooler than in warmer regions. As early as 1847 the physiologist C. Bergmann in fact formulated a rule with reference to birds and animals, which may be expressed in an abridged form as follows: among polytypic species extending over different climatic zones, those races inhabiting cooler regions usually attain a larger body size (as other factors also affect hereditary body size, exceptions will of course be found) [180].

It is an interesting fact – one to which I had already drawn attention in 1935 [179] – that despite all the racial mingling that has gone on since prehistoric times, we can still trace something of Bergmann's rule in the human races of today. Among northern peoples for instance, Icelanders are somewhat taller than southern Swedes (the averages are 173·5 cm for 844 men, and 172·4 cm for 260). These in turn are rather taller than men from the province of Schleswig (169·9 cm for 100). South German (alpinoid) men are shorter still (those from Lower Franconia on average 165·9 cm and from the Black Forest region 161·4 cm). And there is a similar scale for the inhabitants of China; northern Chinese from Chihli (167·9 cm for 114 men) and men from Shantung (165·5 cm for 185) are on average taller than those from the south (164·0 cm for 113 men from Kiangsu, 164·0 cm for 62 from Chi-Kiang). The palaeomongoloid races further south, for instance in the Shan States, are shorter still (158·0 cm for 111 men from Palaung, and 161·6 cm for 60 Cochinese). The same is true also of the American Indians; races north of the Tropic of Cancer have an average height of 163·0-175·7 cm, those between the two Tropics only 153·2-166·1 cm, and those south of the Tropic of Capricorn are rather taller again (154·7-175 cm). M. T. Newman's detailed study [162] of differing build among the Indian tribes of North and South America has yielded similar results. Taking weight as a basis, which to a certain extent also indicates the surface area exposed to cooling, we find correlation among all peoples with the mean annual temperature of the region [202]; to a certain degree Bergmann's rule thus holds good even for present-day man (Fig. 2) (cf. I. Schwidetsky's lucid survey [222]).

According to another climatic law, tropical peoples are usually more heavily pigmented than races inhabiting temperate or cooler zones. Here, too, migration and intermixture have introduced exceptions of different kinds; in general, however, we find the more light-skinned European and Mongoloid races living in the temperate or cool zones in the northern continents, and the dark-skinned tribes in the tropics (Negroes, Tamils, Papuans, north Australians, Melanesians). Brazilian Indians are darker than those from northern North America or Tierra del Fuego. Heavier pigmentation has meant protection for bare-skinned man against the burning rays of the sun, while in cooler zones a lighter colour was no doubt an advantage, for then the ultraviolet rays so important for the synthesizing of vitamin D could penetrate the skin [179].

Probably climatic selection is also responsible for several other racial characteristics of man. A correlation with slenderness of build, for instance, would be in line with Allen's rule, whereby races of warm-blooded animals in colder regions are stockier in build, i.e. their limbs, tails, necks, ears or beaks are shorter. It is a fact that those peoples whose legs are relatively longest inhabit tropical and subtropical Africa, India and Australia [cf. R. Biasutti, 10, and I. Schwidetsky, 222]. Taken all in all, then, the different races of man as well as of animals may be said to have emerged mainly as a result of geographic isolation; and certain rules of racial evolution typical of the animal kingdom have also applied to man. These human racial characteristics are all hereditary qualities, subject to mutation in the same way as the corresponding mammalian ones. And as the rules we have mentioned affect characteristics whose value varies with the climatic zone involved, we may assume that natural selection was operating here as well. Moreover, another process of selection can be seen at work, for the more primitive peoples have been extirpated or supplanted by stronger ones or those whose civilization or technical abilities was more advanced. Furthermore, illness and disease are continually

Fig. 2   Height among Indian and Eskimo tribes of North and South America. Bergmann's rule partially valid; Indian tribes are on average taller in the continental climate of central and eastern North America and in the extreme south of South America. Eskimos, however, are stocky in build (Allen's rule).   Lightly stippled area: an adult height of 155-159·9 cm. Medium stippling: 160-169·9 cm. Black: 170-189 cm. (After Newman, from Schwidetsky.)

operating selectively within individual peoples, as does sexual selection (in line with partly inherited ideals of beauty) (for a fuller treatment, see Chapters 3 and 5). At least during its primary phases, then, man's racial evolution is clearly governed by the same factors as that of the animal kingdom.

We must now deal briefly with certain principles involved in man's evolution which cannot only be observed in the development of races or species. Some principles and rules appear only in a longer time span when new organs and new structural types, and new genera, families, orders and classes, come into being. This evolution, above the species level, like the mutation and speciation that underlie it, is also directionless. It has therefore happened that a great variety of biologically possible structures have evolved. If they were correlated with advantageous characteristics, this has sometimes led to the emergence of excessive or 'superfluous' features. Totally 'unnecessary' structures and functions of this kind include the excessively long tail feathers of some weaver birds and flycatchers, and the giraffe's inordinately long neck. Many vestigial organs are useless relics of formerly important features, which their owners would now be better without – for instance, the python's vestigial pelvis and femur, the whalebone whale's developing and dwindling tooth buds, and man's embryonic rudiment, Jacobson's organ (a smelling organ in the mouth of our reptilian ancestors).

Yet although even in the larger categories the early stages of evolution were in this sense random, long periods of stable selective conditions often meant that it did proceed along definite lines. When a group of mammals became specialized for running, and established themselves in open country, in the course of geological epochs the same or similar selective factors acted upon each succeeding species. Throughout the phylogenetic development of the horse, for instance, it has always been an advantage to have fewer toes, for running at speed. During the Tertiary period we find the original *Eohippus* of the Eocene (with its four-toed forelegs) developing into the three-toed *Mesohippus* of the Oligocene, then into the *Merychippus* (Miocene) with a powerful middle toe and two smaller subsidiary toes, which no longer reached the ground, and finally into the present-day single-toed *Equus* with vestigial splint bones, which are relics of the side toes. The number of toes was also reduced in other running animals (artiodactyls, agoutis and birds such as ostriches). In other cases several toes merged to form a more or less unitary pad (as in bears, elephants and gorillas). This same development has also produced the human foot.

Steady selective conditions led to an absolute or relative increase in brain size in many animal lines of descent. It was almost always an advantage to develop more brain cells; their greater complexity made for increasing division of labour and subtler and more multifarious nervous connections and for much more varied reactions to the environment. A finer degree of response was possible. For instance, an animal receiving a pattern of stimuli through its eyes could react to some relatively insignificant element in the field of vision – for example, a possibly edible insect in a tangle of leaves. With more brain cells it was also possible to store up more engrams as a basis for more complex memories. This, in turn, meant more varied behavioural responses, and inherited instinctive action could yield to activity based on choice. That is why in the course of their phylogeny an absolute increase in brain size can be traced in a very large number of animal groups – insects, ungulates, carnivores, primates, etc. Hence the development of a large brain, which led to the appearance of present-day man, is part of a universal evolutionary tendency among his animal precursors [184]. We touch here the problem of progressive evolution, which is vitally important for an understanding of man's emergence. It will often recur in these pages.

Do mutation, recombination of genes, gene flow and natural selection really suffice to explain all the trends in phylogeny? For a long time this did not appear to be the case. It seemed that one had to assume the presence of some overruling 'directive forces' controlling evolution, at least in cases when orthogenetic changes led to structures or organs so exaggerated that they were a positive hindrance. For instance, in the lines of descent of elephants the elongated incisors continued to grow longer and more massive and eventually became tusks. Among some Ice Age mammoths this development led to the curved tusk growing until the tip no longer pointed obliquely upward but backward or even towards the ground behind (as in *Elephas columbi*). This reduced their usefulness as weapons or tools. Natural selection could not be responsible for this kind of excess, it was thought, for any selection must promote what is advantageous and not something manifestly impractical. But to reason like this is to forget that each characteristic affected by selection has its place within the body as a whole. During the Ice Age it was of advantage for warm-blooded animals in cooler regions to grow relatively larger, since by this process their bulk increased by the cube of their dimensions, whereas the surface area, subject to loss of heat, grew only by the square (see pp. 13-14). As a body increases, however, its proportions do not remain constant. Some organs grow more quickly than the body as a whole (positive allometry), others more slowly (negative allometry). In this case the tusks, growing with positive allometry, were 'automatically' bound to become excessively large in proportion, and since they were curved the tip in time began to point backward. In this manner natural selection, intent upon some chief characteristic (here body size), may involve some side effect that amounts to a disadvantage. Many animals, especially the largest species in their respective groups, often have some excessive structure of this kind. We have already referred to 'superfluous' features, and might also quote the expanse of 'unnecessary' branching antlers displayed by the stag, the apparently almost 'insupportable' overgrown antlers of the Ice Age giant elk (*Megaceros*) or the capricorn beetle's long antennae.

We must also consider some more general principles of evolution above the species level, since they are also applicable to man's emergence. In animal lines of descent well represented in fossil remains, whenever largely novel structural types appear we often find very vigorous adaptive radiation, the emergence of new species, genera and families. On this new constructional basis, the adaptability of a greater variety of forms to the various kinds of habitat was put to the test. These are the periods of 'explosive radiation' (often so called despite the fact that they may have extended over many millions of years). After such periods the number of new branches of the ancestral tree usually diminished. Less suitable types of structures died out, leaving only those groups that had survived a process of continuous selection throughout the countless generations. The pace of evolution slackened, because when the various species had gradually occupied all the suitable habitats, no selective adaptation to new ones was possible. Besides, in many cases a maximum degree of adaptability had then been reached. Such well adapted types often persisted through a long geological period – particularly those with the right level of genetic polymorphism and physical plasticity, which were always able to adapt to continual slight changes in their environment (Homeostasis).

Apparently there were no such periods of explosive radiation in man's phylogeny during the later Tertiary period or Pleistocene epoch. His evolution proceeded fairly steadily, though rather rapidly after the beginning of the Pleistocene. In the last 100,000 years or so we have reached a relatively stable genetic and physical stage, at least in regard to brain structure. On the other hand there is no doubt that many of man's earlier ancestors emerged during periods of 'explosion' – for instance monkeys in the Oligocene, lemurs in the Palaeocene, the first mammals in the Upper Triassic and early Jurassic and early reptiles in the Carboniferous.

It is interesting to find the same sequence of explosive radiation, slackening development and stability, in the history of human inventions. For instance, when the bicycle was invented, several types appeared – the tricycle, the penny-farthing and the bicycle with equal wheels. While the first two 'died out', the last survived and was further modified, though its development gradually slowed down. Improvements were introduced – the back-pedalling brake, the free-wheeling device, ball-bearings, and lighting features. But for some time now it has retained its accepted form, with only a very low degree of 'evolution'. I have not cited this example merely as a comparison but to show that selection is always the decisive factor. Linked with mutation (like the single invention) and new gene combinations (like technical combinations) it calls new species into being and promotes improvement and progressive evolution. The pattern is always the same – explosive radiation followed by the slower development of certain lines that have proved their ability to survive (cf. Chapter 4, section C).

A survey of the entire phylogenetic tree shows that most of the branches that were thrown out died off again sooner or later. As far as we can judge (naturally a difficult task in the case of animal groups belonging to the geological past), extinction has often been the result of too narrow adaptation to particular living conditions. For instance, animals adapted for running grew relatively large and long-legged, reduced the number of their toes, and developed hooves. Later, when their environment underwent a change – e.g. when the steppes became wooded again – having lost the necessary hereditary characters they could not become climbers or burrowers. If, as often happened, animals had specialized to the extent that they had adapted themselves to particular conditions of temperature, humidity and terrain, or to some very special food, they soon became extinct when their environment altered. The Ice Age brought extensive changes in fauna, but when the climate grew warmer again many Ice Age animals died out (among mammals the mammoth, woolly rhinoceros, giant elk, cave bear, sabre-toothed tiger and many others). So it is understandable that phylogenetic development often led to a dead end. While selection is taking place, it is always advantageous to be better adapted than rival types to prevailing conditions. But for the future development of any line of descent it is better not to carry specialization too far. In case of a change in environmental circumstances (lowering of the temperature, disappearance of the customary foodstuffs, the arrival of a new enemy, etc.) it is possible for less specialized forms to undergo some phylogenetic alteration in structure and to adapt themselves anew on a basis of mutations, new gene combinations and selection.

The American palaeontologist E. D. Cope [34] established a phylogenetic law based on these principles, which he called the Law of the Unspecialized. According to this law, only those types of animals that remained relatively unspecialized were likely to continue their line of descent throughout different geological epochs and to develop essentially new and advanced structural types. That is why the mammalian groups today, i.e. those that did not die out, derive from relatively small phylogenetic ancestors with only a minor degree of specialization. Bears, dogs, cats, seals, whales and other carnivores are descended from small creatures, primitive carnivores (Creodonta) with little specialization of dentition or build, and somewhat similar to the proto-ungulates, the slightly specialized ancestors of the hoofed animals. Both these groups derive from small, little-specialized insectivores, from which the lemurs and later the monkeys and apes also descended.

It is important to note that man also traces his descent from a line of ancestors that remained relatively unspecialized. Judging by the numerous fossil findings, man is undoubtedly descended from the monkeys, an order of mammals whose species show little specialization in many important characteristics. They have five-fingered hands, as did their reptilean ancestors. Their fingers are capable of versatile movements, while those of all other groups of mammals are rather limited. Their arms are suspended from two shoulder-girdle bones (the clavicle and the scapula) and can be rotated, whereas animals adapted for running, with only one such bone (the forelegs being suspended from the scapula alone) are practically limited to a backward and forward swinging movement of the limbs. Human dentition is not particularly specialized, and so both animal and plant foods of various kinds are suitable; and this means that the organs and functions of digestion (digestive enzymes, etc.) are also relatively unspecialized. Apes and monkeys are descended from lemurs and these in turn from insectivores – that is from groups of animals that were not much specialized. Furthermore, they were small, and large body size is, of course, a form of specialization that hampers adaptation to completely new environmental conditions.

Finally, another and highly important factor for the understanding of human evolution is the principle of progressive evolution. This process can be observed in many animal groups, and in view of its theoretical importance it has been much discussed, and at times misunderstood. However, it has now been largely explained [98, 181, 229]. Progressive evolution is not simply a matter of 'improvement' or an advance towards 'perfection'. Unremitting selection has made almost every animal group better adapted, and so in a sense more 'perfect', than its predecessors. Yet the phylogenetic 'level' has often remained the same. A saurian that is better adapted to its surroundings – a better swimmer, for instance – is still a saurian. But when a group of small reptiles (Theriodonts) in the late Triassic period first produced true mammals, this was an instance of progressive evolution. So was the development of the earliest fish from their invertebrate lancelet-like precursors.

A closer analysis of many such cases reveals several features, which characterize the stages in progressive evolution:

1 Increased complexity (e.g. more organs or organs developing a larger number of cells).

2 More efficient structures (e.g. by centralization of separate components, such as the emergence of a central nervous system or a central breathing system like gills or lungs) and functions (e.g. by division of labour: digestive tract differentiated into oral cavity, gullet, stomach, intestine and regions for digestion and absorption).

3 Special complexity and 'rationalization' of the nervous structures (e.g. an increase in the number of brain cells, a functional specialization of brain regions, a rationalized arrangement of nervous fibres, and consequently an improved perception and finer reaction to single stimuli – for instance, to finer details of the retinal image – and better memory).

4 Increased plasticity of structures and functions (e.g. greater mobility of the limbs and an increased ability to accommodate the eye to objects at varying distances).

5 Greater independence of the environment (e.g. by becoming warm-blooded) and increase of autonomous behaviour.

6 To be effective, these improvements must not restrict, but should render possible further advance (e.g. development of a nerve centre for reflexes, which can also form the basis of more complex hereditary instinctive as well as memorization processes).

c

Homo sapiens

The particular examples listed above have been selected because they indicate evolutionary trends essential to the emergence of man. They help to explain a seventh characteristic, this time not invariably present but still broadly typical of progressive evolution, namely an approximation of structures and functions to those found in man. We shall have more to say in detail in section D of this chapter about these requirements. For the present, however, this seventh category may serve to illustrate how the idea of progressive evolution is a relative one. We could not assert that the earliest lemurs of the Palaeocene represent a 'higher' stage than the insectivores, had they not continued their advance and developed into more typical lemurs and then into monkeys. Similarly, the primitive Stegocephalia, those earliest amphibians of the Devonian, would rank simply as different in construction from the groups of fish most nearly related to them (the Crossopterygii). We regard them as 'higher' only because their development, instead of resting at that point, led on to more advanced amphibians and reptiles. Whether an organism can be considered as 'higher' or not is often not a matter of the evolutionary step it has actually taken; we have first to look back from the standpoint of some unquestionably 'higher' descendant.

It is clear, then, that progressive evolution has led up to the emergence of man; but we have to ask whether it can be explained by the same factors as the rest of evolution. Can man in the last instance be the product of random mutation, gene arrangements and 'chance' conditions of selection? Or must we assume the existence of some particular directive forces not yet identified? The study of nature has not yet revealed any such regulative factor, such finality. On the contrary, closer analysis has normally traced each process to its cause – as, for instance, even the 'superfluous' growth of the mammoth's tusks mentioned above. Biologists normally try to avoid the introduction of unknown determinant factors as long as mutation, gene combination and selection – all of them rather well analysed – suffice for an explanation of the evolutionary process.

It is necessary, however, to study the characteristics noted above, to see if, and how far, they can be interpreted in terms of random mutation and selection.

(1) Random mutation may easily bring about increased complexity, for instance by additional division of certain cell groups. This may possess a selective advantage, since an increase in cells (brain cells, for instance), like any increase in complexity, makes division of labour possible. (2) More efficient structures and functions may result from random mutation in just the same way as inefficient ones, although the latter occur much more frequently. The far more efficient ones, of course, will possess selective advantages (3-6). Complication and rationalization of nervous structures, increased plasticity, independence of environmental factors, and those improvements that make further ones possible may also result from random mutation; and they have a good chance to survive, thanks to their obvious selective advantages. In time they will prevail. It does not matter that harmful and disruptive mutations are much more numerous, because these are normally eradicated by natural selection (often because they are less viable or fertile).

It seems clear, then, that progressive evolution is explicable along the lines of mutation and selection, and we are not obliged to assume the existence of any directive evolutionary force. At each phylogenetic level a progressive change remains possible, as does a non-progressive change or retrogression. Once any progressive step has been taken, however, natural selection begins to operate in its favour.

Quite understandably, many people feel some distaste at finding the evolution of their own kind traced back to such more or less blind factors as random mutation and 'chance' conditions of selection. But we must remember that we use the word 'chance' in order to circumscribe events that are also governed by laws, but these laws operate on so vastly complicated a scale that man has not yet been able to analyse them. Moreover, these laws are partial effects of the general and continuously acting laws of causality. This overruling causal system is something we can never 'explain', any more than we can 'explain' that, as the world is constituted, the law splits into diverse special laws, to which the biological laws also belong [cf. B. Rensch, 189. 196].

Some groups of the causal processes, certain excitation patterns in the brain of man (and probably also of animals), correspond to psychic processes. When, for instance, light rays of different wave length have effected the transformation of visual substances in the retina of the eyes and have produced excitations running to the visual region of the forebrain, certain sensations like 'red', 'yellow', 'green', etc., correspond to these processes. The sensation 'green', for instance, corresponds to excitation by light rays of 520 mμ wave length. The sensation is not a causal consequence of the excitation but appears at the same time ('instantaneous'). We cannot explain why we have only the sensation 'green' and not 'red' or 'blue'. We can only assume that certain laws of psychic correspondence exist (laws of parallelity in the sense of T. Ziehen [280, 282]), or we can consider the brain excitations and the corresponding sensations as the same (in the sense of panpsychistic identism). The latter conception would mean that psychic laws are also causal laws [more detailed discussion of these problems in my *Biophilosophy*, 196].

As animal evolution has proceeded, these psychological relations have come to affect phenomena of increasing complexity (e.g. more complex processes of thought). We can judge psychic phenomena only from our own experience. We are convinced that others have like experiences – others whom, after all, we can only apprehend through our own sensations and concepts. It is important to realize that the assumption of psychological processes in other beings is only based on conclusions of analogy. Yet since man is phylogenetically descended from animal ancestors, we can assume that the correspondence of psychological and causal phsyiological components also holds in the case of animals. The higher animals possess sense organs and nervous systems very similar in construction and functions to our own. Their reaction to environmental conditions is often much the same; we therefore assume that they are capable of sensations, images and feelings. None of us regards a dog as simply a machine reacting to stimuli. We suppose that it hears, sees, feels pain, has some memory (i.e. primary mental images) of its master and its home, and so on.

The unbroken continuity of phylogenetic evolution allows us to extend the conclusions by analogy to cover more primitive animals; within the limits of their anatomy, learning ability and behaviour we may thus ascribe some simple type of psychic experience to fishes, insects and worms. Even worms possess varied sense organs and a complex nervous system. The further from man, of course, the vaguer the conclusion. For the present, however, all we wish to establish is that a phylogeny of mental components, a *psychophylogenesis*, must be supposed. And here, as in the sphere of morphology, we can go back to the simpler structures of earlier phases. Fish, for instance, can be presumed at least capable of sensations, of feelings, of simple visual, acoustic and other imagery (i.e. of memory), and also of the formation of abstractions. Experiments in training them have shown this to be very probable. In surveying a situation and planning an action, indeed, higher animals like apes may achieve something in the psychological sphere that comes near to human thinking [190, 200].

It is important for man's understanding of himself to make it clear that his mind too has evolved in the course of his phylogenetic history. Protopsychic prestages of lowest organisms and unassociated elements of sensation may perhaps be the basic components out of which his mental world has evolved step by step.

Much the same thing is also true of logical laws. Though these dominating principles appear to have grown in range and complexity in the course of man's thinking itself, they are in fact independent of the living organisms. When we reason as follows: $a = b$, $b = c$, therefore $a = c$, the underlying principle has nothing to do with causality, for a, b and c are coexistent and unconnected by any causal link. We have to do here with a second system of general laws. It makes no difference whether a, b and c are causal components (i.e. 'material' objects such as three atoms somewhere in the universe) or psychic components (for instance, sensations such as three red spots in the field of vision). Logical laws (comprising the laws of probability) obviously held good at a stage when neither man nor animals had yet come into existence. However, man's thought processes had first to be developed during phylogeny before the possible intricacies of logical laws could be grasped and evaluated.

We may consider the whole of evolution as a process of *bionomogenesis*: in other words it is governed by causal and logical laws. Though we can affirm their existence, we have no way of 'explaining' them. We do recognize, however, that in the history of the universe they have brought about a sequence of events of increasing complexity, culminating upon our planet in the emergence of man, conscious of himself and capable of reflecting on all these complicated relationships. At the same time, this progressive evolution, though determined by apparently 'eternal' laws, represents only one possibility out of other ones. It is equally easy to imagine a planet growing cooler or hotter and a process of retrogressive evolution taking place – the whole structure perhaps disintegrating, either gradually or suddenly, and relapsing into a ball of gas [for a more extensive treatment of the subject dealt with in this chapter, see B. Rensch, 182, 189, 196].

C. *Man's physical evolution*

It has been possible to regard monkeys and man as 'related' groups ever since Aristotle (Book 2, chapters 8 and 9) noted the similarity in their anatomical proportions. The English anatomist E. Tyson [251], who was the first to examine a young chimpanzee (in 1699 and 1711), described the animal as *Homo sylvestris*, 'The Man of the Woods', and mentioned forty-eight characteristics in which he is more like man than like any monkey. Linnaeus in 1735 [91] also grouped the anthropoid apes and man together under *Homo*. In a treatise on *Anthropomorphae*, which he wrote for his student Hoppius, he explained at length that anthropoid apes and man are closely related: 'It might seem that there was more difference between man and apes than between day and night. But if you placed a highly cultivated European prime minister and a Hottentot from the Cape of Good Hope side by side, you would find it

28

hard to believe that their origin is the same. . . .' In the Swedish manuscript there is a sentence, deleted before it went to press, to the effect that Hottentots might possibly be hybrids between man and anthropoid apes. Goethe thought that man's frontal cavities were 'relics' of an animal structure. And Kant [105] endorsed the anatomist P. Moskati's view that at some stage man had given up going on all fours.

Thus, long before the beginnings of any definite theory of man's origin, he was considered to be descended from the apes; and in 1784 G. Herder [87] was already inveighing against so 'degrading' a derivation. Later, Lamarck – who despite several forerunners was the real founder of the theory of evolution – expressly included man in his tree of animal phylogeny (1809). But only when works on the subject appeared by Thomas Huxley in 1863 [102], K. Vogt in 1863 [257], Ernst Haeckel in 1866 and 1868 [66, 67] and Charles Darwin in 1871 [39] was lengthy discussion of the problem begun. Findings in comparative anatomy and embryology seemed to show that man must be descended from the apes. Only the Neanderthal fossil remains could be brought forward, which C. Fuhlrott (1859) [57] and H. Schaaffhausen (1858) had already interpreted correctly. Similar earlier findings from Engis in Belgium (1832) and from Gibraltar (1848) were not adequately recognized and examined until somewhat later.

We now possess plenty of fossil remains of man and his ancestors at various levels. Nearly all scholars agree that *Homo sapiens* takes his descent from certain Late Tertiary anthropoid apes. In view of the many intermediate stages that connect man with the anthropoid apes he can no longer be said to derive directly from the lemurs [272, 273] or from any still lower mammals. Some authorities [19, 95, 104, 174] traced man back to Catarrhine monkeys but not the Late Tertiary anthropoid apes. Such an opinion would be in accordance with the experience that many lines of descent branched out at a much earlier period than had at first been supposed. Yet when we consider the intermediate stages that exist and the obvious resemblances that the Australopithecines show to the anthropoid apes, it surely remains much more probable that the Hominids derive

Homo sapiens

from man-like apes of the Late Miocene or Early Pliocene, which had not yet specialized as long-armed 'brachiators', rather than from some of the more primitive types of monkeys.

Clearly, discussion about man's specific pedigree largely depends upon defining what are typically human characteristics, i.e. on differentiating between the Hominids and the anthropoid apes, in particular the Tertiary Pongidae. In the introduction to this chapter (section A) we have already indicated that in recent years these definitions have grown somewhat doubtful and the line of demarcation has become blurred. In view of such obviously intermediate forms as the Australopithecines, most scholars have decided to extend the morphological connotation of the term 'Man' to include them among the Hominids. This category now embraces intermediate forms, which possessed a brain not or not much larger than that of the anthropoid apes, but which walked erect and even fashioned very primitive tools of stone and perhaps also bone. This ability of making tools is generally held to be one of man's chief characteristics. In regard to many important characteristics, then, man might be said to have 'come into being' within a wider group, the super-family of the '*Hominoidea*', which also includes fossil and recent anthropoid apes. It is debatable, though possibly less vital, which group of apes was man's phylogenetic ancestor, the primitive Pongidae or some earlier ape from which both Pongidae and Hominids are descended.

A very considerable number of fossil remains have been discovered up to the present day. Besides those numerous forms included under *Homo sapiens* (the late Pleistocene men of Cromagnon, Combe Chapelle, Brünn, Brüx, Mentone, etc.) and isolated teeth and lesser fragments, larger portions of some 100 skulls or other parts of skeletons belonging to the Neanderthal level, about 70 of the *Homo erectus* (= *Pithecanthropus*) level, and about 70 belonging to the *Australopithecus* level, have already been identified. These 240 finds, which have been intensively studied, extend over Asia as far east as Java, as well as Europe and Africa.

Yet despite this large number, man's ancestry is by no means sufficiently delineated as yet, for one has to assume the existence

30

of several side branches. Springing from some common bough, these lived on for a while beside more advanced types, though geographically apart. Very many finds would of course be required to reconstruct all the ramifications of such a tree; and it is always particularly fortunate when some fossil form is discovered, which can determine or at least suggest a point at which branching has occurred.

Any detailed survey of all these finds would be outside the province of this book. Moreover, a number of modern relevant publications exist [17, 46, 61, 81, 84, 118, 121, 126, 136, 137, 165, 205, 216, 227, 264]. It is sufficient here to emphasize that among these ancestral forms we find all connecting levels between man and the anthropoid apes. An earlier view was that most of these morphological stages followed directly one after another. It was presumed that all the human races of the last 70,000 years, all grouped under *Homo sapiens*, were descended from the Pleistocene *Homo neanderthalensis*, and that he in his turn derived from the *Pithecanthropus* phase and represented a link that led back to the Pliocene anthropoid apes. We now know that man's racial history is more complex.

One established fact is that the skeletal remains of the true *Homo sapiens* and his diverse fossil races all belong to the period when the last glaciation had passed its zenith, i.e. to the last 100,000-70,000 years. Earlier than this, they were either Neanderthal (*Homo neanderthalensis*) or come under a 'pre-Neanderthal' or 'pre-sapiens' heading. But there are certain important differences between these groups. In the first two, though the skull and brain are about the same size as that of present-day man, the forehead is more receding, the brow ridges (*tori supra orbitales*) are more pronounced, the nose is usually broader (and presumably very flat), the jaws somewhat prognathous, the chin receding and the cranial bones more massive. The occiput is more flattened, whereas in *Homo sapiens* the curve is much rounder (Fig. 3). The supporting vertebral column thus joined the head nearer to its centre of gravity, enabling *Homo sapiens* to walk more erect.

These characteristics undoubtedly point to a simian ancestry; and the same can be said of some features in the skeleton that differ from present-day man – the thorax, for instance, is

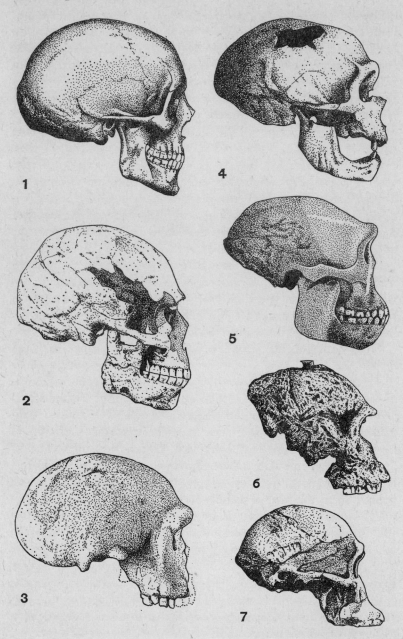

broader, the ribs are wider, and the bones of the limbs somewhat more massive. The numerous finds of Neanderthal men (in a wide interpretation of that term) come from deposits in many European countries, in Asia as far east as China, and in Africa, during the last interglacial and glacial periods. The classical type with rather flattened forehead and flattened occiput was apparently restricted to western Europe eastwards to the Rhine and Italy. The Neanderthal men have shared a fairly primitive Old Stone Age culture. They fashioned mallets, stone borers and scrapers – tools indicating that they prepared animal skins. In rarer cases they also used bone tools. They were hunters, living in caves and possibly also in the open, and they knew the use of fire, often keeping it alive in some sheltered spot. They placed weapons and food in their graves, so they may have imagined some kind of life after death.

Later deposits in Europe have not yielded clear intermediate forms between typical Neanderthals and races of *Homo sapiens*. So we assume that in this continent the former represent dead lateral branches of man's ancestral tree. A few Neanderthal men of the last interglacial period are less rugged in build and a little bit more like the *sapiens* type, perhaps indicating the former existence of a particular Mediterranean race. However, in Palestine (Mount Carmel, Jebel Kafzeh and Amud Cave), in Iraq (Shanidar) and Usbekistan (Teschik Tasch) some skulls display characteristics of both *Homo sapiens* and *Homo neanderthalensis*. It is not yet clear whether we have to do here with a relatively wide range of variability or with hybridization of two

---

Fig. 3 Human and prehuman skulls, approximately similarly reduced, and for ease of comparison all seen from the right (i.e. some reversed). 1 Present-day *Homo sapiens* (after Rauber-Kopsch, reversed). 2 'Pre-*sapiens*' type, Skhul ♂, from Mount Carmel, Palestine (after Snow from Gieseler, reversed). 3 'Pre-Neanderthal' from Steinheim, stippled area added (after Berckhemer). 4 Typical Neanderthal from La Chapelle aux Saints (after Aichel, reversed). 5 *Pithecanthropus* ('*Homo*') *modjokertensis* from Sangiran, Java (after von Koenigswald). 6 *Paranthropus robustus* from Swartkrans, south-east Africa (after Broom, reversed). 7 *Australopithecus* ('*Plesianthropus*') *transvaalensis* from Sterckfontein (after Broom).

races of different levels. It is of interest in this context that the age of the later Shanidar finds is calculated to be 44,000-48,000 years, and that of the skull from Skhul (Palestine) to be 37,500 years.

But there are also earlier Neanderthals, the so-called 'pre-Neanderthals' who show some characteristics pointing to the *Homo sapiens* races. The skull found at Steinheim on the Murr, probably dating from the Mindel-Riss interglacial period, is the best example. The relatively low forehead and heavy brow ridges are Neanderthal features, but the occiput is rounded, not oblate, very like that of present-day man. The specimen found at Swanscombe in England seems to have displayed a similar mixture of characteristics, but the occiput and parietal bones are all that is left. The bones are sturdier than in recent *Homo sapiens*, but the occiput is more rounded and the occipital bone broader than in the Neanderthal skulls. Besides, this is also an earlier find, probably from the Mindel-Riss interglacial period. We possess similar 'pre-Neanderthal' remains from the last relatively warm interglacial period, which come from Ehringdorf near Weimar and from Saccopastore near Rome. The Mount Carmel finds, too, of ten individuals including four complete skeletons, are probably earlier than normal Neanderthal specimens. They, too, already show many *sapiens*-like characters.

In all probability, then, present-day *Homo sapiens* derives from middle glacial period forms, which combined Neanderthal and *sapiens* characteristics. The two racial groups probably diverged in the Holstein interglacial period, some 250,000 years ago. It was from this stage that the typical Neanderthal derived, who died out in the last glaciation. They were thus living at the same time, though geographically separated, as other races with some Neanderthal features but on the whole more like the *sapiens* type. In the present state of research this seems, at least, a reasonable assumption.

The skull from Fontéchevade II in France, ascribed to the later Eem interglacial period, of which all we have is large portions of the parietal and frontal bones, is quite different. The forehead is steeper, the occiput very broad, and there was apparently no brow ridge. What we have here is possibly a direct (indeed the earliest) forerunner of *Homo sapiens*, a 'pre-*sapiens*' type, already in existence when Neanderthal men were still living elsewhere. The finds from Jebel Kafzeh and Amud Cave (cranial capacity calculated to be 1800 cc [240]) in Palestine may also belong to this pre-*sapiens* group.

Furthermore, there is a largely earlier group of fossil men, belonging to the *Pithecanthropus* level, now mostly called the *Homo erectus* level, after the first-discovered form. These were slightly smaller pre-humans, with a noticeably smaller cranial cavity than *Homo sapiens* – approximately 775-1200 cc, compared with 1000-1800 (average 1500) cc for the *Homo sapiens* races (see Fig. 4). In these skulls the forehead is lower than in the

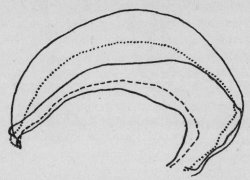

Fig. 4 Profile contours of several humans and prehumans (reading from inside): continuous line, female chimpanzee; broken line, *Australopithecus*; continuous line, *Homo* (*Pithecanthropus*) *erectus*; dotted line, Neanderthal; continuous line, present-day man. (Composite figure from Weidenreich and Le Gros Clark.)

Neanderthal type, the occipital angle sharper, the supra-orbital ridges strongly arched; there is a prognathous snout-like jaw, but relatively human dentition, a markedly receding chin, and very broad mandibular processes. Many of these characteristics recall those of the anthropoid apes of the Late Tertiary. In the Middle Pleistocene specimens from Modjokerto and Sangiran in Java (von Koenigswald's *Pithecanthropus modjokertensis*) the upper jaw has not such a horseshoe shape as in *Homo sapiens* and *Homo neanderthalensis* or in the other *Pithecanthropus* forms;

the jaw is more elongated with almost parallel rows of teeth as in the anthropoid apes. Moreover, in front of the upper canine there is a gap of 6 mm, into which no doubt a much more powerful canine (more like that of an anthropoid ape) could fit. But other *Homo erectus* (*Pithecanthropus*) skulls have only slightly developed canines. In *modjokertensis* the cranium shows traces of a sagittal ridge. On the other hand, in the specimens

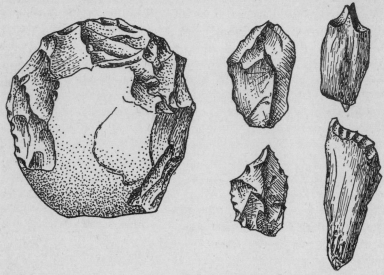

Fig. 5   Stone and bone tools of *Homo* (*Sinanthropus*) *erectus pekinensis*. The bone tools (right) are disputed because the identations may be produced by rodents. (After Pei, Black and Breuil from Oakley.)

of *Homo* (*Sinanthropus*) *erectus* from the Peking region, the forehead is generally somewhat steeper than in the Java forms, and the jaw is less prognathous. *Homo erectus mapaensis*, found in southern China (Kwangtung) in 1958, seems to be similar [28, 84]. Where portions of the leg and pelvis have been found, it is clear that all the *Homo erectus* groups walked upright. In the case of *Homo erectus pekinensis*, primitive stone tools, worked bones (although this is disputed) and the use of fire have also been discovered [18] (Fig. 5). To some degree primitive *Homo erectus* skulls unmistakably resemble those of the anthropoid apes; but by reason of the dentition and other skull characteristics, erect carriage and stage of material culture, the whole group can rank as human ('ape-men'); and we can include them under *Homo*, provided we extend the previous connotation of the term.

In addition to the eighteen or so individuals from Java and about fifty from China, including *Homo erectus lantienensis* from Shensi (without wisdom teeth), the wider *Homo erectus* group includes other finds: the mandible from Mauer near Heidelberg and two mandibles from Ternifine in Algeria (*Atlanthropus* = *Homo erectus mauretanicus* [1]), as well as the upper part of a 360,000 year old skull, *Homo erectus Leakeyi*, found in 1959 by L. S. B. Leakey in the Olduvai valley (Tanzania) together with mallet remains belonging to the Chellean culture. A mandible given the name *Telanthropus capensis* may belong to the same or an older pre-human stage still. The part of a cranium found in 1958 near Ma-pa, Kwangtung (China), from the late Mid-Pleistocene corresponds to *Homo erectus*, but shows some characteristics pointing to the *neanderthalensis* level. The skull of *Homo erectus soloensis* from Ngandong in Java from later Pleistocene deposits has a cranial cavity markedly larger than that of typical *Homo erectus*. At least in east and south-east Asia a direct derivation of *Homo neanderthalensis* from *Homo erectus* seems to be possible, therefore. *Homo rhodesiensis* from Broken Hill, Rhodesia (with excessive brow ridges), formerly ascribed to *Homo neanderthalensis*, is apparently also a race of the *Homo erectus* level. Possibly the same holds good for the Saldhana cranium.

Typical *Homo erectus* level specimens come from the lower Mid-Pleistocene (some 500,000-300,000 years ago). It is doubtful whether the Javanese, Chinese, European and African races of the *Homo erectus* level can be regarded as forerunners of the present-day Australoid, Mongoloid, Caucasoid and Negroid races [see C. Coon's conjectures, 1962, 33]. It seems more probable that man did not split up into the present-day races until the pre-*sapiens* stage.

The south-east, east and central African forms of the *Australopithecus* group show more resemblance to the apes than any

Homo erectus (*Pithecanthropus*) does. As the name ('Southern Ape') indicates, these creatures were at first thought of as anthropoid apes. Today, however, they are regarded as being extremely primitive pre-humans, forming a morphological link between the apes and man. As they fashioned very crude stone tools, they are included in the latter group. We possess skeletal remains of nearly 100 individuals, and, as these vary considerably, they have been given different names – *Australopithecus*, *Plesianthropus*, *Paranthropus*, *Zinjanthropus* – but they represent a fairly uniform stage of development. *Meganthropus* from Java probably belongs to a similar level.

In all these finds the cranial capacity is very limited, a mere 460-600 cc. The brain, then, was no larger than that of the present-day anthropoid apes (*c.* 275-680 cc). Casts were made of the cranial cavities to give an approximate picture of the configuration of the forebrain. G. W. H. Schepers [19] even attempted to distinguish certain important regions of the brain. The drawings of casts in Fig. 6 compare the forebrain of *Australopithecus* (*Plesianthropus*) with the brain of a chimpanzee and of a Negro. It shows how the human forebrain is altogether larger, and the frontal region (stippled) much more highly developed. This is the area containing the main associative centres essential for most complex thought processes. The motor area of speech (Broca's region) in particular is of paramount importance in this connection because it enables man to form concepts and to communicate. The casts do not show whether a small frontal region in *Australopithecus* can have been used as an area of speech. Another feature of the forebrain is that the temporal lobes of present-day man are much enlarged, and these also contain important associative centres.

The jaws are markedly prognathous, showing a similar snout-like projecting line as in a chimpanzee (Fig. 7). The mandibular processes were relatively broad. *Paranthropus* and *Zinjanthropus* both had a well developed bony parietal ridge, to which no doubt powerful masseter muscles were attached (Fig. 8.); and the molars were correspondingly large, in the case of *Zinjanthropus* excessively so [130]. The front teeth, i.e. the incisors and canines, on the other hand, were comparatively slightly developed – a

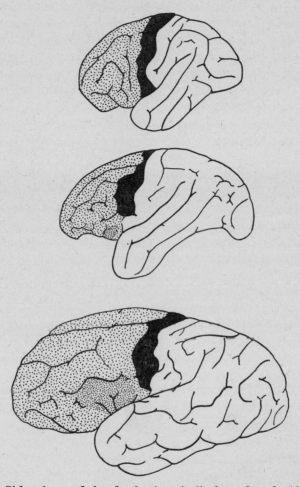

Fig. 6 Side views of the forebrain, similarly reduced. Above: a chimpanzee. Centre: a reconstructed brain, taken from a cranial cast of *Australopithecus* (*Plesianthropus*). Below: a Negro's brain. The motor precentral region is black, frontal brain (predominantly associative areas) stippled. Darker shading indicates the motor area of speech and its rudimentary stage (hypothetical) in *Australopithecus*. (Redrawn, from G. W. H. Schepers.)

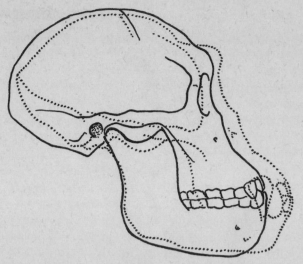

Fig. 7 Reconstructed skull of *Australopithecus transvaalensis*, compared with that of a chimpanzee (dotted line). (From Heberer, after Le Gros Clark.)

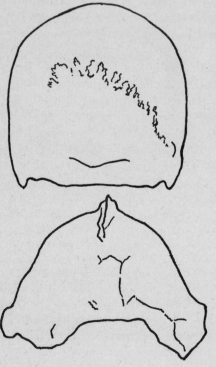

Fig. 8 Posterior view of cranium. Above: present-day man. Below: *Zinjanthropus*, showing flattened skull and parietal ridge. (After Leakey.)

typically human characteristic (though it is probable that a secondary reduction of formerly stronger foreteeth took place [120]).

The structure of foot bones and pelvis proves that Australopithecines walked erect. However, only the shovel-like ileum is hominid, the ischium is more ape-like (pongoid) [264].

L. S. B. Leakey has recently found several remains of skulls in the Olduvai district of northern Tanzania. From the description that he and his colleagues give, these combine certain Australopithecine characteristics with others belonging to the *Homo erectus* (*Pithecanthropus*) stage and some that even suggest later *Homo* forms [131-135]. The cranial capacity is put at 675-680 cc. These extremely important remains, found in association with stone tools of the Olduvai culture, have been named *Homo habilis*. But further examination will be required before *Homo habilis* can be safely ascribed in this way to the extended *Homo* group. It may also be only a new, possibly more advanced female individual of *Australopithecus* [204]. The important point is that this intermediate form probably existed about 1·8 million years ago, and before *Zinjanthropus* or at the same time. Whether remains from Bed II in Olduvai are rightly ascribed to '*Homo*' *habilis* or whether they belong to a primitive type of the *Homo erectus* level can only be decided by further finds. The South African *Telanthropus* and the Lake Chad finds may perhaps belong to the same type.

R. A. Dart [36, 37, 38] thinks it probable that Australopithecines made use not only of pebble tools but also of simple bone and horn tools. The chalk caves of Sterckfontein, where Australopithecine skulls were found, also contained unworked pebbles; these had clearly been collected, probably also for use as tools. In the Chad district, too, 100 km south of Tibesti, Australopithecine-like remains have recently been discovered [35, 127].

Our brief survey of fossil humans and pre-humans has shown a great variety of types; especially in regard to the configuration of the skull, these furnish all the morphological stages required to link present-day man with the higher apes of the Upper Tertiary. It has become increasingly probable that these 'stages' more or less followed one upon the other. As we have seen, *Homo sapiens* descended from 'pre-*sapiens*' and 'pre-Neanderthal' men. It is very probable that these types go back directly to *Homo erectus* (*Pithecanthropus*) forms. The latter may have shared common ancestors, either Australopithecines or some similar type like the new *habilis*. It is also probable that some of the different stages may have been in existence separately though at the same time – Australopithecines, for instance, may have been living in one place while the *Homo erectus* (*Pithecanthropus*) phase was already represented elsewhere by some races; or Neanderthal men may have lingered on after pre-*sapiens* types had evolved. This would make man's family tree look something like the diagram in Fig. 9. To build up a definitive picture, however, we should need many fresh finds, especially those illustrating where the tree branched out before the Australopithecines.

These numerous Australopithecine finds make the kinship between man and the apes still more obvious, but they also throw new light on the sequence of changes in the various characteristics. What chiefly distinguishes present-day man from the apes is his highly developed brain and the enormous increase in its functions. The earlier view of man's emergence had been that this continued enlargement of the brain was the primary factor which led on to his upright gait and the gradual dwindling of typically animal characteristics such as the snout-like mouth armed with large canines. But the Australopithecines demonstrate that the primary factor was quite clearly the transition from life in the trees to life on the ground; they had begun to walk erect. Their build was already human, but their brain was more or less that of an anthropoid ape, or at least not appreciably larger. But their hands were no longer used mainly for climbing; they were free not only to wield tools (as the anthropoid apes and Capuchin monkeys already do [63, 73, 75, 113, 117, 123, 200, 233]) but to fashion them, and they could now carry objects about. The brain that directed these operations gained such importance that any mutants and populations inheriting a larger brain, and especially one with a proportionately larger and more finely differentiated forebrain, were

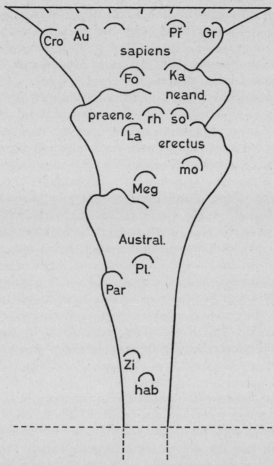

Fig. 9 Diagrammatic illustration of the phylogenetic relationships between humans and prehumans. Dotted line shows the borderline between Tertiary and Pleistocene, about 2 million years ago. Au = Aurignac race of *H. sapiens*. Austral. = *Australopithecus* level. Cro = Cromagnon race of *H. sapiens*. erectus = *Homo erectus* (= *Pithecanthropus*) level. Fo = pre-*sapiens* from Fontéchevade. Gr = Grimaldi race of *H. sapiens*. hab = '*Homo*' (*Australopithecus*) *habilis*. Ka = Neanderthal of Karmel. La = *H. erectus* from Lantien. Meg = *Meganthropus*. neand. = races of *H. neanderthalensis*. Pl = *Plesianthropus* (= *Australopithecus*). Př = *H. sapiens* from Předmost. praene = pre-Neanderthals. rh = *H. erectus rhodesiensis*. so = *H. erectus soloensis*. Zi = *Zinjanthropus*.

43

at a great advantage in the battle for existence, and were favoured by selection. It was only after the brain had improved sufficiently that the hands, now free, could be adapted to more and more uses. Besides, the hands of Australopithecines still show some ape-like traits [264].

The Australopithecines also demonstrate that we need not assume dentition in man to have been first of all of an 'animal' type and then to have grown gradually more 'human' because man began to use weapons with his hands. On the contrary, the growing number of fossil finds makes it probable that as far back as the true apes man's ancestors had a more or less human type of teeth, and the front teeth in particular were always relatively weak. These earliest creatures midway between ape and man only began to spread when they had gained an advantage over animals, that is after their hands had been freed and their brains had improved to make them better able to use and fashion tools. Of course, it is still possible that at some early stage in man's evolution some types may have developed more powerful canines such as *Homo erectus modjokertensis* possessed. This is the more probable as Le Gros Clark [138] could show that the canines of man have apparently undergone 'a regression from a more powerfully constructed canine. . . .'

A further noteworthy point is that in many of their characteristics man's ancestors remained relatively unspecialized. The Australopithecines' incisors and canines were not markedly specialized, and the molars were cusped, as they are in most omnivores. To suit their varied diet of plant and animal foodstuffs, the intestine with its related glands (e.g. the pancreas and its correspondingly adapted enzymes) must also have been rather unspecialized. The hand in man's immediate ancestors retained all five fingers of his reptile forebears and could be put to varied uses. The human hand could not have developed as it did had specialization led to the loss of some fingers, as in the ungulates, or to adaptation of the forelimbs for running or scratching, as in the dog family, the hyenas, the agoutis and others. Man's forelimbs remained unspecialized, too, in the sense that they did not grow longer in relation to his legs, as is the case with present-day apes. During its development in the uterus, the arm in man and ape is proportionately very much the same relative length. It is only after birth that an ape's arms become disproportionately long, growing faster than its trunk or legs (an instance of positive allometry). This shows that apes only acquired their relatively long arms, their 'brachiation', after the two groups had branched off from one another. We see that Cope's 'Law of the Unspecialized' – that there is an advantage in developing without much specialization – also holds good in man's case. Another factor limiting specialization is man's slow pace of development, which slowed the rate of differentiation. The physically and mentally plastic phase of youth, when experience is being stored up, thus became a good deal longer.

Man's evolution, then, has been governed by the same factors and laws as that of any animal species. The variation shown by individuals at fossil stages shows man's ancestors to have been influenced by spontaneous mutation and gene combination in the same way as any animal, and also in the same way as present-day man. And it is at least extremely likely that natural selection was likewise a factor when new and more highly developed races and genera emerged; for we see the less advanced lines of development dying out. Selection was also effective because primitive man was often threatened or in competition with his like or other hordes. Besides, when it came to fighting, hunting or otherwise seeking food, it was the most cunning and not always the most powerful who had the best chance of survival.

But though mutation and selection are 'undirected" evolution in man, as in animals, was also subject to a certain compulsion, certain rules of development. Once man's hands had been freed, those hereditary variants possessing a larger brain were at a special advantage, and as these selective processes persisted, evolution followed a consistent line. As the brain and cranium increased in size, this involved a change in many other correlated proportions of the skull. In its evolution, the brain showed all the features that characterize and determine progressive evolution: increased complexity (more brain cells), increased

45

efficiency (more division of labour and improved memorization), greater plasticity (instinctive actions replaced by free choice, generalized concepts, and actions involving planning and 'insight'). All this led to environmental independence (weapons as a protection from animal and human foes, fire and clothing to keep off cold), and increased autonomy (control of the environment).

We shall see in Chapter 4 that as higher human cultures developed, evolutionary factors that are characteristic of the animal kingdom came to mean less and less, until today there is little possibility for further physical evolution and practically none for that of the brain (cf. Chapter 5, section B).

If we now ask the question – Why did man emerge at all? – we can enumerate many potentially contributive factors; but the problem is too complex for a definite solution to be possible at the present stage. When the decisive step was taken, the advance from animality to humanity, i.e. to the Australopithecines, the forms we have already seen to be the earliest pre-humans, what mattered most was that they left the trees and began to walk on two feet with the result that their hands were now free. Their upright carriage also meant that the vertebral column supported the head more efficiently, and so the brain could increase, in particular the frontal part of the brain which contains the main centres for more complex associations and thought processes. But we know neither why nor where this process was initiated. It may possibly have taken place in Africa, as new findings of Australopithecines from the region of Lake Rudolph are dated at 3·6 million years. This means that these earliest true hominids already existed in the Late Pliocene. Nor do we know whether the first pre-humans came to live on the ground because of better food or shelter, or because they found fewer rivals there; or it may be that the climate of their district changed, the forests receded, and they were forced to take to the ground. Very probably the cooling of the entire earth during the Pleistocene epoch, which, particularly in the northern hemisphere, brought about the 'Ice Ages', may in places have led to conditions of more rigorous selection favouring the development of higher human forms, especially of *Homo sapiens*.

Besides these external conditions leading to the decisive step beyond the animal stage, there were many other factors causing the modification of animal forms to those capable of evolving further and becoming man. To appreciate this we shall have to sum up the various improvements in the structure of organisms that in the course of a long phylogeny have produced man. This will be undertaken in the following section (D). But first we must trace man's ancestry back beyond the earliest pre-humans.

We have already noted several important resemblances between the skull, brain, and pelvis of the Australopithecines and those of the anthropoid apes. At first these have led G. G. Simpson [228], the American palaeontologist, to place the former within the mammalian class as a sub-family of the family of Pongidae, i.e. the anthropoid apes, which, as well as the chimpanzee, gorilla and orang-utan, include the gibbon and the extinct sub-family of the Dryopithecines. Authorities now reckon the Australopithecines as pre-humans, and therefore as belonging to the Hominidae, because of their upright gait and their dentition, because they fashioned tools, thus marking the beginnings of a material culture, and finally because of such intermediate forms as '*Homo*' (?) *habilis*. But that is not to question their close relationship to the Tertiary anthropoid apes. We do not know what were the direct phylogenetic precursors of these interesting intermediate forms that partake of both animal and man. And we cannot as yet with certainty trace the ancestry further back to the lower apes. The reason is that the ancestral tree has different branches, and we do not yet know enough about the fossils already discovered (which represent apes belonging to many different genera) to make any definite pronouncement. But we can at least give some general indication of the probable ancestry. Authorities naturally differ about where the individual genera should be fitted in, and each new find arouses fresh discussion.

Summing up our brief consideration on fossil men and pre-humans, we can state the former existence of many different types representing nearly all the desirable links between the present-day *Homo sapiens* and Tertiary apes. This holds good especially with regard to the skulls and the size and outer structure of the brain. It becomes increasingly probable that the different levels represent a phylogenetic sequence: Australopithecines – *Homo erectus* level – preneanderthal level – presapiens level – *Homo sapiens*. Australopithecines like *Paranthropus* and *Zinjanthropus* and classical west European neanderthals have to be regarded as side branches of the main line of descent.

It also seems probable that sometimes representatives of different levels lived at the same time, but geographically separated. Australopithecines apparently still existed when *Homo erectus* types occurred in other regions, and Neanderthals still existed when presapiens types had developed in other places. The assumption that '*Homo*' *habilis* and *Zinjanthropus* lived together seems not to be proved sufficiently.

Australopithecines possibly derived from types like *Ramapithecus* (from the Siwalik hills, north India) or *Kenyapithecus* (from Kenya). Up to the present, unfortunately, only fragments of lower and upper jaws of these late Miocene or early Pliocene species are known. E. L. Simons [226] found relatively little differences between *Ramapithecus* and the Australopithecines (smaller, shorter face, simpler tooth pattern, foreteeth not so much reduced). Simons therefore includes *Ramapithecus* in the family Hominidae, although this would place the beginning of this family in the late Miocene. It would be of the utmost interest to find remains of pelvis and legs of this genus, which would indicate whether these creatures walked upright or were still climbing apes.

The structure of jaws and teeth of the African genus *Proconsul* (Miocene) also shows affinities to the Hominidae, but these species do not directly belong to the human line of descent. The same holds good for *Oreopithecus* from southern Europe (early Pliocene [95, 217]), which seems to be a representative of a special family (Oreopithecidae).

Our nearest relatives among present-day animals are the chimpanzees (*Pan*, two species), the gorillas (*Gorilla*, two species) and the orang-utan (*Pongo*, one species). They belong to the family Pongidae, which branched off from the more primitive apes of the middle Miocene. Although this consanguinity goes back about 20 million years, we have still very many characteristics in common with chimpanzees and gorillas: the same number and disposition of the bones, in particular the carpal bones (the orang-utan and all other Old World apes have an additional bone here, the *os centrale*), the structure of the frontal cavities, and the type of the eye sockets. Many other traits are also very similar: some of the main sulci in the forebrain, the musculature of the face, the convolutions of the ear, the branches of the main arteries at the arch of the aorta, the structure of the kidney (with a single papilla), the shape of the spermatozoa, the general structure of the chromosomes, the blood groups, and many other biochemical likenesses (such as albumines and γ-globulines). The structure of the chromosomes shows certain conformities, although chimpanzees and gorillas have twenty-four pairs of chromosomes and humans only twenty-three.

The earliest most primitive apes have been found in Oligocene deposits of Egypt (Fayum). The species in question were rather small (corresponding to Cope's rule). A few years ago E. L. Simons [225, 227] discovered a well-preserved skull, which he described as *Aegyptopithecus zeuxis* (Upper Oligocene). It is related to *Propliopithecus* (Lower Oligocene). These finds indicate that the line of descent of apes – together with the Hominidae included in the super-family Hominoidea (G. G. Simpson) – split off from the first monkeys (Catarrhini) very early. The genus *Parapithecus*, only represented by a lower jaw (Lower Oligocene), shows some intermediate characteristics between monkeys and lemurs [cf. A. Remane, 177]. On the other hand some lemurs from middle and upper Eocene deposits of Asia and North America, like *Pondaungia*, *Amphipithecus*, *Anaptomorphus*, *Washakius* and others, have characteristics pointing to Catarrhine monkeys. The 'Protocatarrhines' belong to the *Tarsioidea*, a lemurine group beginning in the Mid-Palaeocene (some 50 million years ago) and themselves deriving from insectivores of the Cretaceous.

As we trace man's ancestry further back into the Mesozoic and Palaeozoic eras, it naturally becomes impossible to refer to individual genera. It may therefore be enough to sketch the broad lines of derivation [30, 74, 178, 205]. The insectivores are descended from the *Pantotheria* (Trituberculata) of the Jurassic period, small mammals with an apparently primitive type of brain. It is worth remarking that in following the line of ancestry upwards, we generally come to smaller and smaller forms; this shows again Cope's rule of increasing body size in the lines of descent, in particular of mammals.

Intermediate forms between the lowest mammals and the reptiles, displaying some of the characteristics of each group, now lead back to the *Theriodontidae* of the Triassic; and these in turn derive from the *Cotylosauria*, the primitive reptile group which existed at least as far back as the Carboniferous. The cotylosaurs developed from primitive Devonian *Amphibia*, and these again from the fish order of *Crossopterygia*. Finally man's ancestry leads back with some certainty as far as the *Ostraco-dermata*, armoured fish, which first appear in the Lower Silurian but which may go back in earlier forms to the Cambrian (though corresponding Cambrian remains have been variously interpreted).

These organisms, which lived some 500 million years ago, bring us to the end of the fossil evidence for our ancestral tree, since their forerunners were most probably small soft-bodied organisms, which in general left no fossil trace. But comparative anatomy and ontogeny of present-day jawless fish (Cyclostomata) such as the lamprey offer quite definite pointers to a derivation from invertebrates. In the larval stage, lampreys show a surprising likeness in many respects to the lancelets. Such similarities include the branchial clefts and the hypobranchial groove in the mouth hole, the vascular system, notochord, spinal cord, liver, segmented muscles and odd fin. Yet these lancelets are not fishes, they are Acrania, a class of organisms without head, true eyes, kidney or vertebrae. These in their turn are related to the Tunicata, many of which are quite unlike any of the vertebrates.

Any attempt to trace our ancestry further back becomes largely speculative. It is quite probable that the Acrania-like ancestors of the vertebrates derived from primitive Hemichordata or a nearly related group of marine animals (present-day hemichordates are, for instance, the strange acorn-worms like *Balanoglossus*, which also possess the gill clefts so typical of vertebrates). These worm-like animals may have been descended from more primitive coelomates which derived from coelenterates of the gastraea type (with only two layers of tissues). Finally, all animals probably developed from unicellular organisms, from Protozoa [cf. A. Remane, 178].

But it is safe to assume that as these primitive organisms developed into vertebrates and finally into man, the above mentioned factors of progress were effective because of their selection value: namely, a tendency to increased complexity, a development of more efficient structures and functions, a greater independence of the environment, and an avoidance of excessive specialization. At each stage, then, all these animal ancestors were structurally relatively unspecialized. They were also comparatively small, and among much larger creatures from other groups and more powerful enemies they showed no sign at all of what their potential powers of development might hold for the future.

At the same time, however, the study of our probably human ancestry teaches us that the great majority of the animals we know belong to other branches of the animal phylogenetic tree from ours, and can only be 'related' to us through very remote ancestors. Carnivores, ungulates, rodents, birds, crocodiles, snakes, frogs, most fish, insects, crabs, snails and bivalves have no direct link with our animal ancestry.

D. *Stages of biological progress in man's ancestry*

We have traced man back through the profusely branching phylogenetic tree of animals. Now we will follow this line in reverse and note the successive advances from the most primitive organism down to man. It is only as we examine this sequence that we come to realize the peculiarities of man, and learn how it was that this line of descent was the only one that could have led to his emergence. As we shall be dealing with improvements within larger animal groups, we shall make no attempt to characterize earlier, and sometimes doubtful, ancestral types, but only to delineate the phylogenetic levels to which these forms belonged. Here too we shall see how progressive evolution brings about more general improvements avoiding narrower specialization and opening up the way for further advance.

It is not yet possible to offer an adequate theory concerning the origin of life on earth. However, at the present state of research it now seems very probable that life slowly developed out of inanimate matter and gradually acquired the characteristic qualities of true organisms [24, 25, 26, 55, 56, 111, 151, 166-169]. A presupposition was the natural formation of very complex organic molecules, which occur in all animals and plants, because they are indispensable for life processes (in the earthly sense): protein bodies and nucleic acids (= polynucleotids). Experiments have indicated that the components they contain probably evolved naturally. In 1953 S. L. Miller [151] succeeded in producing several complex organic compounds, including various amino acids (i.e. the components of proteins: lactic acid, urea, etc.), in a mixture of gases approximating to what it is supposed was the atmosphere when life began on the earth: hydrogen, methane, ammonia, water vapour. He did so by means of powerful electric discharges intended to correspond to the flashes of lightning taking place in the atmosphere at that time. Other researchers also used short wave rays (ultraviolet or X-rays) or high temperatures, which could be supposed to exist when the firm cover of the earth had been formed. Under conditions characteristic of the prebiological epoch of the earth they also succeeded in uniting amino acids to polypeptides and protein-like compounds (proteinoid droplets) and in producing nucleotides, which could be united to nucleic acids [55, 111, 214]. Some of the latter were even capable of incomplete reduplication. These discoveries show that the development of two characteristics of life, reproduction and 'heredity' of a specific structure, can have emerged in a natural way (cf. section B of this chapter). It is possible to assume that many of the complicated organic compounds that developed under prebiological conditions were dissolved in the primeval ocean and partly reacted with one another, perhaps mainly in separated lagoons and pools where a more concentrated 'primeval soup' arose by evaporation.

Prestages of life may then have been produced by the fact that nucleic acids like DNA, capable of reduplication, easily combine with proteins in a certain sequence determined by the sequence of bases in the DNA molecules. If such 'coacervate droplets' [Oparin, 166-169] became surrounded by a membrane (like that of the proteinoid droplets produced by Fox [55]) the basic conditions for the origin of prestages of life would have been fulfilled. But a multiplication of such prestages would have only been possible in the 'primeval soup' when the components of DNA (that is to say nucleotides or sugars, purines and pyrimidines) were present, which could build up the DNA molecule after the double helix had been divided. It seems possible that also adenosinetriphosphoric acid (ATP) and adenosinediphosphoric acid (ADP) could have arisen under prebiological conditions. These compounds, which are rich in energy, were a precondition for the origin of metabolism.

However, the origin of true organisms also implies the phylogenetic development of certain complicated cell structures: a membrane appropriate for intake of specific compounds (food), and ribosomes, needed for the formation of specific proteins. Up to the present one can only speculate about this phylogenetic development in a rather vague manner. But the important probability now exists that under prebiological conditions there was a gradual natural development of organisms from non-living material.

We must suppose that the DNA material of the prestages of life was already subject to mutations – that is to say that occasional failures in the sequence of bases occurred because of short wave rays, heat or chemical effects. This could happen in the same manner as in viruses, which can be regarded as models for such prestages of life. As a result of such mutations different variants arose, and as different environmental conditions were favourable or unfavourable for the supply of components of DNA reproduction, natural selection ensued and new 'species' developed – in other words, evolutionary radiation began.

As the environmental conditions often changed because of

53

climatic alterations, diseases, new enemies, etc., it was advantageous to produce as great a number of hereditary variants as
possible, in order that at least some variants had a chance of
surviving. This necessity led to the 'invention' of sexuality,
which had already emerged in some bacteria and most protozoa. When fertilization takes place, two germ cells or two uni-
cellar individuals fuse to form one common nucleus, thus
bringing about new combinations of their hereditary factors.
As the chromosomes themselves do not fuse, after sexual union
the nuclei contain double the number of chromosomes. This
would mean, however, that the offspring of these diploid forms
would receive a fourfold set, the next generation eightfold, and
so on. A process of reduction-division (mitosis) had to intervene
to prevent this intolerable steady increase in the number of
chromosomes. In this case the daughter cells receive not half-
chromosomes obtained by splitting but whole ones after their
arrangement in pairs (in each case the homologous chromosomes from the father's and mother's sides). Sexuality and
reduction by division have proved such advantageous 'devices'
for unicellular creatures that every higher organism has retained
them. This means that in most cases natural selection weeded
out all variants in which the process of fertilization did not
follow a successful course.

Many of our human characteristics, then, go back to the
lowest levels of unicellular organisms. It would take too long to
enumerate all the others that are found in protozoa and retained
at every stage up to man – for instance, specific enzymes for
converting food substances, the use of oxygen to release energy,
i.e. respiration, the formation of different cell-organelles like
the mitochondria, which contain respiratory enzymes and by
reason of the complicated processes of energy conversion within
them might be called the 'power stations' of the cells.

As simpler multicellular animals came into being, many new
constructions and functions developed; and, as some of them
proved of advantage, they have been retained even by the most
advanced organisms. It proved to be advantageous for a
division of labour to take place by the specialization of cells, so
that nervous, glandular, reproductive or motor functions could

be intensified. This may be exemplified by the gradual improvement of nerve and sense cells which already exist in coelenterates (like polyps, jellyfish, corals, etc.).

It was of great advantage when some cells increased their ability to react to chemical optical or tactile stimuli and became capable of transmitting excitations to other cells by way of long cell processes. This enabled the animal to react not only at the point of stimulation. Once a stimulus was received, groups of muscles elsewhere could be brought into play – for instance, on an optical stimulus the animal could move to avoid some approaching enemy. Then certain patterns of excitation could develop in the course of phylogeny, which on the average led to an appropriate response to useful or harmful stimuli in the environment (deriving, for instance, from food or enemies). Thus reflexes arose in lowest animals. This useful kind of reaction and the corresponding structures were retained up to the human level (cf. Chapter 3, section B). Nerve cells also developed the important faculty of retaining traces of past excitations, and these engrams formed the basis for memory. Experiences could thus be stored up.

All these functions could operate much more efficiently after central nervous systems had been developed (at first in primitive worms). All the diverse excitations were combined and balanced in these systems, with the result that a suitable response could be initiated to each special situation by exciting appropriate muscles or glands. It was also of quite paramount importance that the sense organs reacted in such a manner that very different stimuli in the environment (light rays, sound waves, tactile, chemical and heat stimuli, etc.) became translated into a uniform 'language of excitation' operable at great speed (30 cm-129 m per second) in the nerves. This is how nature made such centralization possible. In the course of animal phylogeny the structure of the most highly developed central nervous system, the brain, became more and more efficient as increasing division of labour took place and an increasing number of different functions could be assigned to individual regions in it.

A similar important device was the evolution of smooth and

E

striated muscle cells. In this case specialized structures considerably increased the normal contractile power of cells. This specialization, which was important in the development of organs of locomotion, heart, intestinal peristalsis, etc., also goes back to the coelenterata. This phylum also first developed a sac-like intestine for storing and digesting foodstuffs. Moreover, several of the lower worms, for example the Nemertea (ribbon worms), Nematoda (round worms), Rotatoria (rotifers) and others, added an important feature, the anal opening, which allowed food substances to pass continuously through the body. Thus division of labour could follow, and the different parts of the alimentary canal could be specialized to break up foodstuffs, produce digestive enzymes, absorb digested material, and eliminate undigested matter. This method by which foodstuffs are passed through the entire length of the body (by no means the only one, for they can also be absorbed through the skin) also proved a success and has been retained right up to man himself.

The system of blood vessels carrying fluid to every part of the body and containing food substances, breakdown products, oxygen, hormones, and so on, is another important phylogenetic 'invention'. It probably originated at the level of the more advanced worms, or rather their immediate predecessors, for we find it not only in the *Annelida* but also the somewhat more primitive *Nemertea*. The worms, too, developed *nephridia*, excretory organs which are forerunners of the tubules that later joined up to form the kidney in vertebrates.

There are other features also which characterize almost all more advanced animals and man and developed at the stage of the multicellular invertebrates. These forms already display bilateral symmetry and so possess many organs in duplicate. Man's two eyes, two ears, the two halves of the nose, two hemispheres of the forebrain, two lungs, kidneys, gonads, and pairs of limbs, are cases in point. There are advantages in this kind of arrangement and it has survived phylogenetically, for the function remains more or less assured even if one part should fail. Besides, two eyes help in appreciating distance and two ears in localizing the source of sound. This duplicate construction is by no means so much a matter of course as it might at first appear; for there are several important unpaired organs such as the intestine, liver, spleen, uterus, descending aorta; moreover, metazoa of asymmetrical build exist, possessing few paired or identical organs – for instance many of the rotifers, bryozoans and ascidians.

This brings us to a further universal feature found in the lowest metazoa and still present in man. All these organisms are 'individuals of a higher order' in that their tissue contains cells leading an independent life, as for instance the leucocytes and lymphocytes do. Such cells move about independently, they are chemicotactically attracted by certain substances and consume bacteria or the debris of tissues. The spermatozoa propel themselves like the flagellata and they are chemically attracted by certain substances, and independently fertilize the ovum.

Some organs and functions first appearing among the earliest vertebrates, the more primitive fish, have been retained – though mostly in a largely improved version – and are also found in man. A few outstanding examples may suffice. We have noted that, thanks to the numerous palaeontological finds, the phylogeny can be traced here in at least its main outlines. We know for instance that the following organs in man derive from primitive fish: the brain, consisting of five functionally differentiated sections, the spinal cord, vertebral column, eyes, heart, liver, pancreas, spleen, thyroid gland and other structures. More advanced fish developed a bony skull, teeth (cutaneous ossifications covered with enamel, homologous to placoid scales), ribs, a labyrinth containing three semicircular canals with sense organs receptive to stimuli of movement and gravity and sound, the mesonephros, fore and hind limbs, and other features. From the amphibians man has inherited the inner ear (Organ of Corti), tympanic membrane, lungs, double auricles of the heart, the division of the anterior extremities into upper arm, ulna with radius, and carpus with fingerbones, a corresponding leg bone arrangement, the development of the scapula, clavicle, etc. And our reptile ancestors developed the metanephros, ureter, alveoli, the amniotic membrane protecting the embryo, the predominance of the forebrain and other features.

57

Homo sapiens

Many of man's component structures first developed with the primitive mammals (probably during the late Triassic and the Jurassic). These include the hair, the stratified cortex of the forebrain with its functional subdivision into regions and areas, an altered accommodation of the crystalline lens by slackening of the suspensory ligaments, the three ossicles of the ear, elastic intervertebral discs, a divided ventricle, mammary glands, and so on. Above all, these mammals became warm-blooded, with regulatory mechanisms allowing all the systems of organs to function far more intensively. The insectivores (dating from the Upper Cretaceous) developed the placenta, an important organ for nourishing the embryo, and the two double vaginae found in the lower mammals (and in reptiles) were merged to form one homogeneous organ.

Our simian ancestors (from the Oligocene onwards) developed teeth with a structure typical of man's, parrallel forward-facing eye sockets separated from the temporal lobes by a bony partition, a single uterus (the lemurs still have two), ears like man's, freely rotating arms, and correspondingly mobile hands for grasping, directly controlled from the forebrain by way of the pyramidal tracts, a pattern of sulci resembling man's, etc. Above all, the gestation period became relatively long and youth a period of prolonged development. Monkeys and apes nursed their young for more than a year and had a social structure in many respects similar to that of more primitive human groups. The prolonged phase of youth was particularly important because it is the phase of gathering experience, and it thus formed the basis on which man's education became a possibility.

The specific characteristics of man's immediate ancestors, the more unspecialized anthropoid apes of the late Tertiary and the prehumans, have already been discussed in section C of this chapter. The main new feature was an upright carriage and the structural alterations that went with this. The pelvis that supports the viscera grew scoop-shaped and the thorax flatter. The scapula came to be sited further back than in monkeys, and this made the arms more mobile. The foot became adapted for walking, the legs grew longer, and the shank muscles more powerful. But the structural changes that made walking easier limited the expansion of the birth canal in the pelvis. To compensate for this, the young were now born into the world at an earlier stage of development, in what might be called a late embryonic state. Now that the hands were free, these completely helpless creatures could be held in the arms. Above all, the vertebral column was held in a more upright position and so afforded the head a greater measure of support. This meant that the brain and in particular the important associative areas of the temporal and frontal lobes could expand [247]. This facilitated the origin and extension of the motor areas of speech, which are of such vital importance for cultural development (cf. Chapter 4). Finally, although there was a relative increase in birthweight, the period of youth was also prolonged [175, 231].

We have dealt at some length, though not of course exhaustively, with these successive characteristic features to show that we can date vital new structures and functions from many of the earlier stages leading up to man, stretching right back as far as the protozoa and their prestages. Without these acquisitions, man's evolution would never have taken place. These successively multiplying 'devices' were not only possibilities of phylogenetic change; they were alterations that brought advantage without involving narrow specialization or hindering further possible progress. As natural selection automatically operates in favour of such structural advantages, the main line of development culminating in man followed what was largely a necessitated course. This is an important point; for the emergence of new forms as a result of undirected mutation, as well as the 'chance' conditions of selection in each case, might suggest that man was the outcome of a succession of 'chance' happenings. But on the contrary, we find that it is evolutionary laws that have determined his emergence. In essence, the word 'chance' is used to mean the cooperation of causally determined components, a cooperation too complex to be adequately analysed and so fully comprehended in its stages. As Voltaire so wisely wrote in his *Philosophie générale*, 'le hasard n'est rien. Nous avons inventé ce mot pour exprimer l'effet connu de toute cause inconnue.'

E. *Monkeys and apes as indispensable prestages of man*

It remains to examine why the line of descent that led to man followed one particular course, a course we can trace, sometimes in detail, sometimes in more general outline, back to apes and monkeys. Other highly developed creatures exist besides man, with good sense organs and comparatively complex central nervous systems – insects, for instance, or cephalopods, birds, carnivores, ungulates, and others. Why have the phylogenetic lines that produced these groups never led up to anything resembling man? The answer is comparatively simple. The insects were too small – too small, that is, to develop a brain large enough, with enough cells, to function as man's does. They remained relatively small because their skin skeleton could not have been sufficiently enlarged, their tracheal system could not have supplied any large body with oxygen nor their open vascular system have been adapted to such a body. Marine cephalopods, with their tentacles and predatory habits, were too narrowly specialized. Besides, warm-blooded animals were the only ones whose metabolism operated intensively enough for anything like man's mental activities to be possible. Birds, too, were unsuitable, because their legs and wings were adapted to locomotion and could not grow into hands that could fashion tools. Among the mammals the only possible groups were those with particularly advanced brains, with anterior limbs that could develop into just such hands – in other words, the monkeys and apes.

In his *Ideen zur Philosophie der Geschichte der Menschheit* (1784-91) [87] G. Herder clearly recognized man's distinguishing characteristics as distinct from those of the animals: a large brain, good eyes and ears, manual dexterity, speech, a prolonged period of youth and therefore of learning, and reduced, though still existing, instincts. Furthermore, he saw the causal connections between these characters quite clearly. In Book 4 he wrote: 'Man by being forced to walk erect acquired free and skilful hands, the instruments of the most delicate operations, and of incessant feeling after new and clear ideas. . . . His reason and improvement begin from speech. . . .' Charles Darwin, Thomas

Huxley, Ernst Haeckel and others have also discussed these same characteristics, and in men's minds today they are still essential attributes that raise man above the level of the highest animals. Let us now examine briefly why the development of these particular features was promoted in monkeys and apes.

Monkeys are descended from arboreal lemurs. They began, therefore, with a body structure entirely adapted to climbing, which was then successively improved. During a period of perhaps over 50 million years, during the whole Tertiary, natural selection helped to adapt them more and more to arboreal life – a circumstance that lies at the root of many of man's distinguishing characteristics. Monkeys are climbing animals; and when at rest they sit erect. With their opposable thumb they can grasp branches and pull their bodies up and along by their arms. This being so, natural selection within this order led to their anterior limbs remaining firmly attached to the trunk by the clavicle and the scapula (whereas carnivores and ungulates lost their clavicles in the course of their evolution). The anterior limbs thus became movable in any direction with considerable rotation at shoulder, elbow and wrist. The hand, however, remained relatively 'primitive', i.e. retained all five fingers and did not reduce their number (as for instance the ungulates did). This made a firm grip possible. But at the same time this flexible hand developed into a highly specialized organ, as it received direct impulses from the forebrain by way of the pyramidal tract. So monkeys and apes use their hands in many different ways, to climb, to catch their prey, to pluck leaves, flowers and fruit, to break open fruits, to convey food to the mouth, sometimes to drink from (by dipping the hand in water and then licking it), to clean the body, to help in defence, to hold their young in their arms, to build their nests, to use simple tools, to throw stones, to beat about with a stick, to poke with a straw at a white ant's nest, etc. Put to such varied uses, the hand naturally developed as an organ of touch; for species or variants were at an advantage if they possessed more sense organs and a finer network of nerves in the fingers and larger centres in the cerebral cortex responsive to tactile stimuli.

With hands put to so many uses, it was necessary to rest with the weight on the pelvis and hind limbs, and therefore to sit in an upright position. This led to the development of physical proportions and an arrangement of many of the organs such as is found in man. In section D we have already referred to the increase in cranium and brain, especially the forebrain, the relative breadth of the thorax and the enlarged ileum of the pelvis. We may now add to these the localization of the lacteal glands in the breasts, the position of the embryo head down in the uterus now made firmer by the cervix uteri. This position was only advantageous if the number of young at birth was normally limited to one. Moreover, it was much easier to transport one offspring clinging to its mother through the branches than to look after a number at once.

These improved conditions now allowed of a longer period of growth for the embryo and so a relatively considerable increase in the size of the animal at birth. This was combined with a slower rate of growth after birth. Besides, selection no doubt also independently favoured this slackening in the rate of growth and prolonged the phase of youth, because this offered the advantage of a longer period of learning and storing up experiences.

Moreover, climbing and leaping adroitly among the tree-tops required the ability to judge distance. So natural selection operated in favour of an enlarged binocular field of vision with both eyes looking approximately parallel.

In several mammalian lines of descent, for instance in horses, dogs, cats and bears, the brain increased in complexity and size, owing to the advantage of reacting with more versatility and remembering more. During the evolution from lemurs to apes, the forebrain was specially marked out for improvement, because versatility of motion was especially useful in a life among the branches (among the rodents, for instance, the tree-dwelling squirrel also developed a brain almost twice the size of that of the rat, an animal of the same weight that lives on the ground). There was also a corresponding decrease in the rigidity of the hereditary instinctive reactions. Moreover, monkeys and apes ate a variety of foods – mostly flowers, fruits, young leaves, insects, small vertebrates – and had to spend most of the day seeking them. This fact and the intensive spontaneous activity of their brain led to the development of a highly exploratory behaviour, which in turn brought them a rich harvest of experiences.

Their exploratory behaviour and ability to imitate one another have sometimes led whole colonies of monkeys to adopt new habits. We shall see (Chapter 4, section A) that an alteration in non-inherited behaviour brought about by tradition is one of the decisive factors in man's cultural development.

So the monkeys and apes – and only these higher primates – had sufficient special characteristics that fitted them to be man's forerunners. We have seen that by coming down to live on the ground they freed their hands to use tools, and this led to the evolution of the Hominidae, i.e. man in the wider sense of the word. We do not yet know why this change in living pattern took place (cf. p. 46). It may be that the increase in body size had some influence. This process has affected almost every group of mammals (according to Cope's rule), and is probably governed by the selective advantages in competition and combat enjoyed by the larger variants or species. But larger animals are less suited to climbing and leaping among the tree-tops. As they grow in bulk their muscular efficiency increases by the square of their dimensions, but their body weight (which they have to raise or transport) by the cube. So the gorillas, with their huge bulk, keep largely to the ground, and the males even sleep there. The foot, with its fairly firm and elongated sole, could easily become adapted to walking. When they are on the ground, anthropoid apes such as gibbons, chimpanzees and gorillas often walk erect, and the mountain gorilla's foot, indeed, is already similar to man's.

Abandoning life in the trees must therefore be reckoned as one of the most important steps towards humanity. As W. La Barre wittily expressed it, 'Man's original sin was not so much the eating of the fruit of the tree as in climbing down from it' [128]. The anthropoid apes had already acquired some use of simple tools; and once on the ground it was useful to improve this ability. Here, natural selection was bound to favour variants with a better constructed forebrain. At first it was merely that some portions of the brain, as a result of mutation, increased the number of cells by an additional division. Then these additional portions were able to take over new functions. Processes of this sort (which I have called postintrogression) appear to have occurred several times during the phylogeny of vertebrates. Amphibians, for instance, have quite a large forebrain in relation to the rest, but its functions have remained relatively unimportant. Only the later developed reptiles filled this enlarged part with more functions [184].

When man emerged it was largely the temporal and frontal areas of the forebrain that increased. A special temporal area, Broca's region, increased and here, too, a postintrogression of functions took place. It received excitations from adjacent areas, especially those associated with sound memory, lip movement and the associative and impulse-giving centres of the frontal lobes; and so it was predestined, as it were, to become the motor area of speech. As speech conferred enormous advantages, natural selection no doubt operated very intensively to improve this region. Later on, in the basal cortex of the frontal brain a region developed which is peculiar to man. In *Homo erectus (Sinanthropus)* it shows only shallow folds, but in *Homo sapiens* it is so much enlarged that deep convolutions resulted. Here, additional functions that distinguish man are located, giving impulses and initiating and maintaining the sequence of thoughts – in other words, functions that are important for planning of actions and creative achievements [232].

CHAPTER THREE

Man's mental evolution

A. *The phylogenetic continuity*

We have noted already (Chapter 2, section B) that mental processes correspond to or are identical with physiological processes taking place within the brain (or also the nerves and sense organs). It seems most probable that the phylogenetic mental development from lower to higher animals and then on to man ran parallel with that of the nerves, sense organs and brain. But as no reliable criteria for mental evolution of animals exist, we are obliged to rely on assumptions based on analogy. What we can deduce from these, however, in some aspects amounts to virtual certainty [181, 195, 196].

Strictly speaking, a man can vouch for only those conscious processes that take place within himself. For any other person, all he has to go upon is sensations aroused in himself through light rays, sound waves and the touch of that person – that is to say, by catching sight of him, hearing what he says, by tactile awareness through contact with him, and also by imaginative processes (the outcome of these sensations) in which all these phenomena combine to make up the other's reality. As we human beings possess a language of communication, we are able to state that the other person has such sensations and ideas as we ourselves have. But we cannot be absolutely certain of this. For instance, we do not know if he sees colours exactly as we do or if he sees at least some shades of colour differently. Doctors testing the sight of adults very often discover weaknesses of this sort in the differentiation of colour and even complete red-green colour blindness. And it is rather more doubtful whether another person's enjoyment of a certain piece of music corresponds to our own, or whether he possibly has similar impulses of volition to ours. We know still less about whether a man of some completely different race – a bushman or a Papuan, perhaps – shares our kind of sensations and mental images. Yet we do not doubt that he does experience phenomena, because even in a primitive language he can tell us about them.

But if we go on to ask ourselves whether we can ascribe sensations, mental images and feelings to a higher animal (an ape or a dog), we are not so certain. We consider it very unlikely that such animals are automata, reacting only to certain light or sound waves without really seeing or hearing. But what are our criteria for assuming that conscious processes take place in animals?

So far as apes and monkeys are concerned we have very much the same anatomical structure as theirs. Our bones, muscles and inner organs, especially our sense organs, nerves and brains, and the structure of tissues and cells are all very similar in construction, and therefore very similar, and partly identical in function as well. Excitations of the brain and sense organs are matched by oscillations of electric potentials exactly similar to those which in man are accompanied by conscious processes. And as these processes function in the same way, the behaviour of animals, their reactions to food, enemies, companions, and so on, and their facial expression of joy, pain, rage and the like, often strongly resemble man's. Moreover, these higher animals have good memories and are capable of abstracting and generalizing. Anthropoid apes, as well as some monkeys, can find out for themselves how to use tools and are able to act according to foresight. When they are planning an action, apparently chains of images of possible future actions are running through their mind before they carry out the action by innervating the corresponding muscles [113, 117, 122, 123, 200, 276]. Given all this varying extent of identity with man's behaviour, it seems quite safe to assume that mental processes similar to man's exist and that the sensations and some mental images and feelings are partly identical with his; indeed, scientists and philosophers from classical times onwards have rarely doubted this intepretation.

But when we turn to vertebrates less like ourselves, such as frogs or fish, are we as certain about the analogy with mental processes, with sensations, mental images and feelings? Is it possible that their reactions to sensory stimulation should perhaps be nothing but 'reflexes', their 'spontaneous' reactions merely instinctive movements without any corresponding conscious processes? To answer such questions we must deal more fully with the above-mentioned criteria in the fields of anatomy, histology and behaviour. Let us first trace the evolution of the nervous structures in animals back through simpler and yet simpler forms regardless of the special human line of descent.

It might be assumed that conscious processes are only possible where a cerebral cortex exists. Many physiologists and psychologists today hold the view that it is here, in this most complex and specialized area of man's brain, that the excitations occur which are paralleled by conscious processes. But the development of this forebrain cortex is confined to mammals. In reptiles (a class of animals from which mammals evolved in the Late Triassic) it is still at a rudimentary stage, and fishes (from which reptiles are descended by way of primitive amphibians) have no cortex at all and their forebrain is mainly a smelling centre. Their midbrain is the most important part for associative processes and is quite different in structure from the mammalian forebrain. Does this mean that fish are incapable of conscious processes? After all, the ganglion cells that constitute their brain are built in a similar manner to those of the more advanced animals, and the structure of the sense cells of the eye in the form of rods and cones is also similar to that of the higher vertebrates. And their nervous excitations are accompanied by similar action potentials. Fish are capable of learning shapes and sounds, and they may retain them over long periods (for two years and eight months in the case of a carp trained in our institute by W. Engels). Like men, they are subject to different optical illusions and also to those brought about by simultaneous colour contrast [50, 88, 89, 90]. During training, if tasks that they have hitherto willingly performed are made harder and finally impossible for them, they may show signs of neurosis, just as a child does when faced with school work that is beyond him. All this suggests that with fish, and so with all the vertebrates, it is relatively safe to deduce the existence of conscious processes, at least sensations, memories and accompanying feelings. And surely most of those who have made experimental studies of the behaviour of fish for some time would agree with this finding. Very probably, then, consciousness is not necessarily connected with the presence of a cortex or a forebrain.

But what of the invertebrates, the insects, crabs, spiders, snails, cephalopods, worms, and so on? They too have extremely complex central nervous systems and sense organs, but these are differently constructed from those of man, and man's behaviour cannot serve as a guide to theirs. The nerve cells, however, and some of the sensory cells that receive and transform the stimuli, resemble those of the vertebrates. So do the nerve impulses, which can be traced by means of cathode ray oscillographs from the brain or eyes of invertebrates. Experiments have shown that cephalopods, crabs and bees are capable of learning visual shapes and they can master three or four optical tasks simultaneously [220, 278]. Bees can be deceived, too, as men are, by simultaneous colour contrasts. When trained to pick out dishes of sugar-water placed on blue paper, they later flew towards grey rings on yellow paper, apparently because they 'saw' the grey colour next to the yellow as complementary [124]. In view of findings like this, coupled with many observations of various other species, it seems extremely probable that behaviour in insects is accompanied by conscious processes at least in the form of sensations and memories, and in all likelihood feelings as well.

If we consider such conclusions by analogy to be valid, we must apply them also to other invertebrates with basically similar, if perhaps more simple, nervous systems and sense organs, which are also capable of learning and retaining [244]. This would mean that on the strength of this more and more vague but quite probable analogy, we could claim that in principle conscious phenomena are possible in all cases where an animal has a nervous system and sense organs. This includes every multicellular organism except the sponges. Yet even the lowest metazoa, the coelenterata, whose nerve cells and sensory cells are diffusely distributed as a network, have been shown capable of diverse sense reactions and possibly also of memory. However, we cannot postulate a 'stream of consciousness' or anything like human 'self-awareness', but at best isolated sensations or images.

'Sense reactions', that is to say reactions to optical, chemical, tactile, thermal and other stimuli, are displayed not only by the lower worms (e.g. microscopic rotifers, gastrotrichs and primitive flatworms), but in a similar way also by unicellular organisms (Protozoa, Protophyta, Bacteria). Among the most highly specialized protozoa, the ciliates, we also find a 'sensibilization' after repeatedly released excitations. It has even been asserted that the ciliates possess some kind of primitive memory; but the claim is based on experiments that can be otherwise interpreted. It is not impossible, however, to ascribe to unicellular organisms very primitive non-associative sensations or some kind of 'protophenomena'. But it must be owned that such deductions, based on the structure and behaviour of these protozoa, are very vague indeed.

An entirely different train of thought, however, brings some corroboration to this reasoning. Throughout a long phylogeny all new species have emerged from previous ones very slowly as a result of mutations, innumerable gene combinations and selective processes. It is almost inconceivable that anything so radically novel as sensations, mental images and other 'psychological' phenomena should have broken in upon this continuous process of development. To be more precise, using the language of epistemology, it seems unbelievable that certain laws of parallelity, existing independently of the causal laws, should suddenly have emerged as an accompaniment to a certain stage in development. It is important in this context to bear in mind that not all psychical processes can be regarded as additional physiological processes, for they show no causal connection with the 'material' processes but appear simultaneously ('instantaneously') with (or parallel to) the excitations of the brain. There is absolutely no temporal difference. It is therefore more reasonable to assume that all matter is primarily 'protopsychic' [arguments for this assumption are discussed in more detail in my *Biophilosophy*, 195, and an additional paper, 199]. In line with such panpsychistic and identistic theories as have been elaborated by B. Spinoza, Th. Fechner, W. Wundt and others, we may then assume that by integration of matter in such complex systems as protein and nucleic acid molecules and in nerve cells and sensory cells, the elementary protopsychic qualities combine to form elementary sensations. For anything like a stream of conscious processes, however, a much more complex nervous system had first to be evolved. And 'self-consciousness' in the human sense presupposes a brain complex enough to have developed a conception of its own 'self'.

But considerations of this sort belong to the realm of speculation, and we do not propose to follow them up here. What should emerge from the above statements is the reasonable assumption that within the animal kingdom the phylogenetic evolution of sense organs, nerves and brains has been accompanied by a gradual psychical development leading step by step to its culmination in man's mental capabilities.

We shall now return to the world of facts. Basing our observations on the activity of nerve cells and sensory cells, we shall consider the growing complexity in the behaviour of organisms from the simplest creatures up to man. This will enable us to appreciate what part of our inheritance we share with the animals and what aspects of our behaviour may be characterized as typically human.

B. *Stages in the development of nervous reactions*

Leaving aside any psychological phenomena that may accompany them, we can establish a scale of behaviour patterns among animals ranging from relatively simple reactions to more and more complex and versatile ones allowing a more advantageous behaviour. It is characteristic of this scale that an increasing number of processes became inserted between stimulus and response. These are especially the processes of abstraction and generalization, associations relating to the future, planned actions, and actions that involve insight.

However complex the biochemical process behind it, a reaction may be termed 'simple' if it concerns a single cell – when, for instance, a unicellular organism contracts on receiving some marked tactile stimulus or moves in a directed manner in response to light stimulus (phototaxis).

The reflexes already occurring in the lowest animals possessing nerve cells are of more importance for the understanding of man's pecularities, for such reflexes also control many essential reactions in higher animals and humans. These processes are fixed by heredity and are largely invariable. A stimulus from outside or within leads to impulses moving along hereditarily determined nerve tracts (sensory nerves) to some nerve centre – in insects perhaps a pectoral ganglion, in vertebrates the spinal cord or some area in the brain, and here the stimulus is switched to other tracts (the motor nerves) mostly leading to muscles, the contraction of which represents the response to the stimulus – for instance, turning the animal in the direction of that stimulus.

The important point is that these reflex actions are normally useful to the individual and that they are not voluntary but automatic, a result of the inherited pattern of the nervous system. In the course of the animal's phylogeny mutations and new gene combinations often introduced alterations and new combinations of reflex pathways, but only those that proved advantageous were retained, because natural selection operated to eliminate unfavourable ones.

It is reflexes that both govern and safeguard the lives of the lower animals to a large extent. In unusual circumstances the reflex response to a situation may often harm or destroy the individual; but that is of little importance, for natural selection is concerned only with average usefulness for the species as a whole. A useful reflex action causes many animals, moths for instance, to move towards light and so to discover the way out of their dark retreats or to find light-coloured blossoms for food. If this light comes from a flame, however, the moth is burnt up as a result of its instinctive reaction. Yet this so seldom happens (especially before the advent of man) that such positive phototaxis has remained one of the advantageous hereditary qualities for these species.

F

Homo sapiens

During the first few weeks of life, most of man's movements are purely reflex ones: clinging on with arms and legs, sucking, swallowing, urinating, sneezing, crying, and so on [51, 176]. As an adult, too, he normally makes many reflex movements: swallowing, sneezing, wincing when his skin is touched, contracting his pupils at a strong light, as well as copulation, birth and much besides. Some are clearly accompanied by conscious processes, others – contraction of the pupils, for instance – are not. In each case it depends on whether the excitation reaches the central nervous system, especially the forebrain cortex, to which the conscious processes correspond.

But many reflexes are not absolutely rigid. Excitation from some other external or internal source may modify it. In some cases the normal ('unconditioned') stimuli may combine with others of a different kind ('conditioned' ones). But only after this has happened many times, the non-normal stimulus may come to occasion the reflex action (a 'conditioned reflex').

When more complex behaviour follows a similar type of rigid and hereditarily determined course in response to a definite stimulus, we talk of instincts. Besides the normal reflexes the so-called 'taxes' are involved, i.e. reflex movements orientated by the stimulus [142, 248]. Instincts are like reflexes in causing reactions of general advantage to the species, though sometimes, in abnormal situations, not to the individual concerned. Three distinct phases can be distinguished in most instinctive responses, for instance in a butterfly in search of food: (1) The animal becomes restless (in this case because hungry), and flies about at random (the phase of appetitive behaviour). (2) It is not necessary to suppose that it is 'looking' specifically for blossoms. But any small distinct bright spot, in a meadow for instance, can act as an inherited 'releaser' and attract its flight. If a second 'releaser' is added, a scent of blossoms, the butterfly settles on these and extends its proboscis (first consummatory act). (3) Only when the proboscis comes into contact with nectar does this chemical stimulus release reflex movements of sucking and swallowing (second consummatory act). Throughout this whole instinctive process, then, the animal may not be acting from experience or with any plan at all. If it flies about

72

long enough, it is very probable to stumble upon some 'releaser'. And the outcome of this 'appetitive' flight differs with the diverse external stimuli it encounters. In every case, what releases the direction of its flight is some specific characteristic or the cumulative effect of a small number of these (a colour contrasting with green, and a definite shape with certain limits of size). This being so, the natural stimuli can be replaced experimentally by very simplified dummies.

The nerve tracts, and presumably also special brain structures excited by a 'releaser', are inherited features, and this explains why instincts have a rigid quality. But instinctive behaviour often varies because the taxes are guided by the environment. Alterations are also effected by influences of memory. Even the consummatory act is not absolutely rigid because of a feedback system: the actions are guided by steady control of sense organs (sucking, for instance, only begins after the sense cells of the proboscis have reported to the brain that nectar is met with).

Another necessary element in instinctive behaviour is a certain 'mood' – one of hunger, mating or the like – induced by the appropriate physiological conditions (e.g. hormone secretion). The mating mood may suppress moods that arouse the search for food. A moth's flight, for instance, may be orientated by the sexual scent of the female, not by the perfume of the blossoms.

Instincts mainly guide all animal life; and it is only with the most advanced mammals that we find instinctive processes partly replaced by actions of choice. But man, too, has retained many varied instincts, which determine to a far-reaching degree his feeding, mating, care of young, family and social cohesion, hierarchical patterns, and so on.

His sexual behaviour best illustrates how these non-rational, inherited instincts affect man. In puberty he begins to experience hitherto unknown positive emotions in relation to the opposite sex, and holding hands or stroking, to which he had been indifferent, now seem pleasant and desirable. Particular characteristics of figure and behaviour operate here as releasers, and we call the most attractive combination of them 'beautiful'.

But this ideal of beauty is based on relatively few of such characteristics; to prove that this is so, we have only to look at very simple experimental models – in this case a few strokes outlining either the human body or even the face alone. If these few lines catch the essential characteristics – for female Europeans or Indians the slender waist, for instance, and the ampler curves of the thighs, – this 'model' will have a similar effect as a releaser, and here too we usually make a sharp distinction between what is 'beautiful' and the reverse [cf. B. Rensch, 192]. Of course aesthetic characteristics such as linear rhythm, hair colour and so on may also be important, but they are not decisive factors.

Such instincts play a much larger part in most men's lives than is apparently recognized. 'Primitive' peoples are not the only ones whose actions are mainly governed by such drives – to eat or drink something pleasant, to possess beautiful women, to tend children, to achieve a certain rank in the community and so on. With regard to the great importance of these instincts we shall discuss them more fully in Chapter 5. However, man has fewer instincts than most higher animals, and they can be modified and even suppressed by actions based on reason.

As we know from experience and can deduce from the behaviour of higher animals, positive feelings (feelings of delight) are attached to the satisfaction of instincts (usually from the moment when the releaser has taken effect), and especially to the consummatory acts. This ensures the necessary course of action. In view of what we have already said about analogies with accompanying mental phenomena, it seems very probable that instinctive processes in lower animals 'down' to the coelenterata are also accompanied by positive feelings. Furthermore, as feelings do not exist independently but are properties of sensations, we may even assume that they are also present in unicellular organisms.

We have now to consider actions governed by choice. These are based on memory, and are consequently quite unlike inherited reflexes and instincts. Memory also presupposes the inheritance of a nervous system, but the experiences stored up have to be acquired by each individual during the course of its life.

Almost every type of multicellular organism 'down' to the coelenterata has been proved capable of memory. At its simplest this amounts to no more than sensibilization and habituation – that is to say, faster or better reactions (as the impulses are conveyed along specific nerve tracts) in response to an oft-repeated stimulus. We noted at the beginning of this chapter that this lowest form of memory can be possibly ascribed even to unicellular organisms (ciliates). Associative memory is of greater importance. Here two oft-repeated responses, either simultaneous or in immediate succession, come to be associated together until what evokes the one arouses the other as well. The histological basis of association lies in the close contact of nerve fibres of different cells within a central nervous system. Such synaptic interrelations may exist either directly or through intermediate nerve cells. In such a way excitations will spread from one cell to another. Psychological components correspond to the course of excitations. When a sensation or mental image is evoked, some associated mental image can be called forth as well.

It is not yet possible to state the material bases of a remembrance, or indeed of any mental image. We cannot tell where to locate the traces of the excitations, the engrams which when stimulated give rise to a mental image, a remembered picture, for example. It is supposed that specific protein or nucleic acid structures are formed in the ganglion cells of the brain. But it is not known whether such structures are to be supposed in the cell bodies or in the fibres.

The so-called 'narrowness of consciousness' imposes a particular difficulty. The excitations to arouse conscious processes, sensations and mental images are mainly those that are perceived with attention. Man's consciousness is experienced as a continuous stream of psychological processes. But many sensory excitations – many incidental features within our field of vision, many unimportant sounds, touch stimuli, and so on – do not penetrate our consciousness at all. On the other hand, once many activities, such as walking upstairs or playing the piano, which began by being conscious, have been repeated over and over again, they end by becoming automatic and then take place unconsciously, 'mechanically', although the excitations in the sense organs and subcortical structures remain the same. There may still be sensations and mental images, but they no longer impinge on the stream of consciousness. In much the same way 'non-associative' sensations may correspond to disregarded areas of our field of vision.

If we are to comprehend the growing complexity and importance of memory in all its phases from the lower animals to man, we must bear all these mentioned points in mind. First we may state that greater complexity of processes of memory implies correspondingly increased complexity of the sense organs; for memory is invariably based on sensations, and even man's imaginative and speculative ideas are formed from components primarily experienced as sensations. We have already noted that unicellular and simpler multicellular creatures are capable of a number of sensory reactions adapted to different stimuli. And higher metazoa also possess various additional sense organs, such as those for hearing, balance, and so on. Above all, in the course of evolution, as the body size increased and its parts became more specialized, all the sense organs grew more complex and came to contain many more cells. This meant that they were able to make better responses to a small part of complex stimuli – for instance, to react to a small detail in the retinal image, which might denote either an edible fruit among a pattern of leaves or a distant enemy.

It was even more important that, as the classes of animals developed, nervous systems became more and more centralized. The worms already possessed a 'brain', representing a superordinate functional centre of the nervous system. And these brains continued, in the course of evolution, to grow absolutely and relatively larger, both in size and in the number of their cells. As every nerve cell of the brain of vertebrates has hundreds of fine ramifications with which it may come into contact with other nerve cells, if the number is doubled in some brain region, then the possibilities of associative connections multiply by geometrical progression. It is therefore conceivable that the brains of vertebrates are often capable of much more complicated accomplishments than their normal life needs. Examples of such astonishing accomplishments will be mentioned in the last part of this chapter. It also follows that the brain has always been pre-adapted to higher accomplishments in the course of phylogeny.

The phylogenetic enlargement of the brains also allowed a correspondingly increased division of labour. A vertebrate's brain consists of five main areas. In fishes and amphibians, processes of memory take place mainly in the midbrain; the forebrain is little involved. In most mammals the memory traces seem to be restricted to the forebrain, its complicated cortex having two to five layers of nerve cells. This cortex is divided into a large number of regions and subregions ('areae') differing not only in the number of layers but also in their functions. In lower mammals such as, for instance, marsupials and rodents, it is divided almost exclusively into (1) the projection fields of the sense organs – that is to say, areas where those fibres terminate which convey excitations from the eyes, ears, tongue, skin, etc., to the brain; and (2) motor fields, which conduct impulses in response to external stimuli – to bring about, for instance, the contraction of appropriate groups of muscles. Besides these sensory and motor fields, higher mammals possess larger cortical regions, especially in the frontal and temporal lobes, in which impulses from various sensory regions are interconnected in various ways and from which extremely varied motor impulses emanate. These associative regions are the basis for the more complex processes of memory, and processes of choice between possible lines of action.

These differences in brain complexity show mainly in the degree of versatility displayed in actions of choice. Already the marsupials and rodents are able to modify their instinctive behaviour considerably in the light of individual experience. A grown rat knows every safe nook of its domain. It knows where to expect either food or danger. It may bolt, for instance, into a suitable hideout, showing more cunning than a young inexperienced rat. But a rat is incapable of planning a line of action several minutes in advance. The highest mammals, on the other hand, are able to make much more use of what their memory has stored up. They possess considerable skill in following

77

through a line of action concerned with the future, and they can often 'plan' something several minutes in advance.

The mental images corresponding to the evoked engrams are mostly accompanied by positive or negative feelings. Feelings are not an independent group of phenomena, but are merely qualities of sensations and ideas. So we may assume that animals have them too, because (as we have seen) they are of importance in safeguarding instinctive processes. This means that animals are also capable of moods and emotions – that is to say, of summations of positive or negative feelings brought about by specific excitations spreading to almost all later series of sensation and mental images. In their causes and effects these states of mind – like rage, fear, delight, sadness – in vertebrates often show a remarkable resemblance to man's.

The already mentioned neuroses, which are found from time to time in learning experiments, also produce a similar behaviour. If we give a child sums to do every day, at first he does them gladly and easily; but if they are gradually made harder, eventually the stage will be reached when the child is unequal to the task, and reacts against it. This state of conflict involves negative feelings. If the harder sums are still set day after day, a neurotic attitude may result. The child is faced with what he feels to be an impossible task: he exhibits mounting distress, becomes agitated and refuses even to attempt it.

Many vertebrates – elephants as well as hens or fishes – behave very much in this way. For example, an animal may have to distinguish between two patterns, a cross and a square, perhaps, one positive (with food as a reward) and one negative (with no reward). If properly treated it will approach its training device eagerly and will gradually solve the problems by trial and error. But if a task becomes particularly difficult, perhaps because a new positive pattern very much resembles one hitherto learned as negative, the animal succumbs to a state of conflict. This happens even more frequently if two negative patterns are presented. The creature turns 'irresolutely' first to one pattern and then to the other, makes a random choice, and is disappointed when no reward follows. If this situation is repeated several times the creature may become so agitated that it runs away, and days may elapse before it will return to training. An Indian elephant we used in experiments, which was generally willing to be trained, ran nervously about, trumpeted, tore off the lid on which the patterns were marked, and stamped on it. Hens made neurotic by experiments might flutter about excitedly, avoiding the choice containers; neurotic fishes often raise their dorsal fins, sometimes change colour, and cease to swim up to the training device. Of course in each case only single specimens showed neurotic behaviour, and it sometimes took different forms, but the basic state of mind seems to have been governed by the physiological condition of over-excitement, and it is very probable that the conflict induced negative feelings.

Such training experiments also show the possibility of ascribing psychological conditions, which in man we should call 'attention', to at least the higher animals. In the direction of attention, the sense organs involved must be made more susceptible to receive stimuli and the mental processes are concentrated in the region where the sensory excitation is aroused or expected. A child learns badly if he is distracted by passers-by – that is to say, by some other mental stimulus – for consciousness is normally indivisible. It is the same with an animal in training; almost any outside distraction leads to an increase of mistakes. As inhibition by distracting excitations is the physiological cause of such behaviour, it is probable that most invertebrates possessing a central nervous system are capable of 'attention'.

We can also ascribe volition to many vertebrates. As this implies the power of choice, and at least a brief sequence of mental images concerning the immediate future, we may assume prestages of volition even in higher invertebrates like cuttlefish and bees. Schopenhauer and other voluntarists regard the will as an unanalysable primary phenomenon. This is a possible interpretation. But it is probably more correct to derive impulses of volition from other mental processes. A dominant, often strongly emotive and purposive mental image takes command, to the exclusion of any rival or distracting chains of association. When we see a newly captured wild animal searching its cage for a way out, we may assume that escape is a dominant notion leading the animal to seek nothing but freedom, and to disregard food or comfortable resting-places. And every dog owner knows that much of what his pet does is so like man's voluntary actions that it seems only natural to think of the animal as having a will.

It is obvious, then, that throughout man's phylogeny many of his nervous and behavioural characteristics go back to his animal forerunners. This implies that they are very probably also capable of the psychological processes corresponding to such behaviour. Sensations will correspond to sensory reactions of animals, mental images to evoked engrams, and we may also presume resulting acts of choice, feelings, emotions and processes of volition. Each increase in the complexity of the brain has mostly been matched by a corresponding increase in the capacity for learning – that is, the quantity of the engrams available for acts of choice – and by the span of retention of associative links.

Compared with the highest mammals, however, man is distinguished by certain particular complicated brain processes, which correspond to quite specific psychic phenomena. He can frame concepts – that is to say, he can extract the common features of many experiences and can then usually form some word to represent them. This is how abstractions and generalizations come to be made. We also form judgements, draw conclusions and recognize laws, and we think and act in the light of this understanding. Among the concepts we frame, one of the most important is that of our own self as an individual. To appreciate man's psychological development it is important to realize that some of these typically human faculties are already present at a rather advanced stage in the higher animals. It will be sufficient to refer to a few of the many significant findings yielded by experiments in this field, because of their great importance for an understanding of how man's thinking has evolved.

We generally use some appropriate word to denote our human concepts. The concept 'cat', for instance, includes sensations and mental images of many animals with distinctive characteristics and varying in colour, size, fur, and so on. Moreover, we frame abstract concepts denoting certain common factors within a much larger number of diverse individual experiences. We may form a word like 'animal', 'house', 'machine', 'brother', 'teacher', or in the realm of more spiritual experiences, 'love', 'judgement', 'science', etc., always embracing what is common to these. Or we may speak of some quality shared by very different experiences and say 'large', 'red', 'unlike', 'valuable', etc. Or we may connect what is common to different activities and happenings, and speak of 'flying', 'working', 'thinking', 'sensing', and so on. Or, finally, we express recognized relationships, especially causal or logical ones between objects or processes, using either some of the mentioned predicates or words like 'therefore', 'because', 'nevertheless', 'if', 'supposing', 'and', etc.

We almost always think in such a way—that is, in words, i.e. in mental images of words. They have the advantage of combining very numerous individual experiences and of being far more stable and unequivocal. This is especially important where the meaning is as abstracted and sharply circumscribed as the symbols in chemistry, physics and mathematics (for example; H_2O, cm, sec, 211; $v = \sqrt{2gh}$, and so on). As a civilization grows more advanced, we therefore find the language becoming richer in grammatical forms and recognized symbols.

When thinking in words in many concepts a faint visual image often accompanies the actual sound of the word. And occasionally we have also purely visual or auditory images without any verbal association, for instance when we are abroad and notice some common flower as typical of the country without knowing the name of it, or when we call to mind a tune. Higher animals also frame a relatively large number of such 'averbal' concepts. Without going more deeply into the theory of abstraction, it may be enough to cite a few examples [190, 195].

A. Meesters [149] has conducted experiments in which he trained sticklebacks and minnows to take food in front of a white square of certain dimensions (e.g. 2·5 cm) on a black ground, and to avoid an adjacent smaller square (1·7 cm) where there was no food. But if this smaller square was presented at the same time as a still smaller one (1·16 cm), the fishes selected to a significantly large percentage the larger square (1·7 cm) – in other words, the one hitherto avoided as negative. This means that instead of merely having learned to recognize a certain characteristic as such, they were aware of the relationship between the two objects and acted as if they had framed the concept 'larger'. Vertebrates have frequently been found to be capable of this kind of relative learning in connection with pairs of objects, especially when the difference belongs to a one-dimensional scale such as 'larger-smaller', 'more-less', 'lighter-darker', 'sharper-blunter', and so on. An Indian elephant which we had trained to prefer a pattern of black and white stripes 2 cm wide (with a food reward) to one of 4 cm (no reward), selected the relatively narrower stripes when the widths were 2 and 1·5 cm, or 4 and 3 cm. Hence it acted as if it had framed the concept of 'narrower' [195].

This kind of averbal abstraction can be carried much further in mammals and birds. For many years O. Koehler [114, 115, 116] and his students [16, 141, 145] conducted careful experiments with doves, jackdaws, magpies, ravens, parrots and squirrels, to prove numerical concepts approximating to those for which humans use words. One raven proved the most adept; it developed averbal 'numerical images' of the numbers 2 to 6, and mastered the following test. Five food bowls were set out covered with round cardboard lids; and on these 2, 3, 4, 5 and 6 pieces of plasticine were placed, their size, shape and arrangement varying with each trial. A cardboard lid was placed in front of the dishes, with pieces of plasticine on it of the number the bird should select. The number of pieces corresponded to that on the lid of one of the food bowls, but the shape, size and arrangement did not. The bird was thus obliged to 'count up' what stood on the indicator and then go to the five bowls and pick out the lid with the same number, even though other lids might look much more like it. If the raven then pushed off the lid, it would find the reward in this bowl. Dolphins even proved capable of responding to the same number of sounds up to ten, which a trainer had called, although they cannot count with the help of different words like 'one', 'two', 'three', and so on [139].

In the course of a long series of experiments we succeeded in developing an averbal concept of 'odd' and 'equal' in a civet cat (*Viverricula*). First, we placed two food dishes before it and trained it to choose the one with two differing black spots on the lid, and to refuse the one with two identical spots. Next, it was given the same training with two triangles. After it had quite mastered both of these, even when the objects were turned at an angle of 90, 180 or 270 degrees, without further training we presented it with pairs of other shapes – irregular patches, crosses, straight lines, and so on – always one with two equal markings and the other with two which were 'unlike'. In most cases and in a significant percentage of choices it selected spontaneously one with the differing markings, even when there were three or more of these [210].

Using a different method, H. F. Harlow [71] has been able to show that Rhesus monkeys can form an averbal concept of 'odd' and 'equal.' He presented them with three objects of which two were alike, and trained them to select the 'odd' one, whether this was on the right, on the left or in the centre. If he presented two circular pieces of wood and one triangular one, the triangle had to be selected, but if two were triangular and one circular, then it must be the circular piece. Once this was learned, Harlow kept offering other objects, two alike and one different. Without further training the monkeys always selected the 'odd' one.

These findings and the results of many other experiments prove that we are justified in saying that higher animals are capable of accomplishments approaching man's thought processes – that is to say, some degree of abstraction and generalization. The psychical processes we can very probably ascribe to them therefore include averbal concepts.

In this sense we can say that animals can also make 'averbal judgements' [181, 195]. In human psychology, a judgement is generally taken to mean that a definite relationship between two mental images or concepts, often the particular correlation of certain spatial or temporal characteristics, has been comprehended. When we train a vertebrate to react in a different manner to black and white, for instance, we humans express the process as 'Black means food – white means no food'. The animal in training cannot judge in this way, for it does not think in words and is ignorant of the predicates needed to link the two concepts. Yet even without using a verb the animal establishes an associative link between the sensation 'black' and the mental image 'food'. All the components required for judgement are present, and it is thus possible to speak of an 'averbal judgement'. Finding no food at a sample hitherto learned as positive, many mammals and birds will show evident disappointment. They often continue in vain to search in the food dish. We may therefore assume that they really 'expect' food to be there and that they have corresponding mental images.

If we find many judgements coinciding in the main, we humans tend to group them as conclusions. Using as we do largely words and grammatical constructions, we might interpret the supposed mental process of Koehler's raven in the above-mentioned experiment [115] as follows: 'The same number of spots as seen on the sample has to be found out on one of the five food bowl lids; then there will be food under that one.' The raven, 'thinking' in visual images as a bird does, experiences all the main components of such a conclusion: the number of spots on the sample, the associated search for the same number on the lids, the food-expectation as a mental image. 'Averbal conclusions' of this sort are present in all the actions of higher animals where we speak of 'planning' or sometimes even of 'insight'. The important point is that there is a complex associative process of excitations, corresponding to a sequence of mental images, which precedes this kind of activity. We must suppose that this is true also of mammals and birds. These images are concerned with possible future lines of action, and lead to a selection of the most favourable sequence. Finally on a basis of experience and judgement a 'decision' is reached. Man thinks it out in words and animals may experience a corresponding sequence of visual images.

This is the kind of process that characterizes the 'discoveries' in the use of tools made by a great number of monkeys and apes, notably chimpanzees and Capuchin monkeys. For instance, W. Köhler [117] placed a fruit outside the bars of an untrained chimpanzee's cage, out of the animal's reach. A few minutes earlier, it had been playing with a stick which lay unnoticed nearby. Suddenly the chimpanzee caught sight of the stick, seized it, stuck it through the bars beyond the fruit and deliberately used it to pull the fruit towards the cage. At other times chimpanzees have used poles to beat down a fruit that hung out of reach, or have pushed empty boxes under the fruit, or piled up several boxes, in order to reach what they wanted. In similar situations Capuchin monkeys showed a corresponding behaviour [113]. It is characteristic of all these actions that the animals seem to have a 'sudden idea', and then consequently carry it out. The only explanation for this is that the animals began by running through a series of mental images of intermediate actions which seemed likely to lead up to reaching the fruit (turning away from the fruit, fetching the stick, aiming, beating at the fruit and so on).

The following experiments carried out together with my former assistant J. Döhl [200] may perhaps show best how far the behaviour of apes may approach human pondering. We trained a young female chimpanzee to survey the complicated paths of a maze and to find out the correct way leading towards the goal. The white paths were inset in a dark board covered with safety glass. An iron ring had been placed on a small elevation in the middle of the rear edge of the board. The ape had to draw the ring towards an exit at the edge of the board by means of a magnet. In the first series of experiments she had to choose between two simple angular paths which were mirror images of one another. One of the paths was blocked at a varying point. If the chimpanzee chose the correct side she could reach the exit, take out the ring and put it into a slot-machine to obtain a reward. In the next series of experiments the paths were made more and more complicated through incorporating more angles and branched blind alleys. As all tasks showed a different arrangement of paths the ape learnt to look first over the maze for some time and to plan the correct action.

After the chimpanzee had solved these tasks in a satisfying manner, the two sides of the maze were no longer kept separate, thus producing very complex patterns of paths. Finally the maze

85

was enlarged to double the size and we could add more exits, of which, however, only one could be reached. When the last series of very complex maze patterns were offered, the chimpanzee looked over the maze for one or one and a half minutes before beginning to move the ring. She normally began to look at different exits first in order to find out which of them she could reach. Then she pulled the ring down to the correct side and drew it to the exit, avoiding all blind alleys. In the last 100 most complicated mazes (Fig. 10) the ape chose the correct path in 86 per cent of the trials and she moved the ring into one of the many blind alleys in only 4·5 per cent of the possible cases.

Fig. 10 Female chimpanzee surveys a complicated maze before pulling down an iron ring to the correct side by means of a magnet and moving it in the sunken white paths to the only accessible exit on the edge of the board without getting into blind alleys. (After Rensch and Döhl).

These astonishing accomplishments can only be explained by the assumption that the chimpanzee compared the mental images of possible actions, chose the correct kind of action and only then sent motor impulses into arm and hand to draw the ring in the correct path. In order to make this assumption more probable we asked six biology students to solve the most complex tasks in the same manner by means of a magnet. They reported that they experienced a similar type of mental image and they also began to look at the different exits first, in order to decide which one could be reached. On the average they needed less than half of the time of the chimpanzee to choose the correct path. However, they were worse than the ape in ten cases, the difference of planning time being 1-58 seconds more.

Experiments of this kind confirm the statement made above that the brains of higher animals are able to accomplish more than their life in a natural state requires. Assuming that apes of the Tertiary, from which our human line of descent branched off, possessed similar abilities, we may say that these animals were preadapted to develop into humans.

Many other experiments with apes and monkeys also prove that these animals are able to grasp causal relations and take these experiences in account in their actions, although of course without comprehending the physical basis. W. Köhler's chimpanzees, for instance, discovered the principle of the lever and used this knowledge to prize up a manhole or dig in the ground [117]. And every monkey that holds a fruit safely in a firm enough grip is showing at least some understanding of the principle of gravity.

Higher animals appear to possess also a rudimentary concept of the self, of their own ego. With human children such a concept only develops gradually, becoming clear about the third year [181, 190, 281]. It is caused by different experiences: (1) certain sensations such as those of touch, pressure, pain, hunger, thirst, only occur when caused by corresponding stimuli to or within the child's own body; (2) sensations of this kind, especially pain, are usually accompanied by much more intense feeling than others (visual, auditory, olfactory) caused by external stimuli; (3) sensations can nearly always be felt on the body; (4) sensations may be felt, when touching, licking or cleaning, or seeing parts of the own body; (5) an uninterrupted stream of consciousness is experienced; (6) the individual recalls experiences he has himself made and learns of his own attributes (his own name, his particular abilities and weaknesses, etc.); (7) the individual becomes conscious of himself as a peculiar member of a social group incorporated among other individuals of higher and lower rank (family, playfellows, schoolmates, and so on).

G

Homo sapiens

We may say that experiences (1) to (5) apply also to those animals for whom we can claim consistent consciousness (while awake), especially for the higher vertebrates whose sense organs and brains function in this respect like man's. But the higher animals, especially carnivores, monkeys and apes, may have memories of personal attributes and abilities or of their own names; so can many crows and (in the author's experience) parrots as well. And even when together with several of their like, dogs know their own names.

The beginnings of an averbal concept of the ego are seen most clearly in the claims of higher social animals within their own groups. There is always a certain hierarchy in a flock of hens, or in a dovecot, a pack of wolves or a colony of baboons. The order is established after some altercation, brief contests, threatening gestures or rivalry over food or mating partners. When this stage is over, the order normally remains undisputed for a long period. The superior individuals in these social groupings are often 'self-assured' and their inferiors timid in manner. This suggests a certain awareness of self. E. Diebschlag [42] has shown this point every clearly in his fine experiments with domestic pigeons. Every pigeon has its own position in the dovecot, which it has to maintain *vis-à-vis* its companions, and which it makes clear by imposing behaviour. The bird highest in rank sits nearest the entrance hole, the lowliest in the darkest corner. Diebschlag took one of these pigeons of inferior rank out of the dovecot, placed it in a cage, and encouraged the self-confidence, which at first it completely lacked, by showing it a stuffed pigeon and then removing it at once when the live bird made as if to defend itself. In this way the pigeon whose position had been so humble gradually lost its fears, and it ended by roundly attacking the stuffed dummy which invariably fell back before it. At first when the pigeon was taken back to the dovecot it remained 'self-assured'. It routed all its former superiors and for a while even rose to the highest rank. But in later disputes its confidence ebbed away and it sank in social status again.

We may state then, that even birds behave in a way that suggests the averbal concept of an ego and a sense of personality, or at least a prestage of this. We may also assume that strongly emotive complexes such as 'courage' and 'timidity' occur among higher animals. This order of rank, the claim to certain resting places and the defence of circumscribed individual domains, is bound up with the development of such notions as 'property' and 'being in the right', though we normally think of these as specifically human. An animal or bird may claim as a 'prescriptive right' some definite sleeping-place or nesting-area which it has won. A monkey often fights to keep some toy, a small mirror perhaps, as its 'property'.

On the other hand, one may assume that higher animals are also subject to a complex that results from 'infringement' of prohibited actions, something we might perhaps even call a 'bad conscience'. A pigeon trained by O. Koehler [114] illustrates this point very well. He offered it several grains of food and trained it to take only three, by chasing it away when it had done so. Once the bird had learnt to 'count' up to three in this way, it used to turn away from the grains even when no longer chased off. On a few occasions, however, it was so eager to go on eating that it turned towards the remaining grains but without daring to peck at them ('expecting to be punished', or 'guiltily'); and then in a flash it would 'steal' one of the 'forbidden' grains and hurry away. One may also see a dog behaving in this way, 'stealing' something 'forbidden' from the table and then crawling 'guiltily' under the sofa. Of course these human, ethical and juristic terms do not adequately describe what is going on in the animal's mind, because it does not think in words or behave according to a standard of morality. But the same factors often determine the conduct of men and animals in this respect. Small children and adults of low intelligence no doubt think largely as an animal does in this kind of situation, in mental images of possible later difficulties or pain, because their grasp of language is insufficient for the abstract concepts appropriate to their conflict of conscience.

The concept of value is another of the abstractions that seem to be characteristic of man but are noticeable in a rudimentary form among the most advanced animals. J. B. Wolfe [274] taught chimpanzees to accept poker chips in place of food as a reward for work done. They put these into a slot-machine and got food instead. For one white chip, for instance, the animals got a grape, and for a blue one they got two; copper chips were valueless. The chimpanzees soon learned to distinguish the chips in value and to see them as symbols of rewards to come. They preferred those that were higher in value and saved several up before going to get their rewards. One of my former students, T. Kapune [107], made a long series of experiments which shows that even a Rhesus monkey was capable of this and indeed of subtler concepts of value. He also learned to regard counters, in this case metal rings of different colours, as a kind of coinage that could be fed into a slot-machine that gave different quantities of food. He got fifteen peanuts for a yellow ring, six for a white, three for a green, one for a blue, and nothing for a red. In the test experiments twelve of these rings hanging on nails on a board were offered. Normally the monkey took the most valuable, the yellow ones, first. If there were none, then he took white ones first, and if there were none or only one of these, he then took green ones. When offered only blue or red ones, he usually after much hesitation chose the low grade blue ones, rarely the red. He generally played for a while with the rings before exchanging them at the machine for food. This experiment shows that even monkeys can learn to regard counters as 'currency', as symbolic substitutes for food to be obtained later – which implies mental imagery referring to the future – and to distinguish five grades of value accurately. Even a lemur, using another training device (three boxes which had to be opened, with different patterns of black and white on their lids), was able to distinguish three grades of value, with a significant degree of success. All these actions based on concepts of value are also evidence of a limited 'insight'.

It is astonishing to find also aesthetic factors having a positive effect with apes, monkeys and crows comparable with the effect in man. When we humans look at different black and white patterns, feelings of aesthetic pleasure are based in the main on three basic conditions: (1) symmetry, (2) rhythmic repetition of similar component parts, and (3) consistency of curvatures.

To test the effect of these factors on a Capuchin monkey, a green monkey, a jackdaw, and a carrion crow, the author [183, 185, 194] many times offered them six small white cardboard discs to play with. These were arranged in a circle, three having a rhythmic, symmetrical or otherwise aesthetically effective pattern in black, and the other three a similar but irregular pattern. As it could be assumed that a pleasing pattern would be more often taken up in either hand or beak, in each case it was the first choice only that counted. As a general rule, the rhythmic or the symmetrical pattern and the one with consistency of curvatures were preferred to the irregular ones, and the results were statistically significant. It shows that with these animals, as with man, the greater facility to apprehend a design, the details of which are rhythmically repeated or otherwise more easily apprehended, the 'complexibility' is connected with positive feelings and arouses aesthetic pleasure. The same holds good when chimpanzees and a Capuchin monkey were trained to fit coloured cubes together. They preferred to combine the same colour instead of adding a different one. In similar experiments my former student M. Tigges [246] found that jackdaws preferred pure colours (red, blue, yellow, green) to equally bright mixed ones (orange, brown, violet, lilac). Certain basic aesthetic feelings may also be concluded by an analysis of 'drawings' and 'paintings' of apes and Capuchin monkeys. These products often show a clear tendency to centralization, a certain balance of the right and left half of the sheet, and an adaptation of the direction of the lines to the shape of the sheet [154, 188, 194, 198].

Chimpanzees, orang-utans and Capuchin monkeys like putting scarves, ribbons, chains, etc., round their necks and running about with them on. They may quite possibly be enjoying dressing up. Aesthetic factors would then be involved. It is even more likely that birds find aesthetic pleasure in repeating tunes they hear from other birds or from humans, and in 'composing' new melodies from phrases either learned or already known.

An increase of curiosity has probably also played an important part in the course of phylogenetic evolution. My former student A. Wünschmann [275] has conducted experiments at our Zoological Institute in Münster to compare species of different phylogenetic levels. Fishes, hens, jackdaws and a chimpanzee were tested under the same or similar conditions, and the results were quantitatively assessed and compared. A series of the same pattern was presented for fixed periods (usually between 10 and 30 minutes), and then each fourth or fifth pattern was replaced by a new type. It was noted how long and how often the animals turned towards them and towards the patterns they had been adapted to before. Young carp showed no reaction to the new pattern, *Carassius* a little; quails showed a marked interest, jackdaws more, and the chimpanzee intense curiosity.

To round off what has been said on the abilities of chimpanzees, we may refer briefly to observations made by C. and M. Hayes [73, 74] on a young animal adopted when three days old and brought up by them like a human child. Vicki, as she was called, learned to wash herself, brush her teeth, get dressed, drink from a cup, and eat off a plate. She took over a number of human activities purely by imitation, and without any coaching: dusting, washing dishes, filing her nails, opening bottles, etc. She used to take up the telephone for fun, dial a few numbers, listen, and if she happened to get through somewhere, she would call 'Boo!' and ring off. At the end of three years she had imitated seventy different activities. It was obvious that she framed averbal concepts, for she was able to recognize objects when she saw small reproductions of them. When she was first shown an object and then two pictures, she always chose the one that represented that particular object. She could recognize cars and chairs in pictures, even types she had never met with in reality.

Like human children, Vicki appeared to be capable of imaginative thought processes, for she was once observed playing with nothing but apparently pretending in imagination to pull a toy along on the end of a string, losing the string and taking it up again. Once she was seen pulling in the 'string' hand over hand, though in fact there was nothing in her hand at all.

She also learned to obey fifty different words or phrases,

such as 'Fetch your doll', 'Shut the door', 'Go into the bathroom', 'Kiss me'. As a rule she had clearly understood the words, for the situations in which the commands were given were not always the same, and the actions required of her differed accordingly. It cannot have been, then, that the mere sound of the words released impulses in certain motor nerves, as a trainer's commands do. As in every deliberate act, what happened was that the words when heard evoked mental images inducing appropriate behaviour. In this sense we can say that anthropoid apes 'think', using images of the sound of words. The same is probably true in some measure of other 'trained' mammals and birds as well. We cannot of course know whether when she remembered her doll, the chimpanzee sometimes also experienced some image of the words as spoken. But this is quite possible, for images linked by association may easily evoke one another.

Reviewing the findings described in this chapter, we find the behaviour of vertebrates, especially warm-blooded animals, throwing light on the evolutionary progress leading to the origin of man. Some of their achievements seem very strongly to suggest complicated mental images of a kind generally regarded as typically human. Higher animals appear to be capable of very many averbal concepts, visual and auditory, which can lead to simple judgements and conclusions. Their discovery of how to use tools and their ability to plan actions proves that they can act with 'foresight' or even 'insight'. They are able to grasp and take into account certain causal relations (the effect of gravity, for instance, or the lever principle) and they are also subject to complicated and strongly emotive complexes – what we would call 'fear', 'rage', 'jealousy', 'pleasure'. They possess a rudimentary concept of the self and prestages of concepts of right and value, they have basic aesthetic feelings and a certain degree of imagination. With man, all these phenomena take much more complicated and specialized forms because he thinks in words. His imagery and purposive thinking, too, have a very much longer span. But at the same time, mental processes in the higher animals are so close to man's that it is possible to understand how his particular qualities have developed. 'Man', in this sense, of course includes early forms of the *Homo erectus* (*Pithecanthropus*) type and the much more primitive Australopithecines. What we know of their culture does suggest mental processes only a little more complicated than those we can ascribe to present-day anthropoid apes.

So it is obviously by no means easy to draw a clear distinction between man and the animals, not, at least, when we go back beyond the present and consider the past stages of our phylogenetic evolution. The mind, like the body, has gone through a very gradual process of development. This fact leads most recent research to define man in terms not merely of physical characteristics but of mental ability. And here we can apparently draw a rather sharper line of distinction at the point where the making of tools begins – that is to say, the artificial alteration and improvement of natural implements such as stones or sticks. Of course, there are intermediate stages here too. Quite clearly, Australopithecines sometimes used rough pebbles or pieces of bone as tools, such as those found heaped up in the caves near Sterckfontein. Some, like '*Homo*' *habilis* or perhaps *Zinjanthropus*, also produced very primitive stone tools. Apes, on the other hand, not only often use sticks and stones as tools; they sometimes make little improvements here also. A chimpanzee biting off the side twigs of a branch to use it as a stick is surely 'improving' his material in this way. And the chimpanzees that piled up an erection of two or even four boxes to reach a fruit hanging from a height, and the one that W. Köhler [117] observed fitting together short pieces to make a longer stick, were obviously beginning to fashion tools.

What fundamentally distinguishes present-day man from even the highest animals, the anthropoid apes, is the spoken word, the ability to speak. Apes have not developed a speech centre in the forebrain. During their research, the Hayeses [73, 74] undertook the important and difficult task of teaching their young chimpanzee Vicki to speak certain words (helping her at first to move her lips). After considerable trouble the animal learned to say in a somewhat inarticulate manner 'Mama', 'Papa' and 'cup', connecting the words with roughly the correct mental images, although with a rather more limited

94

connotation than that of man. 'Mama' and 'Papa' did duty in a general way for her human 'parents', while 'cup' meant any drinking vessel, or just the act of drinking itself. For instance, Vicki would hold her empty cup out beside the coffee-pot, saying first 'Mama' and then 'cup'. When she saw a drinking-vessel in an illustrated magazine she also said 'cup'. Her failure to speak more words would seem to be because larynx and vocal cords had not an adequate structure and the speech centres in the brain were undeveloped. Clinical investigation showed a resemblance between Vicki's imperfect articulation and the symptoms of aphasia in humans, when the motor region of speech is destroyed.

Quite recently R. A. and B. T. Gardner [60] proved that a young chimpanzee was able to learn a kind of deaf and dumb language. After twenty-two months of training the ape could master thirty-four appropriate gestures and used them to a certain degree in a purposeful manner. Chimpanzees living in the wild have apparently no need to develop such abilities because their inherited gestures and sounds [122, 129] are sufficient for their mode of life.

What prevented anthropoid apes, then, from developing primitive culture was that they lacked speech and so were incapable of abstract thinking in words. It is possibly correct, therefore, to rank the Australopithecines as only a little higher than the present-day anthropoid apes, for the brain, and in particular the frontal part of the forebrain, was not larger and had probably only a little better structure than that of anthropoid apes. It was only after the human ancestors began to walk upright, to make much greater use of tools and to work together in groups that the forebrain rapidly developed and a primitive culture emerged. Tool using and tool making were matters of such vital importance for these comparatively defenceless pre-humans, who lacked powerful canine teeth, that natural selection operated in favour of the variants or tribes which had the better brains. Such selection pressure probably caused the improvement of larynx and vocal cords, the development of the motor areas of speech and abstract thinking in words. This gradually produced men of a higher level of culture, their

95

actions becoming less guided by present sensations and more by ideas. They could now 'run through' possible actions experimentally in their brains before carrying one of them out. They were able to balance one action against another, and this led to more and more 'freedom' of decision, until they reached a stage where they displayed a wide measure of what seems to be 'free will'. However, present-day civilized man is not truly 'free' in his thoughts and actions, for hereditary disposition, education, experience and present sensations, feedings and mental images always determine the course of his thinking (cf. Chapter 5, section C).

C. *Some epistemological problems concerning the phylogenetic development* of mental powers

It must continue to be a source of wonder that living organisms came into being on our inorganic planet and, in time, developed into man, distinct from all animals in his ability to comprehend not only this process but also the guiding principles and laws of the universe. A better understanding of man's unique position in the cosmos can be reached by considering certain specific and far-reaching problems of cognition. Within the limits of the present work, however, it is impossible to offer more than a rapid outline, designed rather to stimulate reflection than to provide a solution.

(1) The latter part of Chapter 2, section B, dealt with the fact that various physiological – that is to say, causally determined – processes in the brain and sense organs correspond to certain psychological phenomena, in particular to sensations and mental images. In section A of this chapter we saw that psychological processes in animals can only be postulated by conclusions from analogy, which in the case of the higher animals are almost certain but grow progressively vaguer with lower animals. It is extremely unlikely that psychic elements have suddenly sprung into being because they are not causally connected with the corresponding physiological processes. A panpsychistic and identistic conception is therefore obvious

which assumes that even molecules and atoms possess elementary 'protopsychic' qualities. But it is only later, after a nervous system has developed, that they are bound to become integrated into a kind of animal consciousness components. This hypothesis is all the more probable because it is the material hereditary factors, the DNA molecules in the chromosomes, that transmit special psychic characteristics, for instance artistic talents, to the next generation [196, 199].

During the course of progressive evolution in the animal kingdom the protopsychic components have been integrated to form more complex psychological processes, sensations and mental images. More complicated nervous systems have led to such new and complex phenomena as acts of volition, feelings, the framing of concepts, generalization, conclusions, insight, and logical thinking.

This poses a very important question. Do these apparently new phenomena, corresponding to phylogenetic evolution, really represent something entirely novel? Or has the increase in psychological complexity simply followed from the combination and integration of more primitive components? In our opinion the latter interpretation is quite possible, because the sphere of matter shows corresponding integrations. Matter has obviously evolved by stages from plasma to atoms, molecules, complex molecules, and then to the even more complicated structures of living cells. But the combination of the basic components was not merely additive. As the structure of every molecule shows, their integration gave rise to entirely new qualities. Different modes of integration of carbon, oxygen and hydrogen produced the characteristics of cellulose, sugar, alcohol, acetic acid, and so on. In a corresponding manner we can imagine the integration of protopsychic components to form entirely new qualities of sensation or mental images, acts of volition, and so on. Psychic phenomena realized by such processes or integration could, however, only be 'experienced' when they entered a stream of consciousness.

It is very probable that all progressive evolution – including what has led up to man – took place through mutation, gene combination and natural selection. This means that it was based on causal laws. In my *Biophilosophy* [196] I have enumerated more than one hundred phylogenetic rules.

Man's psychological evolution, then, must also have been regulated by these laws, although in the present stage of our knowledge we cannot resolve these problems finally. But it is something gained if we realize that they exist, and they are of immense importance in assessing the strange evolution of the creature known as *Homo sapiens*.

The identistic and panpsychistic conception is also important from another point of view: the development of psychic phenomena can be regarded as a process directly corresponding to the continuous 'material' development of the earth and the lower and higher organisms. It is sufficient to suppose successive causal processes, and it is not necessary to assume the appearance of something absolutely different in principle, the 'psychic', a speck appearing in the brains of higher animals although not existing in thousands of millions of years during which our planet system evolved. Although we would deprecate any intermingling of scientific findings and religious beliefs, we might point to certain parallel ideas in the works of the Jesuit priest Teilhard de Chardin [242].

(2) Some more specialized problems of cognition can be treated more concretely. During our earliest years of life, we humans gradually build up a universal idea of a three-dimensional space; that is, we act as though 'absolute space' were a reality, with matter or complexes of energy disposed within it. We arrive at this homogeneous idea of space because most of our sensations have spatial properties. The details of our field of vision follow a spatial arrangement. Small children, and those who were born blind and then operated upon, apparently start with two dimensions and then quickly learn to add that of distance. Touch, and to a certain extent hearing, are also spatial experiences. We find that the spatial properties of all three modes of sensation correspond, being homogeneous and consisting in a three-dimensional continuum round any zero point. Thus our tactile, visual and auditory fields soon fuse to form the idea of one homogeneous space. Moreover, the uni-

formity of spatial properties convinces us that space exists as a reality independent of living organisms and that such absolute space is very similar or more or less identical to the space we experience. We build up an idea of absolute time in the same way, on a basis of the corresponding temporal properties in our sensations and mental images.

Some philosophers doubt whether space and time really exist in such a way. Kant, in particular, has stressed their subjectivity (we are not concerned here with the physically demonstrable relativity of space and time, as this does not correspond to the idea of them we derive directly from experience). So it is particularly interesting to establish how experience of space and time has developed in the course of mental evolution. Here also, of course, we have to work by analogy with the reactions of animals at different phylogenetic levels. Unfortunately comparatively few serviceable findings are so far available in this field.

The behaviour of the highest vertebrates shows that they act as if they indeed had an averbal concept of a three-dimensional space. A monkey jumping through the tree-tops hardly looks at the branch itself at the moment when his hands grasp it. He is using his eyes to map out a route. His eyes and the organs of touch on his hands and feet could not work together in this way unless visual and tactile space had fused to form a homogeneous experience. W. Tellier [241] has conducted experiments with monkeys that make this probable. She trained a monkey (*Macacus sinicus*) to pick out cubes from among pyramids, cylinders and other shapes. Once the animal had learned to do this by sight, the objects were all put into a sack and it picked out the cubes by feeling them. Next, it learned to select painted crosses of various sizes and patterns from among spheres, pyramids and cubes. After mastering this, it usually managed to pick out crosses shaped out of wood, feeling for them in a sack also containing spheres, cubes and other shapes. This shows that monkeys are apparently capable of experiencing absolute space. When we come to lower vertebrates it seems uncertain whether the spatial properties of visual and tactile sensations fuse to form a concept of a homogeneous space. Quite possibly they do; but this is not necessarily so. For instance, a sea fish such as a Moray eel, threading its way among the stones in small caverns, may perhaps never combine the spatial qualities of his tactile sensations with the spatial qualities of his visual sensations, particularly as these last are connected with the time it spends outside the caves.

With invertebrates the case is still harder to determine. The flight of a fly, directed by its eyes and halteres, and possibly its wing sensillae, suggests that the spatial properties of these organs may be fused. But the formation of a mental image of three-dimensional space is very improbable. With worms such as the marine polychaeta, with primitive eye cups and a decentralized nervous system, it is likely that tactile and visual space may still be completely independent. A praying mantis, in the grip of another and larger one, which is eating away its hind-quarters, may still be eating a fly it has caught. We may assume that these creatures possessing nerve centres in the separate segments of their bodies do not experience even tactile space as a unity.

In estimating how the concept of time developed it is important to establish the phylogenetic level at which we can say that animals distinguish past and future in their mental images. We can postulate this ability at least in such birds and mammals as can act according to plan – that is, whose brains are capable of running through a series of mental images concerned with the future before acting accordingly. To make such a plan, the animal must be able to distinguish between past images (memories) and future ones (intentions, expectations). Although lower animals may possess a sense of the past (memory), nothing about them suggests that they are aware of the future.

The point of these brief remarks is this: on a basis of analogy we may assume that man's lower animal ancestors experienced space and time, not yet in the way we do, but only as properties of their individual sensations and mental images. As higher, more advanced animals developed, it is probable that their more complicated brain functions and corresponding psychological components grew more adapted to absolute space and absolute time. This is a vitally important matter for any epistemological theory of the extramental existence of space and time and also for man's understanding of himself.

(3) An extremely important stage was reached in the phylogenetic advance of mental functions when the higher organisms began to distinguish between subjective phenomena and objective reality. For instance, when a fish has learned to look for food in a food tray placed under a cross, but not to look under a circle, it has established an associative perceptual link between the search for food and the impulse needed to approach the trap. However, this does not mean that the fish regards the trap as a 'thing' outside of its own body. That kind of distinction presupposes an imaginative differentiation between one's own body and the world outside, and the most a fish can possibly be capable of is a very rudimentary form of this. It is a distinction that can only become clear when the idea of self begins to emerge, as this is the case in higher warm-blooded animals (cf. pp. 87 ff.).

We have seen that a fully developed concept of the self is only possible in civilized man. His greater capacity for abstract thinking In words, and therefore for generalizations and conclusions, leads to a clear differentiation between object and subject. Very young children only distinguish between two groups of phenomena. In our first years of life we very gradually begin to frame a clearer idea of 'material things'. We develop concepts of different objects by learning to discount variable properties, different coloration in different lighting, varying size and configuration of things seen at different distances and from different angles. But even the man of average 'culture' is far from being consistent in eliminating all qualities of things when he is thinking about matter. For instance, he still includes its colour, though he may realize that the experience of colour is only a phenomenon due to excitation in the visual cells or the corresponding brain cells, stimulated by certain electromagnetic oscillations reflected by the object. Only a man trained in epistemology and scientific thought abstracts the colour, hardness, smell, etc., from a 'thing', and so arrives at a more accurate distinction between objective 'things' and his own subjective ego and an adequate definition of matter.

Experience of matter, then, develops like that of space and time – by gradual adaptation of brain accomplishments to a transsubjective reality. What this means in a philosophical sense becomes clear when we express it the other way round and make the following deduction: that cognitive adaptation to a world outside the subject, the ego, has gradually taken place in the course of progressive phylogenetic evolution, that we have come to apprehend what reality is, shows that the 'things' around us are not mere 'appearances'. Objective 'existence' must be supposed independent of any living and percipient organism, though the average man still fails to understand its true nature and the specialist trained in philosophy and science is only gradually in process of establishing it by eliminating secondary properties and analysing primary properties of matter (what is said here in no way throws doubt on the possibility that all 'matter' is already 'protopsychic') (cf. pp. 196 ff.).

(4) To sum up, we may state: during the whole course of evolution, natural selection has ensured that the behaviour of animals is adapted to the laws of the world they live in. Mental images, generalizations and thinking based on insight have likewise developed, always adapted to the conditions of the world that are governed by causal and logical laws. Any insufficiency or lack of adaptation in development or in reaction was a disadvantage in competition. The fixed laws of a world which is independent of the living organisms perceiving it, and which existed before they emerged, have controlled the course of physical and mental phylogeny.

These reflections lead to a further interesting conclusion. If living organisms have developed on other celestial bodies under similar conditions to those on our earth – and among the 10,000 million solar systems in the Milky Way and in about 80 million galaxies (spiral nebulae) like it, there is ample likelihood that, in consequence of corresponding evolutionary laws, organisms and their mental faculties, thinking and cognition, must have followed a similar course of development to our own.

CHAPTER FOUR

Biological aspects of man's cultural development

A. *Hereditary and non-hereditary bases*

True Hominidae came into being some 4 or 5 million years ago, at about the end of the Pliocene. Later we find '*Homo*' (*Australopithecus?*) *habilis* or *Zinjanthropus* fashioning the first extremely primitive tools [36, 37, 126, 130, 131, 133, 134, 135]. By the *Homo erectus* (*Pithecanthropus*) stage, man was making quite a number of still rather simple stone tools. In north-west Africa, for instance, *Atlanthropus* was making primitive stone hatchets and choppers. *Sinanthropus* (China) had learned how to chop pieces of quartz to provide himself with large blades and borers, and to make bone implements for piercing and scraping [18]. Hence for a million years progress has been extraordinarily slow.

It was not until *Homo sapiens* appeared, some 70,000-100,000 years ago, that a new period of cultural advance began. It became rapidly faster and since then it has been steadily gaining momentum. Summarizing all known facts and simplifying the matter we get the following brief outline of this development. From the first primitive tools to the manufacture of improved and more specialized ones in the Aurignacian, we have a period of over 1·7 million years. From the beginning of the Aurignacian to the first more advanced civilizations, about 50,000 years. These civilizations date from some 6000-7000 years ago. The revolutionary 'machine age' began some 200 years ago (the steam engine was invented in 1769); and the no less revolutionary atomic age opened about 35 years ago.

How is one to explain this regularly quickening pace of

H

cultural evolution since *Homo sapiens* appeared, in such sharp contrast to the conspicuously slow development among his fore-runners? At the beginning cultural development depended upon enlargement and improvement of the forebrain – that is upon a hereditary change effected by mutation, gene combination and natural selection, a process in which any noticeable progress normally takes anything from 10,000 to 100,000 generations. Counting twenty years for each generation of pre-humans and early types of man, we can reckon that it took about 85,000 generations for the brain found in *Homo sapiens* to develop. Considering the hereditary improvements achieved, this is rela-tively fast. As it is unlikely that the mutation rate increased – and in any case this would only have led to more 'random' variation of brain structure – it follows that natural selection must have been operating most intensively. And indeed this is very likely. Lacking either powerful canines or claws, early man was rather defenceless compared with many larger animals. But his large and complex brain gave him an advantage enabling him to invent tools to defend himself or to obtain his food. At the same time he was able to store up more experiences. He was now better able to think and act according to each situation as it arose. Selection grew more intensive, too, as pre-humans and early man quickly spread, thus constantly encountering new and different conditions. Moreover, initially they lived together in fairly small groups, in which selection produced changes more quickly than in larger populations.

As the forebrain increased in size, the most significant improve-ment was undoubtedly the development of the motor area of speech. It improved communication within the family and the group, and also allowed the development of abstract thought and the further cultural advance that only tradition ensures. *Homo sapiens* made his appearance. Up to the last centuries he has still been exposed to the same natural selection, in particular to selection between whole races, which has sometimes led to the virtual extermination of culturally and technically inferior ones (such as the killing off of American Indian tribes by Europeans) and to the spread of superior races. But the heredi-tary characteristics of the brain had already arrived at a structural optimum in all races, and selection has largely or wholly ceased in this respect during the last few thousand years.

However, while the inherited brain structures remained constant, selection was now furthering the non-hereditary knowledge based on tradition. The stone and bone tools that one generation had made served as models for the next generations, who went on to develop similar and eventually improved types. When speech was more developed, experiences could be transmitted in a more general manner to children, and they in turn could communicate their wider experience to the next generation. The store of experience could grow steadily and rapidly because it was independent of hereditary mutations, which could only very slowly produce favourable alterations. And in the beginning natural selection probably also worked to the advantage of such individuals or tribes as could better learn and were better 'educable' because of their inherited brain qualities.

So it was the particularly favourable hereditary equipment that determined *Homo sapiens*'s cultural development. The inherited structure of his highly complicated brain with its 12,000 million nerve cells was the decisive factor; for this brain could retain a very large store of memories, and showed enormous versatility in linking up excitations and corresponding sensations and mental images. As in the higher animals this brain was capable of very many more accomplishments than were necessary in the course of normal life. Man's brain was preadapted to evolve a culture. The mounting improvement we have outlined could only come about because the store of knowledge continued to grow as each succeeding generation added what the individuals in it had learned by experience. Julian Huxley was the first to recognize the full implications of this important problem, and his remark that 'Man added tradition to heredity' dates from 1929 [96]. Among animals traditions also occur, but they do not lead to an increasingly complicated behaviour in the succession of generations. Some species of birds learn their specific song by tradition and pass it on to the next generation. The starlings, returning in their tens of thousands to their special roosts in the heart of London,

Berlin, Paris, New York and other great cities, offer another instance of a tradition handed down from one generation to the next. Ants and termites use and add to the same nests for years or even decades.

Among Japanese monkeys (*Macaca fuscata*), however, the spreading of acquired traditions could be proved by experiments in the wild. One troop, living on Koshima Island, was regularly offered sweet potatoes. Once, a female of one and a half years old began to wash the tubers in a streamlet before eating them. Soon this method was adopted by other members of the troop. After nine years 75 per cent of the adult monkeys were washing the tubers in water, and also in the sea. Later on the monkeys were fed with grains. To begin with the animals picked them laboriously out of the sand. Then the above-mentioned female, by then four years old, made an innovation: she threw the sand and grains into the water, thus easily separating the grains. During the next years one third of the members of this troop had adopted this new method. The Japanese researchers rightly speak of precultural or subcultural behaviour in this case [108, 109, 152].

B. *Development of culture by accumulated tradition*

'Speech alone has rendered man human. . . . By speech alone we attain to reason and by tradition to speech.' These words are taken from Herder's *Ideen zur Philosophie der Geschichte der Menschheit*, 1785, Part II [87]. And this enlightened theologian went on to give an equally accurate estimate of the importance of writing: 'All nations which have been destitute of this artificial tradition have remained, according to our ideas, uncultivated.'

We can do no more than surmise how human speech originated. It seems very improbable that the Australopithecines were able to express their individual experiences in words and make them known to other members of their number. If this had been the case, very primitive stone tools would hardly have shown so little improvement over more than a million years. It is most likely that watching their production was sufficient to maintain the tradition and for small improvements. We do not even know if men of the *Homo erectus* (*Pithecanthropus*) level reached more than a first prestage of true language. When Ernst Haeckel postulated the existence of this ancestor of ours, his first name for him was *Pithecanthropus 'alalus'*, 'the speechless ape-man'. This may have been accurate; any language these early men may have had must have been limited to a few words, or rather sounds, for otherwise cultural development would not have remained so slow for several hundred thousand years. G. R. H. von Koenigswald [121] supposed that *Homo erectus* could speak because a spina mentalis was already developed in his lower jaw. However, D. Starck [234] emphasizes that full speech is also possible in Recent man, in whom the spina mentalis is occasionally lacking. The fact that the first rapid and steady advance of culture falls during the Upper Palaeolithic (Aurignacian) suggests this as the period when real speech began. Certain sounds or sound sequences were probably used as symbols to express not only moods and individual objects but also actions, qualities and causal or logical relationships (regular successions and consequences, equality and the like).

Man became able to think in mental images of sounds of words symbolizing former visual experiences. This was very important because thinking could run on without being disturbed by visual sensations, which nearly always prevail. Apes and other higher animals on the contrary can only have successions of visual images of former visual experiences, and these can easily be disturbed or suppressed by visual sensations, which are normally very much stronger than mental images. But our human thinking can be disturbed by strong auditory sensations. Strong noise makes reflection nearly impossible, as Schopenhauer has observed.

For what was probably a long time, such words remained few in number and very restricted in connotation. Even today some primitive tribes still have a vocabulary that is disproportionately limited. In Europe, too, the lowest social classes used a vocabulary of no more than 400-500 words at the beginning of this century.

Homo sapiens

Marked progress in the use of language and the beginnings of a more advanced civilization have usually gone hand in hand. In the more complex and specialized life of larger communities more numerous and abstract concepts were needed. Moreover, as men increasingly began to act and think with insight and to grasp the laws of nature, they had to form grammatical constructions, to be able to express causal and logical relationships between individual words as precisely as possible. Besides, the exact connotation of all words had gradually to be established.

This improvement was helped forward by the invention of writing, an invention made independently by several nations and coinciding more or less markedly with the beginning of an advanced culture. The Sumerians, indeed, dated their own civilization from the invention of writing. As far as our present knowledge goes, this oldest known writing originated in the fourth millennium B.C. (the Uruk period). At first it took the form of pictures, impressions on clay tablets, designed to evoke the memory of certain objects and activities. The Sumerians and Akkadians (Babylonians) developed this into the cuneiform script. The oldest documents consist entirely of lists of objects. It was not until many centuries later that written signs became differentiated grammatically, and sentences could be framed [11]. The Egyptian hieroglyphs, which also began as a purely pictorial writing, are earlier than the First Dynasty, about 3000 B.C. Chinese writing, which clearly also derives from pictorial symbols, can be traced back to the second millennium B.C.

Traditions were much more easily established once the language came to be fixed in the written word. Written signs lasted for many generations, whether carved in stone, stamped on clay and then hardened, or painted on papyrus or wood. They could be copied over and over again, as was often done in Egypt's Old Kingdom (*c.* 2700-2200 B.C.). This laid the foundation of historical records and so of historical thought. As writing, and the meanings attached to the symbols, had to be learned, some kind of scholastic training became a necessity. So ideas came to be handed on in a traditional form.

Man's way of thinking, and therefore the nature and significance of his traditions, have been greatly influenced by the particular manner in which writing has developed in different countries. For instance, the Egyption hieroglyphs started merely as symbols for objects, animals and men, and for man's activities. Soon, however (as early as the Old Kingdom), they began to be used for sounds or groups of sounds apart from any object, and this paved the way for an alphabet composed of letters, by which much more specialized concepts and relationships could be conveyed and defined. But it was the Phoenicians who first evolved an alphabet of letters (possibly about 1500 B.C.). Via Greece and Rome this has come to be used for the European languages of today. An almost endless variety of concepts could now be expressed, but no new symbols were needed, and it was much easier to learn. In Chinese writing, on the other hand, the written symbols have always represented whole words. In time thousands of them came to be needed, and the craft of writing became limited to 'scholars'. As well as its large number of symbols – amounting to over 40,000, though generally only 3000-4000 were used – this 'word-writing' had the disadvantage that it did not allow any grammatical construction to develop. The result was that many logical and causal relationships could not be expressed with any precision. Presumably this is why philosophy in China, like the exact sciences, was largely limited to its more practical aspects (ethics, architecture, medicine) until well into the nineteenth century.

The invention of printing represented a further significant advance. This time the first country to develop the art was China, where single sheets go back to the second century A.D., and books to the tenth century A.D. The invention of book printing in Europe in the fifteenth century led to much wider and more rapid dissemination of important theoretical works. Many books were preserved and studied for decades, and indeed for centuries, and important paragraphs were read and reread, were used to instruct the young, and could also be revised. In consequence, more and more of the older established lore reinforced by new experiences and knowledge of all kinds was accumulated. The circle of those engaged in storing up tradition grew wider. Since then we have added colour reproduction, the preservation and circulation of lectures and music on records and tapes, and of events on films, which can be broadcast over large parts of the world by radio and television.

From a biological point of view, this accumulation of knowledge in the form of scrolls and books represents something fundamentally new. Mankind has, as it were, created a social superbrain: his literature and his libraries. We now spend years in schools and colleges stuffing our brains – often to satiety – with the knowledge and experience of former generations. In the course of living and aspiring to new knowledge we find ourselves making use of countless trains of thought, which we could never hold in our memories but which are at all times at our disposal in the books we read. In timetables or cookery books, in manuals for constructing complicated appliances, in scientific works, in lexica, in monographs on art illustrated in colour – in all our reading we can link up with the author's train of thought and so make use of knowledge beyond that which our own brains alone could retain. In this way – by what I described in 1947 [181] as 'extra-cerebral chains of association' – literature immeasurably enriches our capacity for thinking.

In the electronic computer, science has created an appliance which can do more than man himself. In a few minutes it can complete a complicated calculation that would take a man several years. Moreover, as such results are often of practical use only when applied to control some rapid process (e.g. guiding rockets) involving intervention measured in fractions of a second, there is some justification for describing its achievement as 'suprahuman'.

Yet we must bear in mind that all this knowledge amassed through writing, print and other means of reproduction could only have been accumulated because at the same time larger and larger human communities have grown up. These have made increased division of labour possible, making much fuller use of the special gifts many individuals have for particular activities. As long as pre-humans and early men lived in family groups or small bands sharing a common cave-dwelling or hearth, all the adults of the same sex were obliged to do more or less the same tasks. It was only when *Homo sapiens* settled in one spot that larger communities came into being, with such limited division of labour as one can observe today among primitive peoples (Papuans, Congo pygmies, Brazilian Indians and others). *Homo sapiens's* late Palaeolithic brain appears to have been like that of present-day races – at all events its structure, judged on the base of casts of the brain cavity, does not hint at any important differences. In other words, between 20,000 and 50,000 years ago men may well have possessed special aptitude for higher mathematics, theoretical physics, complicated languages, music, and so on. In the small communities of those days, however, they had no possibility either of discovering or of making use of it. Division of labour probably began with more skilled individuals carrying out specialized tasks – preparing stone and bone implements, for instance – while those with superior mental ability assumed leadership. It is only when we come to more civilized communities that we find division of labour to any appreciable degree. Use is made of special gifts fostered in youth by special training adapted to these specific capacities.

Nowadays human communities have grown enormously, and extensive specialization has led to a division of labour which has produced much greater efficiency in all sizes of groups. At the same time, the invention of quicker and easier means of travel and communication has brought international cooperation in almost every cultural field. Personal contacts, the spread of books and broadcasts, the continued exchange of material and cultural assets, have produced a kind of uniform global culture, which continues to expand. In particular, almost all important inventions – railways, cars, the telephone, the wireless, the refrigerator, the camera, scientific appliances, and also novels, plays, and works of art – are shared by nearly every inhabitant of the globe. Exchange of findings is most lively in the field of scientific knowledge and especially in the natural sciences. One has only to look at the bibliography of any scientific publication with its references to writers of many nationalities. Scientific libraries in particular already constitute a kind of global superbrain. And to match this, a global standard of knowledge has developed, beyond the aspirations of even the best single human brain. Even the most brilliant intellects cannot link up any longer with all the 'extracerebral chains of association' – that is, the trains of thought in all branches of knowledge – for a very complicated language of symbols and technical terms has naturally been evolved to deal with intricate problems, above all in mathematics, physics, chemistry and many branches of biology.

The cultural development brought about in these ways led very rapidly to a mounting mastery over nature, while at the same time individuals as well as entire nations grew more and more independent of their environment. In a more advanced civilization, life became determined less by such elementary needs as food, protection from the climate and so on, but to a greater degree by more abstract ideas – values, ideals and supra-individual aims. Ethical and nationalist ideals, religious values and scientific aims developed and largely dominated both thought and action.

Yet we must not forget the overriding influence of technical advance. Palaeolithic man could not have survived without primitive weapons. Fire, the wheel, the plough, the use of metal – all these led in turn to new and higher cultural stages [140]. Later, machines used in supplying clothing, houses, means of transport and so on also determined the cultural progress. Without microscopes, physical and physiological appliances and the application of chemical knowledge, our expectation of life would still not exceed thirty-five years, for we would know almost nothing of how our organs function, what causes disease and how to combat it. The course of political history, too, has been largely determined by technical inventions. It was thanks to their superior arms and military techniques that the Romans conquered many less civilized peoples. Guns and cannons enabled Europeans to defeat American Indians, African negroes and others. Today the atom bomb and the long range rocket are decisive factors in the struggle for political supremacy.

This development of modern weapons capable of wiping out mankind, however, has led to second thoughts on technical achievements as a product of culture. We find this ceaseless technical progress often described today as something dangerous and far from desirable. Besides, faster trains, cars and aircraft, the telephone, radio, television, films and so on have placed an alarming strain on man's nerves, and they are clearly tending to undermine his health and shorten his life.

Yet technical progress is an inevitable development and its pace cannot be halted (see section C of this chapter). Unfortunately, however, it is proceeding too rapidly for man to adapt his ethical concepts and customs or his social and political patterns to it. A reasonably stable tradition is needed to foster these elements, otherwise crises may occur which release man's dangerous potentialities. During the most recent millennia the hereditary good or evil latent within him has not changed significantly, because natural selection has been much less active in this field. The latest decades have shown us that Europeans are capable of the same cruelties as were perpetrated in the Roman arena, the medieval torture chamber, by the Inquisition, by slave-hunting, or during the Thirty Years War. Instead of lightly casting off the bonds of ethical tradition, we ought to be relaxing and adjusting them to meet a rapidly changing technical environment, mainly by abolishing wars, which formerly ranked as ethically defensible instruments of policy.

As man's cultural qualities are not hereditary in the biological sense, throughout his life each individual has to acquire them. There is a certain parallel here between child development and the historical development of civilization. In our first years, learning is mainly concerned with customs and manners connected with elementary essential needs, introducing us to the limited world of family and neighbours (eating habits, usages in dress, respect for one's elders, writing, counting, and other elementary 'accomplishments', simple religious ideas and practices). Only gradually do we move on to more advanced aspects of civilization (technical skills, science, ethical ideals, aesthetic principles, and so on). And the highest and most precious cultural values are appreciated only by adults – and indeed are beyond many belonging to even that category.

Individual development (ontogeny) echoes phylogenetic

stages in much the same way in the sphere of biologically inherited peculiarities (the 'biogenetic law'). But in this case the
genes, which remain constant during tens of thousands of
generations, ensure that these characteristics will develop. Not
so in the cultural field. If tradition is broken, if the rising
generation receives no cultural instruction, those values may
be lost again, and we may fall back into an earlier cultural
stage. Man's history offers many instances in which the decline
of a people has meant the destruction of countless and often
precious traditions. One has only to recall how the civilizations
of Egypt, Babylon, Greece and Rome fell into decay. Much of the
valuable knowledge and tradition belonging to classical antiquity did not come to light again until the Renaissance. Even
a change in the political system, or in scientific or religious
tenets, may mean the extinction of important cultural values –
instances that spring to mind include the decline of science in
the first fifteen centuries of our era, in consequence of the
supremacy of orthodox Christian convictions, the collapse of
historical studies and pictorial art in the Nazi period in Germany,
and the falling off in religious practices in many countries
today. Civilization is a treasure that may increase or dwindle
at any time, and in the event of global atomic warfare might
vanish entirely. Growing international cooperation in every
cultural sphere holds out the only hope that cultural values
may be less likely to vanish completely.

C. *Laws of cultural development*

It has become increasingly probable that evolution depends on
purely causal processes. Although the origin of mutations can
be explained only in certain groups of cases because of the
enormous complication of the biochemical processes in the cells,
relevant research has always proved that here too only causal
processes are operating. Natural selection, which is so important
for the progress of phylogenetic development, shows cause and
effect more clearly. Hence the development of human beings
has also apparently been determined by causal processes and fits
in well with the whole development of life and of our earth.

However, humans normally presume that their appearance caused a suspension of the laws of nature because free will is capable of directing the brain processes which correspond to their thoughts. But this assumption meets with many difficulties. Surely it is not possible to prove definitely that free will does not exist. The processes in our brain and the motivation of our thoughts and actions are much too complex to be analysed sufficiently. However, it is at least possible to deduce that free will is improbable. We will come back to this problem in Chapter 5, section C [more detailed treatment: Rensch, 193, 196].

If we admit that human will, thought and action is determined, then the development of human culture and history must also be a determined process. The philosopher Kant [106] made such an assumption. In 1784 he wrote: 'Whatever one's metaphysical concept of the freedom of will may be, its manifestations, human actions, are like every other occurrence in nature in being determined by the universal laws of nature . . . although the causes may be deeply concealed, we may nevertheless hope that, when considering the play of freedom on the whole, we may discover its regular course. . . .'

Is it possible to demonstrate that human culture develops according to natural laws? Do at least some laws or rules exist, even though this development is based only on tradition and not on hereditary changes? I believe that this is the case to a much greater extent than is normally assumed. The importance of these questions may serve as excuse for a biologist to be concerned with them. He is well aware that it is difficult to evaluate the basic prehistoric, historic, ethnological, cultural, political and economic facts and relations and to survey the relevant literature. But it is natural to discuss the problems because the rules of cultural development run parallel to the rules of causally determined phylogenetic rules to a surprising extent. A series of examples may show this.

(1) As already mentioned in Chapter 2, mutation and recombination of genes are the basic conditions of evolution. In cultural development non-hereditary new ideas and new

combinations of mental images follow a similar course, as they also appear regularly, or more precisely in a manner proportionate to time. They have led to the invention of new tools, better machines, better communications, new types of administration, scientific discoveries, works of art and so on. And, like mutations and new gene combinations, new ideas appear as individual events, which spread if they are favourable or if they are at least accepted by the population, corresponding to gene flow.

(2) Just like hereditary variants, new ideas are subjected to natural selection. However, selection of hereditary characteristics is an extremely long term process, which normally took hundreds of thousands of years to produce any appreciable change among man's forerunners; whereas with non-hereditary human cultural elements, selection operates a great deal more rapidly.

This process can be seen at work in everything that man has devised – tools, machines, buildings, state systems, scientific or religious ideas, as well as language, music, etc. Bows and arrows have been superseded first by the crossbow and then by the muzzle-loader; then came the breech-loader, the needle gun and after them the machine gun. The goose quill was abandoned in favour of the steel nib in a penholder, then followed the fountain pen, ball-point pen and typewriter.

Here, as in animal phylogeny, two different types of selective process are at work, differing chiefly in intensity. First we have gradual selection (as already described) between more or less advantageous rival variants within a community (corresponding to infraspecific selection); and secondly, rapid and intensive selection, possibly trade rivalry, competition or even war between whole communities or peoples (corresponding to interspecific selection). Many technically less advanced peoples, such as American Indians, African negroes, Australian aborigines and Melanesians, have been defeated in war by Europeans. Their culture was then largely destroyed and replaced in part by European institutions. But even when rivalry between peoples has been peaceful, the change in cultural patterns has been no less rapid, especially when the products of a more advanced civilization could be distributed in a more primitive area. In many countries the people have discarded the loin cloth for European dress, primitive carts for cycles or cars, grass roofs for corrugated iron ones, their own fallible native cures for European medicines, the tribal system of chiefs for an administration modelled on that of European countries or America.

The invention of the internal combustion engine has changed the whole world. Cars involved a rapid expansion of the road systems, and in this process the countryside was soon ravaged. Horses were replaced by tractors, which were cheaper to run. The land formerly needed to grow fodder could then produce food. Cars and planes brought nations into closer contact and intercourse was freer.

(3) But natural selection by no means always had the effect that variants in an animal population became totally replaced by a new variant. Small groups of the weaker variants may survive in special 'niches' (annidation). In a corresponding manner older ideas and implements were normally not totally replaced by better ones. And when the environmental conditions changed, the older variants sometimes proved to be more practicable and soon prevailed again. When electrical and gas mains were totally destroyed in many towns during the Second World War, oil lamps and candles proved to be favourable once again. In autocratically governed countries normally weak and suppressed democratic groups still existed. As soon as living conditions fundamentally changed they soon increased and prevailed.

(4) Alterations in animal species are often brought about by a change of organic function, because this is a quicker evolutionary process than the origin of quite new organs. The forelimbs of former reptiles, for instance, have been transformed into wings of birds and bats or fins of penguins and whales. Bones of lower and upper jaws of reptiles became auditory ossicles in mammals. Human establishments and concepts have gone through a similar change of function. At first an 'obolos'

was a little metallic roasting spit which had a certain exchange-value. Later on this concept was carried over to denote a coin. An 'idiot' was formerly a 'private man' or a 'layman'. Only in the seventeenth century did the concept acquire its present meaning.

(5) During animal phylogeny, such structures as have lost their functional significance have undergone gradual retrogression. They often remain as functionless rudiments, such as the vestiges of pelvis and hind legs in the Greenland whale and giant python, or man's vermiform appendix. Similar rudiments can also be found among human tools, clothes, institutions and customs. The buttons at the back of a tail-coat were originally put there to fix the tails back when riding. Nowadays they are still there as functionless rudiments. Sleeve buttons have a similar history. Many women in Egypt wear an equally functionless modern black veil; its mesh is fully an inch wide, and it does nothing to shroud the features of the wearer. There are other examples: the 's' in the word 'island', or the circumflex in 'bête' and 'tête', which marks the lost 's' of the Latin 'bestia' and 'testia'. A German 5 *Pfennig* piece is often called a 'sechser', although the real coin of that denomination has long been obsolete. And a relic still remains of the former Slav custom of acquiring a bride by capture: not many years ago two armed youths used to drag her to the altar at the wedding ceremony.

(6) In view of the laws governing both animal and human evolution, it is not surprising to find parallel and convergent features in concurrent but unrelated lines of development. Swallows, swifts and terns, though not related, are similar in flight and so have developed very similar wings and tails. Parallels exist in man's cultural history: medical science and operating skills among ancient Egyptians, Incas and Chinese, for instance, or the invention of writing in Egypt, Sumer, China and Mexico, and construction of a calendar, the development of monarchy in different countries, and so on.

(7) Evolution often follows a definite line of development (orthogenesis), because natural selection often favoured the same trend

during a long period. Among running animals, for instance, those were favoured that possessed particularly long legs, powerful muscles at the shorter end of the lever (i.e. in the thigh), reduced numbers of toes, a tendency to walk on the toes or tip of the toes, and well developed eyes and ears. In the same way, man's instruments and machines frequently developed for long periods along some definite line. After stone tools had been invented by the first hominids, they have been continuously improved by sharper cutting edges or better points. Similar trends of continuous improvement show in the development of fire arms, locks and bicycles, and also of methods of administration, etc.

(8) With humans, as with animals, evolution in any fixed direction sometimes led to the development of 'excessive' structures. The stag has 'unnecessarily' large branching antlers, and the capricorn beetle's antennae and the giraffe's neck are 'needlessly' long. Mankind, too, has produced exaggerations. The excessive profusion of curls and the wasp waist of the Baroque period, or later the guardsman's busby, the dress with flowing train, the Japanese warrior's elongated trouser legs, and the more recent stiletto heels. In the literature of the past two centuries we have had the vast involved sentence, and extremes of political despotism have arisen in every age.

(9) One important characteristic of animal phylogeny is its irreversibility. Single genetical alterations can be reversed by back-mutation or by a reversal in the trend of selection; but the main evolutionary steps cannot be reversed. The reason is that at any one time there is a steady production of mutations, some of which are retained in the ensuing generations. Evolution flows on in a steady stream. So a repetition of former conditions of selection cannot possibly result in the same structure again, because selection has to deal with an organism that is no longer genetically the same. For instance, the earliest known bird, *Archaeopteryx* of the Jurassic, and also the toothed birds of the Cretaceous (Odontornithidae), still had real teeth, while all later birds have only weak embryonic rudiments. Subsequently,

when it again became advantageous to have teeth – as, for example, among the fish-eating mergansers – these teeth developed in quite a different way, as outgrowths of horn from the edge of the beak.

The main steps in human civilization are irreversible in the same way, and it moves steadily forwards. The same needs or the same historical situations may recur, but as the cultural basis has altered meanwhile, what emerges – however similar – is never precisely the same. For examples, medieval soldiers used to protect their heads with iron helmets; but in later centuries more comfortable leather ones were preferred. Then in the First World War, when the need again arose for some metal protection for the head, methods of production had meanwhile changed and protection was now required against projectiles, so the steel helmets then made were quite different in construction. The Polish state has more than once been brought into being, but never twice in the same form, for the system of government and the political boundaries have varied. Houses built in Greek or Roman style in Europe were not exactly like those of ancient Greece and Rome, for in the meantime building materials had come to be treated in a different way and could now be put to other uses and adapted to new purposes. Continuous and varied alteration is typical of all historical processes, and irreversibility therefore governs phylogenetic evolution as well as cultural development.

(10) After a variable period of structural improvement, many animal structures and organs entered a prolonged phase of relative stability (stasigenesis). In mammals the heart, lungs, liver, eyes and other organs are very similar in structure and function; and as they surely go back to before the Tertiary period, this means that they have existed as 'permanent structural types' for over 60 million years. In the same way, once a functional optimum was reached, human implements have often varied very little. For example, after some initial modifications, we find practically no change in such things as spoons, bottles, pots, cycles, vacuum cleaners, the telephone, and so on, or in the alphabet, figures and musical notation. Furthermore,

accepted mathematical propositions, physical laws and many religious tenets, in particular in Buddhism and in Mohammedanism, have remained virtually unaltered for centuries.

(11) Hybridization represents another common feature. As we saw in Chapter 2, sexuality is a device that has enabled diverse organisms to go on producing new combinations of hereditary factors, and so to include numerous variants in a population; and with the frequent changes in the conditions of selection at least some of these had a chance of surviving and preserving the species. Secondary hybridization also occurs in established animal races, and this makes for still wider variety and the emergence of new types. All man's appliances and institutions display these same characteristics, owing to 'hybridization' of ideas – that is, new possibilities of modification and improvement being transferred from one variant to another. Improvements to wristwatches, for instance, have included luminous figures, a watertight case, built-in shockproofing and other features. After the steam-engine, and later the internal combustion engine, had been invented, cars and boats acquired new driving mechanisms. Languages also form a very clear case in point: they are always gaining in subtlety and expressiveness by borrowing words. Something rather like 'secondary hybridization' is illustrated by words of mixed origin taken from quite advanced languages – such as 'ex-king', 'vice-chancellor', 'hyper-intelligent', 'omnium-gatherum'.

(12) One of the most important rules of animal phylogeny is that of progressive evolution in many branches. We have already noted (pp. 22 ff.) that the 'higher' animal forms can be distinguished by the fact that their structure and functions are more complex and also more efficient. This is achieved by division of labour and by centralizing important functional groups (brain, heart, kidney, and so on). Therefore, higher animals can react in a more flexible manner; they are more independent of the environment, and as individuals they are more autonomous. Mutations and gene combinations involving greater complexity or more efficient and more adaptable

functioning of structures or organs are rare, but they may occur on all phylogenetic levels. Where this happens, natural selection normally operates in their favour, whereas harmful mutations (which are much more common) are eliminated. In most phyla this has inevitably led to progressive evolution [181].

Human cultural development, though non-hereditary, has followed a very similar course. Culture became increasingly complex and the different functions also grew more complex. Here, too, an increase in centralization is characteristic. As human communities expanded, settlements, villages and townships were formed. Specific needs were met in specialized centres such as workshops and factories, schools and universities, post offices, ministries, law courts, hospitals and churches. The advantages were obvious – economy in personnel, possibility of using specialists for different tasks, multifarious individual needs now registered and reconciled. Moreover, it was useful for many of these centralized institutions to be grouped together. Urbanization followed, and is still rapidly spreading in our day. In the numerous larger cities that have grown up it is easier to conduct business, bigger fortunes can be made, there are more opportunities for further education, and wider sources of entertainment and relaxation are available. So towns will no doubt continue to expand until 'saturation point' is reached, at some 60-80 per cent of the population in an industralized country (cf. Chapter 7). Table 1 illustrates the spread of urbanization in every continent, the rate being slower in countries already largely urbanized (Australia, not included here, has 64 per cent town-dwellers).

Increased independence of the environment and greater individual autonomy represent other features running parallel in animal phylogeny and human cultural development. The most advanced animals, the warm-blooded mammals and birds, are largely independent in this respect, and many types can winter and remain active in temperate and cold zones. Civilized man's ability to produce fire, clothing, houses with artificial heating or cooling systems, lighting, and transport of all kinds, has enabled him to live in more and more varied and difficult conditions. The higher vertebrates already reveal a measure of individual freedom. Their actions may involve choice based on experience, and even some planning on the basis of foresight. Man's cultural development has brought him much more

TABLE I Percentage of population living in cities and towns (or town-like communities) with percentage increase in recent decades. *Source:* United Nations, *Demographic Yearbook,* vol. 4, 1952.

Country	Year	Urban pop.*	Recent increase
Germany (1937 boundaries)	1939	69·9%	13·8% in 39 years
West Germany (today)	1950	71·1%	0·6% in 11 years
Sweden	1950	56·3%	34·8% in 50 years
England and Wales	1951	80·7%	3·7% in 50 years
France	1946	52·9%	11·9% in 45 years
Spain	1950	60·5%	28·3% in 50 years
U.S.A.	1950	26·6%	2·1% in 50 years
Canada (excl. New-foundland)	1951	62·1%	24·6% in 50 years
Mexico	1940	55·1%	1·6% in 10 years
Argentina	1947	62·5%	25·1% in 52 years
Brazil	1950	36·5%	5·3% in 10 years
Japan	1950	37·5%	19·4% in 30 years
India (1931, before partition)	1951	17·3%	6·2% in 20 years
Ceylon	1946	15·4%	3·7% in 45 years
Egypt (excl. nomadic tribes)	1947	30·1%	5·0% in 10 years
Union of South Africa	1951	42·4%	19·2% in 47 years
S.W. Africa	1951	16·0%	2·1% in 5 years

* According to a standard estimate of urban communities.

autonomy because he has gained insight into the laws of the universe and can act according to complicated plans, giving an impression of 'free' will in thought and action.

Man, like animals, continued to incorporate successively new features that proved particularly useful. Chromosomes, mito-chondria, cells, the arrangement of cells into larger units, nerve cells, central nervous systems, muscles, intestines, blood vessels and other features, once 'invented', were then retained. So too were such fortunate inventions as pottery, weaving, metal work, the wheel, the cart, ships, steam-engines, motor power, electric appliances, planes, writing, printing, mathematics, and so on. Once invented, they have been preserved.

What a wealth of successive single inventions has gone, for instance, to make up the bicycle of today! Iron smelting, wheels, cogs, gears, braking systems, ball bearings, lamps, reflectors, production of rubber, the pneumatic pump, the use of enamel, and so on. More practical versions were continually replacing less useful ones. This is how our knowledge in every field has developed, as each cultural stage has made and handed down its contribution. The cell theory is a case in point. It dates from the seventeenth century, when it was discovered that organisms are made up of cells. In 1839 T. Schwann established the nucleus as an essential component. During the latter half of the nineteenth century the types and functional significance of the different cells were distinguished: epithelial, muscle, bone, nerve and sensory cells, and so on. In 1875, O. Hertwig discovered that fertilization depends on the fusion of two cell nuclei. A few years later various researchers found how cells and chromosomes divide. Since the invention of the electron microscope it has been possible to study the microstructure of the cell wall, the nuclear membrane, the mitochondria, etc., and to discover much about the functioning of these organelles. Finally, now the molecular structure of the nucleic acids is known, we have come nearer to understanding the transmission of information which the chromosomes hand on to the cytoplasm. And this whole series of successful discoveries and findings have been kept and combined in present-day cellular theory.

All these parallels show that the development of human culture was subjected to similar rules as are recognized in animal phylogeny, the common guiding principle being the general law of selection and ultimately the causal law (assuming that no free will exists, as the author believes). In this way cultural development is directly combined with and annexed to the evolution of organisms and of our planet. The knowledge of these rules of cultural progress is important because it may form a basis for predictions of man's future and for corresponding planning. However, such planning will normally be limited to a few decades (cf. Chapter 6).

It is not so easy to see 'phylogenetic' laws in political history. Mankind's thought processes are so complicated that hereditary dispositions, education and contemporary and environmental influences can only account for a small part of the ideas and decisions either of the leaders or those who follow them. Most historians deny such laws or rules because they are convinced that man's will is free. Some recognize at best a sequence of youth, prime and decline among states [233, 250], although just as many exceptions to such rules exist as in the phylogeny of animals. However, as the principle of selection also operates very clearly in the realm of politics, and as the mentioned rules of cultural development also influence political actions, at least the following rules of political history can be established.

(13) The stronger nations subdued the weaker, either incorporating them or holding them in subjection, by payment of tribute, by establishment of colonies, or by keeping these countries in a state of dependence.

(14) The general tendency in prehistory and early history has constantly been towards larger and more unified communities. This has continued in the main (though by no means invariably) in more recent times. The collapse of colonialism has naturally led to the establishment of many small new nation-states, but it seems as though large political entities, such as the United States, the Soviet bloc, Communist China, Indonesia and India, will also develop in other parts of the world. There are at least signs of this already in western Europe, the Pan-Arabian countries and the federations of African states. This is the principle of centralization, which, with its many advantages, has always ranked as a positive selective factor.

(15) An unmistakable global tendency towards increasing democratization exists. As this is a logical outcome of the spread of

education, it can be traced back to the invention of writing and printing. Democratization expresses itself in juridical equality among all citizens, a general right to vote, equal possibilities of education and of medical treatment, and a certain levelling of all social classes. This process is, of course, more advanced in socialistic countries.

D. *Independence of conceptions and institutions beyond the level of the individual*

Man's cultural development has brought him to the point where much of what he has produced and conceived goes far beyond the span of any single individual's life. This has meant that many traditions have taken over control and now direct man's life. Even during the last century the complaint was frequently heard that machines ruled man, not man the machines. And this could now be said of many cultural institutions. Nowadays man grows up amid a framework of long established traditional institutions: the state, the town, the nation with its traditional language and writing, customs and views, fixed laws, recognized religion, and so on. These traditions have all grown so powerful that the individual is usually quite ready to be ruled by them. In our day, life is not lived with the *aid* of all these cultural achievements so much as for their preservation and the welfare of a state, a town, a branch of knowledge, a business undertaking, a journal, art, the Christian religion, and so on.

By improving his brain accomplishments, man has gained greater freedom; but he largely pays for this as an individual by his subordination to tradition. We have the clearest proof of this: not only is he ready to live under the domination of certain ideas and 'ideals'; he is even prepared to die for them. The hero or martyr has abandoned the elementary instinct of self-preservation. His animal counterpart is the ant or the bee, which will die in defence of the colony.

This biologically remarkable phenomenon, the abnegation of individual autonomy, also reminds us that all human life on earth is one in origin and homogeneous in character. Like all other living organisms, every human alive today derives from

126

the one common stream of life, and all are bound together by the germ tracts, the unbroken chain of living cells (see Chapter 2, section A).

We ought not, then, to rate our own individual importance too highly. But neither should we help forward the 'stereo-typing' process, which is mainly caused by the rapid increase of mankind. On the whole man appears indeed to be tending towards increasing autonomy. And it is certainly extraordinary that *Homo sapiens* emerged from the animal world at all. For he is the only species to gain self-knowledge as well as an appreciation of universal laws, to look to the most distant galaxies and into the heart of the atom, to comprehend the world's course and to begin purposefully to direct his own future history.

CHAPTER FIVE

The biological uniqueness of man

A. *Physical features*

Like any other organism, man has his own place in the dimensional scale that stretches from the atoms to the stars. Strangely enough, this fact has received very little attention hitherto. The individual ranges in size from the 0·2 mm of the fertilized egg to the 1·50-2·10 metres of adult man; but the achievements that distinguish man from the animals are not made until the individual, at the age of perhaps one to two years, is fairly large in relation to the full extent of his growth. As child and as adult, man must undoubtedly rank as one of the larger 'animals'. We know of very few indeed that are larger (some cephalopods, fishes, saurians, crocodiles, ostriches and a few mammals).

Man has the most complex brain of all the larger mammals, and so it is relatively large in proportion to his body. As his most essential characteristics – speech, insight and purposeful actions – depend upon the development of his brain, it is apposite to ask whether these typical features could have developed had his size been different. It seems that they could not. Thought based on insight requires a high grade ability to differentiate perceptually, to retain innumerable impressions and to forge corresponding associative links. This requires a centralized system of thousands of millions of nerve cells. The brain must also be functionally specialized in many sensory and motor centres, as well as in extensive associative regions. This subdivision, it seems, was impossible as long as the brain remained small. None of the smaller mammals has produced such a specialized structure.

The 'invention' of cells, nerve cells and central nervous systems probably developed more or less of necessity along lines

determined by selection (see Chapter 2, section D). Cells, however, are governed in size by the effective range of action of the
cell nucleus. This range in turn is limited to microscopic proportions by the chromosomes, i.e. by the shape and dimensions
of the DNA molecules, and ultimately by the limited reach of
the genes, which control the biochemical processes of the cell.
There are, therefore, certain fixed lower limits to the size of
the brain and to the accumulation and functional grouping of
the several thousand million ganglion cells required for insight,
planned action, the invention of tools and the development of
culture. As brain size and body size are correlated to a certain
degree, size and proportions of man's body are fixed within
the order of magnitude of existing creatures. And any being on
another planet capable of complicated thought would necessarily be of a similar order of magnitude – subject, of course, to
variations determined by the particular conditions, especially
gravity, and by the special structure of whatever organs of
thought he possessed.

We might, however, wonder why man did not grow considerably larger, for greater land mammals exist and they have
a much larger brain (elephants 5000-6000 g, man about 1000-
1800 g). But these giant animals are usually rather clumsy,
because, although their body volume and weight has increased
by the cube of their dimensions, this mass is supported by bones
whose efficiency has increased only by the square. Giant animals
thus have disproportionately massive bones and are incapable
of the mobility that has been a prerequisite of man's evolution.
Besides, natural selection operates on a limited scale in present-
day civilized man (see section B). Further hereditary increase
in size along the lines of Cope's rule seems to have been largely
halted. Moreover, giant animals show a less favourable metabolism than related smaller species [21].

The development of man's other specific features was just as
little a matter of 'chance'. The laws of evolution operated here
as well, tending to bring about progressive structures. As we
have seen (in Chapter 2, section E), it was not 'chance' that
made Tertiary apes the ancestors of the human species.

If, in an attempt to estimate man's place among living

organisms, we examine the physical features that distinguish him, we find that *Homo sapiens* might be described as a superior mammal, different mainly quantitatively from the anthropoid apes, the animals most closely related to him. The following are among present-day man's chief distinguishing features.

The upright stance leaves the hands free for grasping food, using and fashioning tools, and carrying about objects such as the young, as well as for defence. The hand, that of a climber, is unspecialized in so far as it still retains the five fingers of man's reptilean forerunners, and the opposable thumb of his more recent ancestors. But it is specialized in that it can rotate in any direction and that the nerves are more directly connected to the forebrain by the pyramidal tract. The elbow and shoulder joints are also extremely flexible in many directions. The pelvis and legs are adapted to walking on two legs, with the related *glutaeus maximus* and calf muscles well developed. The five-toed foot clearly reveals its origin as a grasping foot. It is similar to that of the mountain gorilla. An upright stance shifted the weight of the intestines from the belly to the *pelvis*, and this became adapted by its broad scoop shape. Man's parallel vision, taken over from his simian forerunners, helped to develop the sense of distance so vital when eye and hand work together. The cranium is considerably enlarged, while the facial bones are more reduced than in the prognathous apes. The front teeth are relatively weak, and there are no large canines. Nor are the teeth much specialized, so they serve for both plant and animal food, while the relatively long intestine is also suited to a partly vegetable diet.

But the chief distinguishing feature in *Homo sapiens* is undoubtedly his forebrain; and the striking development here was made possible because his more vertical spinal column gave better support to the cranium. In particular, the associative centres in the frontal and temporal lobes could be much more highly developed than in the anthropoid apes (In *Sinanthropus* and *Homo rhodesiensis* the temporal lobes were still rather narrow). The most significant new regions were, however, parts of the basal cortex of the frontal brain and the motor area of speech, particularly characteristic of the human brain.

It was this marked development and greater complexity of the forebrain that made possible the cultural evolution that, mainly since the origin of *Homo neanderthalensis*, has set man apart from all the animals.

The number and structure of the chromosomes also distinguish man from the anthropoid apes [70]. In the haploid set – that is to say, in the mature sex cell – Macaque monkeys (as far as present research tells us) have 21 chromosomes, gibbons have 22, the orang-utan, gorilla and chimpanzee have 24, and man has 23. Thus the anthropoid apes that are nearest to man have one chromosome more.

Some further characteristics are connected with the marked slackening in the pace of individual development. Human pregnancy (*c*. 266-267 days) is a little longer than the chimpanzee's (237) but as long as that of the gorilla's. Man's average weight at birth is about 3·6 kg, whereas the anthropoid ape's is only about 2 kg. Man's prenatal period could not be extended beyond the present limits because the bony pelvis forms a canal through which it would be impossible for any larger infant to pass. Nor could an enlargement of this canal have taken place in the most recent phylogenetic phase, for it would have conflicted with the adaptation in the pelvis to walking on two legs. Although heavier than the anthropoid apes, man is less fully developed after birth. During the first months of life the medullary sheath surrounding many nerve fibres in the infant's forebrain is still maturing. Indeed, the child is nearly a foetus – during most of the first year its organs and frame are still growing at a rapid foetal rate [174, 175]. Rhesus monkeys continue to grow for six and a half years after birth, chimpanzees for eight to ten years, and man for an average of over nineteen years. The rapid growth in puberty is, moreover, a typically human trait. Man's cranial bones unite at a comparatively late stage, and slight cranial growth continues until an advanced age.

In view of this long prenatal period of development, it is normal in man, as in almost all the apes and monkeys, for only one child at a time to develop in the uterus. And there is a correspondingly longer period at which the child is still completely dependent on parental care.

In line with this, we find many characteristics displayed rather earlier by anthropoid apes and only later, if at all, by man. Body hair is one of these. Anthropoid apes have little hair at birth, though it soon grows, but in man it is limited to certain races, especially Europeans, and to the male. In anthropoid apes, whose foot is still a grasping organ, the big toe is opposable; in man it is not. The skull of a young anthropoid ape is more human in shape because the cranial part is relatively large, the facial portion small, and the jaw less prognathous. In youth the facial portion then grows more rapidly than the cranial part. Especially in the males, the jaws project like a snout. Only fossil races and species of *Homo* show a similar development. In the embryonic state the nose in both man and the apes is broad and flat. Among many human races it later develops a pronounced curve. But among mongoloid races, and also some of more primitive physique, it remains flat.

Because of his gradual and prolonged development man has, with some exaggeration, been called a 'foetalized ape'. It would be truer to speak of 'prolonged juvenescence'. But although this term is in line with those characteristics just mentioned, it is in no way applicable to man's important new acquisitions, to his additional brain regions, to his speech, or to the structural change in his limbs, pelvis and other organs. The increase of age corresponds to the slackening of the individual development. On the average apes live to 35-40 years, men to 70-80 years. *Homo sapiens* ranks with the few warm-blooded species that reach a similar age, like the elephants, for instance. A prolonged period of youth has led man to live in *long term family groups*. We have already noted that this tendency to join together into family and larger groupings was a major essential for the evolution of speech and culture.

None of the characteristics, mentioned even the more complicated forebrain, had led the Australopithecines and the *Homo erectus* races much beyond the animal stage. For more than 1·5 million years there was relatively little cultural progress. Real culture emerged only some 50,000-60,000 years ago.

When discussing the physical characteristics of *Homo sapiens* we must not forget to mention his relative structural and functional perfection. We have noted (pp. 54 ff.) how progressive evolution in animals has generally been bound up with an increase in adaptively functioning structures. Man as the highest animal has reached a certain maximum in this respect. Those structures that were 'devised' at different phylogenetic stages and then retained allow the organism to cope with every environmental situation and with the many necessary physiological reactions within the body. It is interesting to note here that the body fluids of man (and he is 60 per cent water in terms of volume) are near chemical neutrality. This makes their reactions extremely sensitive to acid or alkaline substances and they are able to respond quickly to changes inside or outside the body. The heat generated by metabolism is largely retained, and several regulatory mechanisms keep the relatively high temperature stable. According to van t'Hoff's rule all reactions therefore pass off very rapidly.

Most regulation is done by hormones and by the very rapidly reacting nervous system. Many of these adaptive functions operate according to the principle of feedback, in which some stage or result of a process acts as a message to a centre to regulate the activity of that process. For instance, if the blood pressure is too high, pressure builds up on the walls of the first part of the aorta, exciting the delicate sensitive termini of the *vagus* nerve. Through centres in the brain stem this causes the peripheral vessels to expand and so bring about a lowering of the blood pressure. During an instinctive process, when for instance an infant is seeking with its lips for the mother's breast, messages are continually being sent back to the central nervous system, and only when the lips touch the nipple are sucking reflexes set up. In a similar way, the body temperature is controlled by the expansion or contraction of the skin capillaries and by the varied output of hormones which regulate the metabolic rate. The type of food acts as a stimulus, which affects the amount of saliva and the different enzymes in the pancreas. We see similar feedback processes where the composition of the blood plasma is regulated by the liver and kidneys, in the control of heartbeat and breathing, and in the regulation of egg maturation and reproductive instincts by sex hormones.

The regulating mechanisms of the eye are extremely sensitive. The human eye, like that of most mammals, can vary the curve of the lens for near or more distant vision (accommodation), and can alter the length of the visual cells where they penetrate the pigment layer (adaptation) in response to changes of light intensity. The size of the pupil can be adjusted for bright or dim light. There are so many visual cells that many diverse excitations can be transmitted from the retinal image to the visual areas in the forebrain, where the numerous neurones can set up subtle and sensitive reactions to small details of the picture. The visual cells have reached a maximum of perfection. They can react to a single quantum of light and 10-14 quanta are sufficient to produce a sensation. The auditory cells in the inner ear respond no less perfectly. If they were any more sensitive, indeed, we should be disturbed by a sound of molecular humming.

The human brain is extremely adaptable. The hereditary instincts can be suppressed or released at will and most actions spring from learning processes – that is to say, from experiences gained by each individual or his predecessors. This gives him insight and ability to plan ahead, and enables him to adapt his actions to all current situations and needs.

Yet with all its subtlety of structure and function, the human body has also certain imperfections, which are not less characteristic of this highest of organisms. A few examples will suffice. First man has some organs, structures and functions that are now meaningless, as they are vestigial structures of earlier phylogenetic stages. The vermiform appendix is apparently better removed than retained (although it has some unimportant lymphatic functions). The hair, which develops at a late embryonic stage and disappears again before birth (*lanugo*), is an 'unnecessary' retrogressive structure, as are the embryonic vestiges of Jacobson's Organ for smelling within the mouth (which still functions in reptiles), and also the central wrist bone, the *os centrale*, fully developed in the orang-utan and lower apes and occasionally seen in a vestigial form in adult man. The nipples, too, are entirely superfluous in the male. And so is the cutaneous reaction that causes 'goose flesh'. In man's animal ancestors it caused the hair to stand on end and so gave extra warmth.

When the hominids adopted an upright stance, certain structural weaknesses resulted. Flat-footedness often follows when too much weight bears constantly upon the soles. Carrying heavy loads may cause the metatarsal arches to break and pressure on sacral or lumber vertebrae may lead to disc or hip injury. Women often suffer from visceroptosis and varicose veins.

The long growing period in youth has led too to a disadvantageous discrepancy between sexual maturity and full growth. Girls in particular reach sexual maturity, in Europe at eleven to fourteen years, while they are still growing and are therefore not always able to bear a viable child. Moreover, the child would not be adequately provided for, since the young parents cannot yet guarantee sufficient food and protection. Among further imperfections one might include the fact that child-bearing is accompanied by pain, and the menopause often by years of physical disturbance.

If natural selection plays such a large part in shaping the organism's hereditary characteristics, why have these and many other structures and processes persisted, when they are unprofitable, imperfect or superfluous? The reason is much the same as that given in connection with 'excessive' organs (pp. 18 ff.). The individual characteristics are not inherited independently; various correlations are involved, depending partly on linkage of the genes (localization within the same chromosome) and partly on morphogenetical or physiological interdependencies. Natural selection cannot act upon each genetical characteristic singly. It often alters total correlative systems. For instance, if the growth period from birth to maturity were to be slowed down and further prolonged, then countless proportions would have to be altered, for many structures grow faster and others more slowly than the body as a whole. As man's jaw has become relatively shorter, there is less and less space for the back molar. A prolonged growing period has led to a discrepancy between sexual maturity and end of growth, because there was no firm correlation between the two. Superfluous embryological or

K

adult vestigial structures are sometimes not important enough to affect any process of selection.

Moreover, natural selection could not eliminate detrimental characteristics except before or during the reproductive period. Unlike most animals, however, man and especially woman lives on well beyond this stage. So selection cannot affect any harmful developments during the years of change, nor could the variants it favoured build up hereditary resistance against such diseases of old age as cancer, arteriosclerosis, cataract, long-sightedness and so on. Man has been no more able than any other animal to develop as a fully perfect organism.

B. *Polymorphism and the restrictions of further phylogenetic development*

Two further outstanding organic characteristics call for some consideration because of their special importance for man's present and future condition. Firstly, there is the phenomenon of polymorphism; secondly, there are the restricted possibilities of further evolutionary progress. Despite their different origins, the two are connected in certain respects.

We must begin by recapitulating certain factors that have governed the evolution of animals; mutation, recombination of genes, spread of genes (gene flow), isolation, effects of population size, random changes in the frequency of genes within a population, and natural selection. There can be no doubt that these factors were involved in the emergence of *Homo sapiens* from his pre-Neanderthal forerunners. But now that civilizations have arisen, altering man's whole way of living, are these factors still important? Has natural selection, in particular, still any considerable meaning?

In man's twenty-three different chromosomes (the haploid set plus the y-chromosome) it has formerly been estimated that there are about 20,000 genes (or loci) on the chromatids or chains of DNA molecules. Now that we understand the structural complexity of such DNA molecules, and a little about their effect on the process of protein synthesis within cells, it has been realized that the number of loci may be very much larger. The more recent estimate is somewhere between 60,000 and 6,700,000 [62, 256]. Furthermore, after a long period of tens of thousands or hundreds of thousands of generations, during which it reproduces itself identically, every gene may be subject to mutation and these mutants can combine in the most diverse ways; hence the number of possible individual variants is astronomical. Except for identical twins, every human individual can be said to possess his own combination of hereditary factors, distinct from that of any other.

The new mutants that survived gradually spread over large sections of the population in which they arose, and entered other populations by gene flow. In small populations they may have relatively quickly gained a preponderance by genetic drift (the Sewall Wright Effect, cf. p. 12). Moreover, populations frequently became isolated and thus subject to special conditions of selection. Such geographical isolation has led to the emergence of numerous races and sub-races of man.

At the same time, however, races have tended to mix as a result of wars, migrations or friendly contact between neighbours. In war it was a frequent practice among many peoples to kill off the men and absorb the women into the tribe. Many mixtures of races resulted from the keeping of slaves, especially female slaves, or a harem including also women of foreign stock. And in more recent times improvements in transport and communications have furthered racial intermingling. There are only a few nearly pure races in existence today; in their place we have peoples of mixed racial stock. The process of racial differentiation is now on the whole becoming reversed.

Hybridization among sharply distinct geographical races of animals often results in offspring of diminished fertility; but this does not appear to be the case with man. Indeed, there are some districts of Central and South America where people of mixed race now make up the majority of the population.

On the other hand, there are factors that militate against any widespread racial intermingling. Although easier communication has meant an increase in mixed marriages, in most countries it is still more usual to marry within a small community. Differences of caste represent another restrictive factor. For instance, despite official abandonment, this still largely operates in India. Occupational or social strata, like the aristocracy or the middle classes, and religious communities also tend towards exclusiveness.

All these limitations have resulted in a distinctive development of hereditary characteristics in relatively small populations. Few new genes came to them from outside, certain mutants arose and special conditions of selection were effective. Marked random variation and homozygosis in such populations produced distinctive arrays of hereditary characteristics. What emerged were not new sub-races but genetically distinct though not easily definable reproductive communities (gene pools). When the period of isolation ended, these contributed and will continue to contribute to an increase in polymorphism.

The language difficulty hinders sharply differing races from mixing. 'Language barriers are marriage barriers', wrote I. Schwidetzky. So languages common to several peoples always facilitate mixed marriages. This is not only true in the Anglo-American countries, but also of the English widely spoken in India, Indo-China, Japan and other lands, as well as of Russian, Chinese, Spanish, Malay, Swahili, etc.

Homogamy is a further factor operating as a hindrance to racial mixture. Similar variants often tend to mate with each other within one race and this preference is still more obvious when the choice is between a member of their own race and a member of some very different one. Europeans in Africa and Americans of European stock in North America rarely marry Negroes – not from racial arrogance but because of a native instinctive insensitivity to what is admired as beautiful in a race so different from their own (cf. section C). But in the case of half-breeds, quadroons and octoroons, these barriers are progressively diminished, and it is mainly they who bring about a definite mixture of very different races. Yet almost every mixture adds some abiding element, for the new hereditary factors normally persist. Even today in Europe traits introduced during the great migrations of the fourth and fifth centuries can still be recognized.

Finally, polymorphism will continue to increase in proportion as man, like every other organism, produces new mutants. In animals, natural selection eliminates most mutants, but in man its influence is greatly limited (see below). This too makes for more variety in *Homo sapiens*.

Altogether, polymorphism is steadily on the increase. And in our day, with its democratic tendencies and its creed of universal equality before the law, the pace of growth is likely to quicken. The advantages of specific cultures may cause this to be regretted, but the process cannot be halted. And it must be remembered that intermingling and an increase in polymorphism may have the following three positive advantages.

(1) The harm caused by inbreeding is much lowered. Investigations into a great many marriages between cousins have shown that among the factors inherited by every European or American, many are detrimental and between three and five are even lethal – that is, they may cause the death of the embryo or infant [156, 157]. These factors are normally harmless, however, and go unperceived, because they are recessive. It is only when the detrimental recessive factor is homozygous, in other words when a marriage brings it in from both sides, that the characteristic shows itself. This is most likely to happen among near relatives, and is therefore commonest in small communities or limited castes and strata (for example, the upper nobility).

(2) Increased polymorphism continually involves new hereditary combinations. This may lead to favourable effects due to heterosis, with new combinations of genes displaying greater adaptability and the population as a whole demonstrating a greater variety of forms. New types of hereditary physical ability and all kinds of new talents may then emerge.

(3) The mixture of races and peoples lessens the likelihood of conflict. Exaggerated nationalism, the political root of all evil, is commonest in peoples who live shut in upon themselves.

What has just been said must not be wrongly interpreted. There is no suggestion that there should be general racial intermingling. We have simply attempted to assess the import and consequences of what has already taken place, and what can confidently be expected in the future.

It is obvious that man is still evolving, though the phylogenetic changes are now largely limited to the fusion and fresh combination of hereditary factors. But what of natural selection, which determines the direction of further evolution in the whole animal world? In consequence of rivalry among individuals and species of animals, and the premature elimination of some 95-99 per cent of most offspring, selection ensures that the species shall continue to meet the varied challenge of existence.

During the 100,000 years since *Homo sapiens* appeared, there is no doubt that the selective factors have undergone progressive modification. In particular, the rise of more advanced civilizations has led to radical changes. As long as man lived in small groups, such hereditary conditions as extreme myopia, malformations of the jaw, diabetic tendencies, feeblemindedness, or physical debility might have easily proved fatal to the individual. The hereditary factors in question have thus been eliminated. In states with a high degree of civilization, however, weak or short-sighted or feebleminded people have been able to survive and even produce large families. Today no enquiry is made into whether anyone proposing to found a family is suffering from extreme myopia or diabetes. Those with short sight are provided with spectacles, diabetics are treated with insulin, the community protects the feebleminded and often finds some suitable occupation for them. Hardly any attempt is made to prevent them or anyone else afflicted with hereditary disease from having children and passing on injurious traits. On the other hand, modern medicine has found cures for most of the non-hereditary infectious and often epidemic diseases which used to prove fatal. In other words, among civilized peoples, natural selection of resistant variants is much reduced.

It might seem indeed as though natural selection had almost ceased to operate. But a closer look will show that this is not so. Many factors of this sort are still at work.

In the first place, underdeveloped peoples still exist in which the lives of individuals with serious hereditary defects cannot be saved. Infectious diseases of all kinds still claim countless victims; and this amounts to a form of selection of resistant variants. Some tribes even kill any weak or ailing infants soon after birth, as the civilized peoples of antiquity did, and as Tacitus tells us the ancient Germanic peoples used to do. H. Sick

[224] reports that the Xingu Indians of Brazil still carried out this practice up to fifteen years ago. No doubt that is why, despite difficult living conditions, the tribe gives the impression of being an extremely healthy one. H. Bernatzik [6] writes that life is so hard for the Phi-Tong-Luang, a nomadic tribe from the forests of Thailand, that although efforts are made to rear them, weak or deformed children almost always die.

To some degree selection also operates in this way in civilized countries [45]. Quite a number of individuals die of infectious diseases before the age of reproduction. The same is true of such hereditary diseases as lead to a high percentage of deaths among young people. Haemophilia is one of these (50 per cent of haemophiliacs in the U.S.A. die before the age of fifteen), and sickle-cell anaemia is another (most homozygotes die before puberty) [68, 69, 236].

Selection has always operated whenever settlers have come to a new region. The Europeans who emigrated to America, Australia or South Africa were mostly vigorous, enterprising and unemotional men. These characteristics are no doubt at least in part hereditary and have shaped the outstanding traits of the new peoples that emerged there. The Americans are of mainly European stock, but they are noticeably more enter-prising and progressive than Europeans, and on average less gifted artistically. In Oriental and especially Muslim countries one positive selective factor, though a minor one, has been that the leading men, who presumably represent the ablest strains, kept large harems and had more numerous families than their less wealthy contemporaries.

There is also negative selection. For instance, among some peoples, outstanding men may voluntarily renounce offspring and choose to exert influence as Roman Catholic priests, Hindu hermits or Buddhist monks. It seems, too, that hot baths can be an involuntary cause of sterility. If the testicles remain at a temperature of 40·5 to 41·0 C for some minutes, sterility may ensue for the next 22-25 days. Hot baths that may have had these effects were a custom in ancient Rome, as they are in many countries today – in Finland (the sauna), Japan, Pakistan, Morocco, North America and elsewhere. It is possible that the practice may lead to a slight though perhaps negligible drop in the birth rate. Finally, war always acts as a markedly negative selective factor, as the young and healthy enlist and are killed off, whereas the weaker and ailing individuals stay at home and often escape.

Voluntary birth control is an entirely new selective and apparently fairly efficient factor in Europe and America, which is now spreading to Japan, India and other countries. Many families who might formerly have numbered six to twelve children now have between one and three, not from sterility but from choice. Moreover, it operates selectively in affecting the higher social strata in particular. This factor selects against hereditary aptitude (cf. Chapter 7).

Present-day man is subject also to new selective conditions as a result of what Julian Huxley [100] calls 'post-maturity', the long post-reproductive period of later life. Older men often occupy leading positions or acquire a fortune, which gives younger members of their families a greater sense of security. This in turn may affect the size of their children's families [47].

Sexual selection, however, remains the strongest selective factor in all peoples. Once puberty is past, every normal person reacts to the opposite sex with emotions, mental images and actions, which vary as its members approach a certain ideal of beauty. Each race has its own definite and distinct characteristics of face and figure which release erotic feelings (see also section C). These are not only limited to primary or secondary sexual features – the woman's softer contours, more delicate form, absence of facial hair, the lines of bust and hips – they are also concerned with something quite apart from sex: the regularity or 'normality' of the whole frame. If the chin is too short, the nose too long or thick, the figure too heavy or abnormally tall or short – that may be enough to diminish or exclude all possibility of marriage and the production of offspring. This is true especially of women. The chances are still further reduced in the case of pathological deformity. Sexual selection thus acts as a check on defects such as stunted growth, club foot, albinism and so on, at any rate in so far as they are hereditary. E. T. Mörch's investigations in Denmark into achondroplastic dwarfs show that they have only one fifth as many offspring as do people of normal growth. Man's native instincts thus ensure the continuance of a regular build, one that corresponds to a 'releaser pattern' varying slightly with different races. It is worth noting that this unlearned ideal of beauty accords with the slender frame of a young and reproductive person. This fact has also been borne out by the author's own experiments in which the subjects·had to choose between several simplified models of human faces and figures [192].

Schopenhauer recognized the full implications of this connection between man's instincts and the preservation of a certain build. In his *World as Will and Idea* he wrote: 'In fact we possess a very definite, distinct and even complicated instinct, enabling us to make a delicate, serious and determined choice of some other individual for our sexual satisfaction. . . . This dominant attraction of beauty is what preserves the specific type; that is why it acts so powerfully. . . . What in fact guides man – though he thinks he is merely seeking enhanced pleasure for himself – is in reality an instinct that favours what is best for his species.'

These factors, especially sexual selection, are still operative today, but on the whole they have no more than a stabilizing effect. They do little to further evolution. It seems impossible that in future natural selection should suffice to preserve the present level of fitness, for it does not do enough to hinder the accumulation of hereditary detrimental characteristics. If this is so, then one could even say that sexuality has largely ceased to be essential to man. Clearly, nature 'devised' and retained it for almost every plant and animal, because in view of constant and stringent selection it was an advantage to have as many different types of gene combination as possible. Even in abnormal conditions there was then a chance that some resistant variants of the species would survive. Present-day man, at least in more civilized countries, is no longer subject to this kind of selection. Yet as reproduction is connected with fertilization, however, we cannot of course dispense with sexuality.

Non-hereditary characteristics are normally not involved in the preservation of any inherited norm. In recent years, however, these factors have increasingly modified the stringency of sexual selection. Such 'tertiary sexual characteristics', as they may be termed, are often of considerable importance, for they may correspond to or enhance the native ideal of beauty, the instinctive 'releaser pattern'. Among women, they include such things as attractive clothes, dainty underwear, artificially waved hair, powder and lipstick, special clothing to accentuate the figure, high heels to draw attention to the feet, and the former Chinese custom of binding them. Among men, they may include such things as padded shoulders and sporty clothes. A cultivated manly air, and a position of social importance, may also be advantageous. Skilfully employed, all such characteristics can do much to make up for a lack of hereditary assets and so thwart natural selective 'intentions'.

So far we have considered only selection between individual variants; but selection also operates between whole peoples – more or less what in the case of animals is termed interspecific selection. This is particularly intensive in times of wars, which are decisive for the decay or rise of peoples. Many tribes have been completely wiped out by nations superior in size or technical abilities. Europeans have exterminated tribes of American Indians and Australians, while hordes under Ghengis Khan and his successors destroyed several Mongol tribes, killing off the outstanding men and their children, and incorporating all the rest into their own armies. In other instances the conquered have been so weakened economically that their population then increased more slowly than that of their conquerors. Even in normal economic rivalry one finds successful nations increasing and expanding while weaker ones diminish. This is obvious in the different rates of increase and the constantly shifting balance between them (cf. Chapter 6).

To resume, then, we may repeat that many selective factors still combine to favour certain gene combinations and mutants, but in general this makes mainly for stability in the hereditary characteristics. These factors have often changed, especially during the century before our own. And as the size of communities and the intermingling of tribes and races steadily increase, some evolutionary processes continue to affect the whole of mankind. As for their direction, all we can say is that some degree of genetic compromise between the races is being aimed at, and that sexual selection has ensured the continuance of a normal physique. But as there has been a decrease of natural selection against genetically defective individuals, and against those with reduced resistance to infection, whereas the regular mutation of the genes has been maintained, we must expect an increasingly high proportion of recessive detrimental variants. Man's hereditary stock may therefore be in the process of degenerating. For the present this may not be apparent, since increased contacts have meant less inbreeding. Individuals are less frequently homozygous, and the detrimental characteristics, being recessive, go unperceived. However, such detrimental hereditary characteristics will increase. Appropriate eugenic measures may perhaps be taken in the future to deal with this threat (cf. Chapter 6).

But there is so far no indication that man's evolution is going to continue along the lines that have led to *Homo sapiens*. There is unlikely to be any further increase in the forebrain, any new development of sense organs, or any heritable improvement in mental faculties; selection is no longer operating in that direction. Man's main physical structure will meanwhile remain much as it is. The man of the future will not be the bulbous-headed superman so often depicted and caricatured. No one need regret that. Present-day man with his highly complex brain is already capable of the loftiest achievements. If he is to develop to the full, however, he must diminish the increase of detrimental hereditary characteristics by stronger eugenic measures. And he must also match his ethical code, which is naturally relatively stable and slow to modify, to rapidly expanding technical skills and scientific knowledge, which are developing at an overpowering rate. It seems that building up new non-hereditary traditions and ideals can only help him in this task.

C. *Man's mental characteristics*

We have noted the extremely large and specialized forebrain and the high adaptability of the nervous processes as distinguishing *Homo sapiens* from other living organisms. Present-day man can run through several possible lines of action 'experimentally' in his mind and then carry out the appropriate one; in other words, he is far superior to the apes in thinking and acting according to a long range plan. In consequence of his own extremely varied experience and cultural traditions his thinking became adapted to the universal causal and logical laws. During his most recent phase of development, he has grasped the essence of these laws and is capable of real 'insight' in the spheres of thought and action. But he has learned all this. What he has inherited is merely the ability to do so. Left to his own resources, brought up in utter ignorance like Kaspar Hauser, he would have a very meagre stock of experience and his thinking and action would not even equal that of Mesolithic man. In addition, however, man is guided by drives, by instinctive actions. Being hereditary, these are relatively rigid, especially in their largely reflex final phase. These instincts govern human life much less than the life of higher animals, but they are stronger than many of us would like to admit. We must therefore consider them rather more closely.

Their very rigidity makes us think, quite rightly, that these drives are 'animal' in nature. We often are even ashamed of such instinctive processes, though they are also necessary for our preservation, since feeding, reproduction and social structures all depend upon them. Besides, they pervade the whole of our mental life. Our plays, novels, poems and many of our films deal with problems connected with love between the sexes. These sexual relations are given spiritual expression among most peoples through love poems. Only in Western countries do they descend to the level of elementary reproductive drives in the form of pornographic literature, films and pictures. The main reason for this development is apparently not so much the intention to help natural drives to develop properly but to make a financial profit. For the fact that every normal human possesses inherited sexual instincts which remain active during a long period of his life can be exploited for profit. The responsible authorities seem not to consider the overexcitement of the sympathetic nervous system of young people and all its detrimental sequels. Gorillas and chimpanzees in the wild are not so obsessed with sex as Western peoples.

Only to a minor degree is life governed by instincts bound up with social order, fighting and hunting. However, here too Wild West and thriller films and books show that one can exploit these instincts. But also our everyday life is subjected to influences of subliminal sexual, feeding, fighting and cleaning drives and instinctively based claims of social rank. It is characteristic that our actions based on choice and 'insight' often come into conflict with inherited drives (examples of this will be found in a later section). This conflict arises because the urge to instinctive action is so often linked with a powerful access of emotion, which may override rational considerations.

It is worthwhile examining man's instincts, therefore, before passing on to his highest achievements, the 'free' play of his mental abilities. The essential qualities of instincts have long been recognized. Being hereditary, they follow a relatively rigid course, and they help the species to survive. N. Tinbergen [248], whose research into instincts has furnished us with comprehensive and accurate analyses, defines an instinct as a hierarchically organized nervous mechanism which is susceptible to certain primary releasing and directing impulses of internal as well as of external origin, and which responds to these impulses by coordinated movements that contribute to the maintenance of the individual and the species. Instincts are subjected to a hierarchical order. To give an instance, we may note that in vertebrates a male sex hormone arouses the reproductive instinct, and this releases various subordinate lines of action, such as display before the female or combating other males. In the former case the most common sequel is that the sexes approach each other and engage in the final reflex stage of sexual activity.

The different instincts are also arranged in a changing hierarchy in which their positions are determined by their relative intensity, and by their corresponding ability to suppress others. An animal in mating mood normally heeds only certain specific 'releasers', for instance, physical characteristics in the other sex; it ignores any that would lead to feeding, for example. A hierarchy of this sort undoubtedly exists for man as well. His sexual instincts are the strongest, and then follow instincts for social rank, feeding, cleaning, and eventually hunting and collecting. We have evidence of this hierarchy, too, in the fact that love causes many more suicides than do questions of social rank (demotion, wounded pride, etc.). Hunger is yet rarer as a cause, while unfulfilled urges towards cleanliness or collecting are surely negligible factors.

We shall begin, then, by examining the sexual instinct, already mentioned in Chapter 3, section B (p. 73) as determined by the same hormones in man as in other mammals. After puberty, young people like to wander about visiting cafés and dance halls, where they can meet with members of the other sex. This unthinking urge corresponds to appetitive behaviour in animals. The emotional reaction aroused by the 'releaser' characteristics of the opposite sex is experienced as a pleasurable sensation, not at first consciously connected with any desire for sexual actions. We have already noted that such releasing characteristics usually belong to a youthful physique. And here, too, as with animals, models or 'dummies' can be used to arouse the same emotive response – in this case wooden or stone figures, paintings, drawings or even sketches in very simplified outline. Artists and their public unfortunately often confuse this kind of effect with aesthetic values. The 'pin-up' girl on the cover of the glossy magazine is proof that 'supranormal releasers' with unlikely proportions are particularly effective, just as in animals. And in section B of this chapter we also mentioned the enhancing effect of dress and make-up as 'tertiary sexual characteristics'.

The instinctive effect of the female 'releaser' on the male sex first shows itself as 'imposing behaviour'. The young man displays his manliness by his commanding tone and air, by strutting about, driving his car at a reckless pace, and so on. He is not doing this deliberately, or at least not primarily so. It is an unconscious instinct just like the behaviour of many of the higher animals in a like situation. Indeed, the resemblance is so strong that Konrad Lorenz, the famous ethologist, found he could always evoke bursts of spontaneous merriment when he showed a film of comparable behaviour in grey lag geese and other animals.

The female animal usually responds by 'submissive' behaviour, which protects her from possible attack by the male who in the first place may be seeing her simply as a rival at the feeding ground and may not realize why he is attracted to her. Women of every race make the same instinctive response by modest and submissive behaviour. This instinct can lead to difficulties when it comes to questions of equality between the sexes. It is not uncommon, for instance, for an intelligent young woman to marry a less gifted but possibly very manly husband. She continues to look up to him as long as love is 'blind'; but later she realizes her superiority, and this may lead to conflict. With the advance of education and the stronger accent it places on the individual personality, conflicts of this kind are likely to become more frequent. The submissive behaviour counteracts the aim of equality between the sexes. But definite equalization seems also to be difficult because women of Western countries strive too much to exaggerate their releasing characteristics by all kinds of make-up, colouring their hair and uncovering their legs, for instance.

Yet man's reactions are usually so intermingled with actions of insight that his inherited relatively rigid instinctive attitudes may go unnoticed. But the instinctive basis often becomes conspicuous when conflicts with established customs arise. We have noted that because of his prolonged period of growth, sexual maturity has ceased to coincide with the age of marriage. In many European countries a young person at the age of puberty is still thought of as a child and even his shy approaches to the opposite sex are frowned upon. In many areas of Polynesia, on the other hand, these conflicts are avoided by the custom whereby the young people after puberty live together under one roof and erotic relationships are freely permitted among them. During the last few years a certain propaganda for such freedom of young people has been started in Western countries. But it must surely be remembered that we are no longer children of nature. In the present state of civilization any exaggerated sex propaganda may easily lead to a tendency to *la dolce vita* and

149

an overexcitement of the sympathetic nervous system, and it may endanger later family life.

Again, conflict may result when one partner's physique does not correspond to the ideal image of a mate which is built up and serves as a 'releaser'. A plain girl and a pretty one both form much the same ideal of a handsome man, but it is usually the pretty one whom he 'chooses'.

Instinctive bonds within the family are not nearly so strong. Apart from the 'Oedipus complex', an inherited reaction that attracts mothers more to their sons and fathers more to their daughters, the only indubitable one is that between mother and infant. During first months of life the infant feels the drive to cling to something warm and soft. It makes stereotyped movements in search of the breast, rocking its head to and fro, with its mouth open, and as soon as a nipple or dummy is put into its mouth it makes stereotyped sucking movements. Once satisfied, it then rejects the nipple. The mother's 'releaser' takes the form of an 'infant pattern' comprising certain features: a relatively large head, a bulging forehead, a rudimentary chin, a chubby form, short fat limbs and rather blundering movements [142, 143]. This bond is evidently an instinctive one, for maternal behaviour in animals, especially in monkeys and apes, is very similar. It depends, in both cases, on the female luteotropic hormone (prolactin), which ensures the supply of mother's milk after the infant is born. The maternal instinct of childless women may be satisfied to some extent by 'dummies' in the form of cats, lapdogs, and so on. Little girls of three or four already display it also, pressing their doll or some pet animal instinctively to their breast as they will do with their own child in later life.

Failure to satisfy this instinct may lead to serious conflicts, as when a mother steals some other child. A lack of the instinct (possibly through a deficiency of prolactin) may cause a mother to reject her own offspring. An inherited drive is here overriding obstacles produced by the normal process of 'thinking out' an action. But on the other hand it must be remembered that normally the instinctive basis of maternal behaviour is considerably overlaid by various psychological relationships between the mother and her child, as well as by ethical notions.

Monogamy, the practice in most countries, is not (or at least not primarily) based on instinct. It is largely dictated by custom and is often bound up with religious ideas, such as the Christian sacrament of marriage. It is natural, then, to find some peoples adhering to quite different customs [245]. Polygamy is fairly common, usually in the form of polygyny; among Mohammedans, Australian aborigines, and many American Indian and African tribes, a man is allowed several wives. Or, as well as the official wife, there may be second wives or concubines. In China this practice was usual when the chief wife grew old. Polyandry is not so common, but in Tibet, the Marquesas Islands and among the Todas of India it is customary for several men to share one wife. The Nayars of Malabar used to go through a form of pseudo-marriage, which was then dissolved at the end of three days. The children of the different fathers were then brought up by their maternal uncle. Whatever the type of marriage, the custom has always taken a definite form. There has never been absolute promiscuity. But as there is no hereditary instinct to support these various customs, conflicts have often arisen, sometimes resolved by such drastic measures as veiling the women or shutting them up in seclusion.

In man as in animals, the relationships between the sexes, and the conception and care of offspring, are regulated by inherited instincts. In man these instincts are overlaid and complicated by customs, morals and other psychological interactions. And here man is subject to many conflicts unknown in the animal world.

Like every higher animal living in a social group, man possesses instincts of social rank, and these considerably influence his way of life. Nearly everyone has them, and they may override other motives and operate even against reason. As among animals, this attitude often leads to struggles over 'order of precedence' followed by a relatively long period when an individual's position in the group is generally recognized. Precedence between the sexes is basically a matter of instinct, the female normally occupying the inferior position (with 'submissive' behaviour).

Although many more non-instinctive elements are mingled

L

with attitudes based on precedence than with sexual behaviour, the instinctive basis finds expression in the social hierarchy, the desire for higher status and its symbols (crowns, sceptres, marshals' batons, badges or rank, titles, orders and the like). Although a higher status naturally brings other advantages, in particular a better style of living, these play no part in the instinctive element of ambition, which simply involves the feeling of having achieved some higher position, some distinction or title, even if purely honorary.

Such social instincts are fundamental to the development of complex human societies. They explain why all the early civilizations – Egyptian, Sumerian, Akkadian, Chinese, Inca – evolved independently along similar lines to produce a state headed by a sovereign and ruled by an intricate hierarchy of officials and dignitaries. As with the animals, but here on a basis of tradition rather than of heredity, a strict 'code' was elaborated to avoid unnecessary dissension and strife by setting up definite rules and gestures of precedence. Those in a superior position usually express themselves by 'threatening gestures', a commanding presence, stern looks or words of command, while underlings bow, curtsey, bare the head, kowtow, kiss the hem of the robe, and so on. These subservient gestures have just the same meaning as the symbolic actions made by the weaker of two dogs (standing and looking away, exposing its bared throat to the stronger rival), or the 'treading' (rapid stamping up and down) by which a younger lizard symbolically indicates flight before an older one. Social rank is further accentuated by the development of such adjectives as 'majestic', 'noble', 'proud' and 'dignified', or verbs like 'command', 'direct' and 'obey'. The need for appropriate deportment might even go as far as it did with the poet Ludwig Tieck's teacher, who stuffed his coat with a cushion to provide the portly presence then considered to be dignified.

The struggle for precedence has always acted as a spur to great deeds in the community or state. Unfortunately, it can also be a source of evil. It may lead to jealousy, envy, vanity, arrogance, driving ambition and despotism, and to strife, intrigue, conflicts and even major wars. Its biological significance belongs to man's animal and pre-human stages, and because it is hereditary it cannot be stamped out. All that man can now do to avoid the dire consequences of this drive is to guide it into harmless channels. Thus it is useful for as many people as possible to be given some social or professional position of authority, some honorary post, to distinguish themselves in sport, or in the community, or to have some title or order. It would be better still to inculcate moderation in the young, to develop ethical ideals that would brand excessive ambition as an evil particularly dangerous to a civilized society.

Further instincts can be considered briefly, because more exact research is still lacking in this field. The combative drive, linked with sexual instincts and those of social rank, is doubtless connected with male sex hormones. This has been established experimentally: when mammals and birds are castrated, the combative drive subsides. When they are then injected with male sex hormones, it is revived. We may assume that the same holds good for man as well, for in this respect his anatomical structure and physiological functions resemble those of the higher animals. The combative instinct is often clearly expressed in friendly sparring aimed solely at 'working it off'; but it may also lead to more serious differences, whether physical or intellectual. The impulse is so strong and the motives for fighting so powerful, that men usually prefer to appear unreasonable rather than cowardly. Fortunately, sport has provided an outlet for this instinct. It is not only good for the health but helps to prevent the brawling and fighting that seems to have been so much a feature of life in the past.

Feeding is also based on instinct. Unlike animals, man no longer finds that certain plants or animals act as a 'releaser', but he still feels a generalized impulse to seize on plant or animal food when he is hungry, or to slake his thirst with water. He may also have vestiges of a hunting instinct. Quite a number of people appear to have an innate tendency towards hunting, whether stalking deer or chasing butterflies. Boys tend to like bows and arrows and air guns. They enjoy playing at Indians or 'cops and robbers'. Like other instincts, hunting can also cause conflicts because it is often inconsistent with rational considerations – for example, when there is a feeling of pity for the doomed or wounded animals, or when there is an obsession for poaching.

Collecting is very probably another of man's vestigial instincts, for it often prevails against more reasoned counsels, as when too much money is spent on collecting stamps, coins or pictures. Non-instinctive considerations may also, of course, be present or even dominant. There may be aesthetic aims in collecting pictures, or intellectual ones in amassing autographs, first editions, coins or beetles. But great collectors are 'born collectors'. And the fact that men are more strongly addicted than women suggests an instinctive basis. Men and boys are almost the only customers in stamp shops; and they may pay astonishingly large sums to complete the sets in their albums. No doubt there is also an innate instinct for cleaning and care of the skin. Most of us react sharply to sticky hands.

All these statements show that human life is governed by a number of instincts, hereditary traits ensuring the survival of the individual (feeding and cleaning), of the community (social rank) and of the species (reproduction). We have no cause to be ashamed of these qualities we share with the animals. We ought rather to extend our ethical concepts to find a natural and suitable place for them. Instead of castigating sins and so making existing conflicts worse, we would be better to recognize Nietzsche's primal 'innocence of the senses'. Furthermore, we can continue to blend these instinctive impulses with our culture – sublimating love as poetry, or stressing the ideal aspects of precedence – for instance, by honorary positions in the community. In the Western world at the moment, there is regrettably little sign of any such trend. On the contrary, we seem to be sinking to the level of medieval lansquenets. Instead of loftier aims and idealized love, the mainspring of many men's lives is self-indulgence and sex.

We have already noted that the influence of instinct is obviously much weaker in man than in the higher animals. Instincts are still present, but their effect can be modified or suppressed by reasonable considerations. Many of the conflicts so typical of *Homo sapiens* spring precisely from this ambivalent motivation. We cannot yet form any clear overall judgement, however, for we still lack a more exact psychological and physiological analysis of several drives and research into their heredity (along the lines of other investigations already made with identical and non-identical twins).

All research into instincts is of special importance to man, for it elucidates the part played by higher psychological abilities, which he alone has developed. We have noted how the increased complexity of the forebrain, with its 12,000 million or more nerve cells and its specialized functional areas, has made for very subtle perception and retention on a wide scale. Moreover, the wide expansion of purely associative centres has led to a positively astronomical number of differing associations and so to a comparable range of possibilities for thought and action. What is of particular importance here is man's much more pronounced volitional thought processes and his wide range of abstraction and generalization, as well as his capacity for imagination and speculation, so essential for all planning, invention and the advance of his civilization.

Homo sapiens is the first species to be capable of envisaging his own ego as a significant concept and of seeing himself objectively against an extramental background. This has enabled him to measure matter, space and time, and to recognize causal, logical and psychological laws. These are all based on experience and are the result of inductive reasoning. In this process they are often helped by testing the truth by thinking experiments – the paradigmatical conclusions that, for instance, make us 'certain' that a mathematical theorem or an axiom is correct. It has only been during the last 6000-8000 years of his long history that *Homo sapiens* has come to an unique state of self-knowledge and to an understanding not only of his own phylogenetic evolution but also of the structure of the universe from the most distant galaxies to the interior of the atom. And he has done this through language, writing and printing, which have enabled him to hand on tradition and to develop a supra-individual memory and a global range of knowledge.

Moreover, man is the first living creature to enjoy aesthetic and intellectual pleasure and to set up aesthetic, ethical, scientific and religious standards. These have governed his way of living but, like other traditional, supra-individual institutions, have also served to reduce his individual autonomy.

In Chapter 3, section B, we noted briefly that man's thought and actions appear to be based on a large measure of free will. It is doubtful if this is really so. During the phylogeny of higher vertebrates the brain has grown steadily more complex and more efficient. The hereditary reflexes and instinctive reactions have increasingly become overlaid by what memory has retained. At the same time, higher animals have developed wide powers of abstraction and generalization, of planning and voluntary activity, so that some of them, especially apes, appear to have some degree of free will. In the last resort, however, physiological processes in an animal's brain are causal processes. Inherited brain structures, engrams of experiences, conceptual images and voluntary processes may make these mental activities extremely complicated. We can therefore detect causal connections only in partial processes. In view of man's simian ancestry, it is obvious to assume that all his physiological brain and thought processes are also causally determined. Admittedly this can never be proved since it is impossible to say which of the countless memories and feelings are effective when an action is 'thought out' and planned in advance. But it is quite conceivable that, despite their complexity and apparent freedom, man's thought processes are determined solely by inherited traits, training, instruction and present environmental influences. Yet we are entitled to retain such ideas as 'freedom', 'duty', 'conscience' and 'guilt' in their usual sense, for they are dominant determinants in our thought and action; in other words, they represent advantageous causal components.

There is another reason, too, for considering it unlikely that man's will is really free. As far as we can tell, for the thousands of millions of years of our solar system, causal and logical laws alone have determined the course of events, the creation of the world, the appearance of life on it, the progressive evolution of the animal kingdom, and the emergence of the Hominids. It is unthinkable that in the comparatively short space of 70,000-100,000 years since *Homo sapiens* first appeared these laws should suddenly have ceased to hold good and 'free will' should from then on be determining the course of brain processes and thus infringing the law of conservation of energy [for a more detailed consideration, see B. Rensch, 193, 196].

In considering the attributes typical of man, we must now, however, confine ourselves to those of modern civilized man. At the present time, a Papuan from Central New Guinea shows many of the latter in only a small degree. Even a peasant from some remote corner of Europe is on a very different psychological and mental plane from a man of worldwide culture. This great disparity itself is yet another typical trait of that unique polymorphic species *Homo sapiens*. One could enumerate several other such traits, like his consciousness of history and his receptiveness. For the most part, however, these are direct consequences of other attributes already discussed.

There is still one further peculiarity of man, one that has both positive and negative effects. *Homo sapiens* is the only species that has managed to alter the nature of the earth's surface to an appreciable extent. By so doing civilized man has gradually created his own environment. His artificial dwelling places, with all their technical appliances, have made modern civilization possible. As we have seen, however, this new man-made environment has largely eliminated natural selection. Natural selection has made *Homo sapiens* genetically suited to life in natural surroundings as they existed some 100,000 years ago, but not to his present milieu. It is only because he is structurally and functionally so adaptable that he can live under such unnatural conditions. We modern men, especially the city-dwellers, are not in the least suited to the sort of life we are leading. We spend most of our day in artificial caves (our houses), by artificial light (mostly deficient in ultraviolet rays) and we stay awake long after sundown. Nature did not fit us to travel in cars, trains and planes where speed no longer permits a normal appreciation of the hurriedly changing surroundings, or to look at films, straining our nerves to keep pace both with the pictures and with their emotional content. It is biologically unsound for us to be exciting our nervous systems by listening to the radio or watching television, communicating by telephone, or reading and writing, with every leisure moment filled with some excitement. It is appalling to think of all the stimuli overexciting our sympathetic nervous system, which innervates our stomach, intestine, liver, heart, and especially our endocrine glands. Diabetes results from damage to the Islets of Langerhans in the pancreas, rheumatism of the joints from injury to the adrenal cortex, and other forms of disease are known to be caused by stress. We can only wonder how we manage to survive this new kind of life at all. Selection of hereditary characteristics may perhaps help us to adapt ourselves, but it will take thousands of generations, and most of the ailments of civilization attack us when we are past our prime, and are therefore beyond its influence.

Similar changes have taken place in our foodstuffs and stimulants. The food we eat is boiled or fried, artificially salted or seasoned; artificial seasonings incite us to eat more than we ought; we also eat much more fat than is 'natural'; we drink coffee, tea and alcohol, which act as strong stimulants on the sympathetic nervous system; we take pills and tablets; we flood the body with nicotine as it passes into the mouth, nose, lungs and stomach; we breathe exhaust fumes. With regard to new foodstuffs and habits, the human body again shows an amazing power to adapt itself. But we have clearly begun to overstep the limits of endurance. The diseases of civilization – lung cancer, circulatory troubles, neuroses and so on – have increased alarmingly, in spite of scientific and medical progress. And so far it seems sheer optimism to imagine that by realizing this biological danger we have taken the first step towards averting it.

D. *Man, the demigod*

For men who are as yet scarcely touched by modern civilization, such as some Papuan, Melanesian, and Brazilian peoples, the world is full of ominous, mysterious powers. Lightning and thunder, earthquakes and eruptions, illness and death are the work of gods, spirits or demons. When one of these primitive animists encounters a creature capable of understanding what causes all these happenings, capable of interpreting world history far back over hundreds of millions of years, familiar with the most distant stars and the elements of the invisible atom, capable of applying his vast knowledge to construct complicated technical devices to harness nature's energy – what wonder that he regards such a creature as a demigod. Despite this enormous disparity, however, primitive man is also *Homo sapiens*.

The Book of Genesis reports that the snake said to Eve with regard to the fruit of the tree of knowledge: 'the day ye eat thereof, then your eyes shall be opened, and ye shall be as gods' (Genesis, 3, 5). Since then man has indeed eaten many fruits of knowledge. But, in spite of the great mental difference, a primitive man is quite capable of becoming just such a demigod, if educational facilities enable him to absorb the traditions of several thousand years of culture.

We are quite rightly brought up to think modestly of ourselves, and in particular not to overestimate the results of our scientific progress. But when we study man's phylogeny, it must also seem to us extraordinary that this species, *Homo sapiens*, with his 'godlike intellect', as Charles Darwin called it, has emerged as the crown and culmination of the whole process of evolution.

> The Universe can live and work and plan,
> At last made God within the mind of man.
> Julian S. Huxley, *Poems* [97]

Not only has this strange *Homo sapiens* come to an understanding of himself and the universal laws; he has developed further godlike qualities, creating his own new and complicated environment, changing almost the whole face of the earth, decimating or exterminating numerous animals and plants, promoting the dispersal of others, himself creating new forms of cultivated plants and domestic animals.

Moreover, man is the only creature that can make long-term plans for the continuation of his own existence, for the development of his institutions, and for the attainment of other such aims beyond the scope of the individual. Civilized man has carried this so far, indeed, that he 'lives' less in the present than in the future and, thanks to memory, in the past. For those engaged in creative intellectual work this has an important result. As all planning has a purpose, a meaning, it seems to follow that the whole of existence must have a 'meaning'. Besides, man is conscious of the fact of death as the inevitable end of life, and knows that because his own thought reaches out into the future he must fear that end. So religion seeks for the 'meaning' of existence in the life of the soul beyond death, in a heaven or a land of spirits, or in absorption into a Nirvana. Men without religion usually confine themselves to temporal aims. It is of interest that the question of the meaning of existence did not arise before the advance of civilization and that even then it only gradually emerged. It is quite possible to disagree even with the formulation of such a question. Existence is in a state of flow but it need not necessarily have any ultimate 'aim'. A few thousand years ago the problem did not even exist, and primitive men today are scarcely conscious of it at all. Even a large proportion of the so-called intellectuals in every nation still live largely as Goethe counselled:

> Ours not to brood upon our own small fate;
> Life is a duty, were it but a moment.

Quite apart from any religious ideas, however, certain humbler aims do exist. They are of man's own making, and are those connected with the desire for ideal human communities, with the advance of scientific knowledge and artistic achievement – in a word, with the establishment of all kinds of values and standards.

The heading of this section may strike some as unseemly, but men have often referred to themselves as gods or demigods. Rulers among the Egyptians, Romans, Chinese, Japanese and Incas have done so; and the high priests in several religious communities have ranked as God's representative on earth or as the incarnation of a Buddha – for instance, the chief Lama of Tibet, the Panchen Lama.

Finally, there is one further parallel, one which may have some theological significance. As we saw in section B of this chapter, man's evolution will continue, although probably not in the direction that in the past has led up to *Homo sapiens*. His body and brain are unlikely to undergo further alteration; for in this respect man, this most fully developed of creatures, has apparently reached the end of his phylogeny. Modern Christian theologians see its whole course as determined by God, but proceeding causally, quite in accordance with biological findings. This gives the fact that *Homo sapiens* apparently represents a final stage, a special interest, for Genesis refers to man as created in 'God's image'. Christian theology and biological thinking seem to converge at this point in a way that, though it should not be overestimated, ought to be taken into consideration by theologians.

CHAPTER SIX

The future of mankind

A. *Factors in a possible forecast*

The scientific study of mankind, his biological nature, his phylogeny, the development of his culture, is still in a rather imperfect state. On the other hand, so much material has already been gathered together that we have surely reached a stage when some assessment of his future evolution might be attempted. Civilized man is accustomed to think in advance, and often to make long-term plans years ahead. If science today were to make some authoritative statement about man's more immediate future, we would be able to take appropriate measures. We could try to avoid inevitably unfavourable features and exploit any advantageous tendencies.

Prophecy is known to be a doubtful business. But forecasts based on science are relatively securely grounded in a series of recognized laws. And laws imply the possibility of certain forecasts. Yet in the spheres of biology, history and cultural development, events are so interrelated that it is nearly impossible to analyse the interreaction of individual laws. All one can do is to draw up a 'balance sheet', to establish certain 'rules' and to attempt a forecast with a percentage of probable exceptions. Within these limits it seems that some lines of development can be laid down – at least as far as the near future is concerned – provided there is no unexpected interference from other trends. But for the remoter future, especially in the cultural sphere, any prophecy is bound to be indefinite, for all kinds of individual factors may intervene, leading to entirely new stages of integration, with unforeseeable consequences. The effect of mutation, selection and hybridization in producing physical changes is so gradual and slow that one can reckon the next hundreds or even thousands of years as the 'near' future. But in the cultural sphere forecasts are limited to the next few decades.

As a basis for any forecast we must begin by considering what might be regarded as provisionally permanent and invariable aspects. These include the structures and functions of the human body and in particular the inherited reflexes, instincts and corresponding psychological processes governed by brain and nerve structure. The future effects of different factors will then have to be assessed: the influences of mutation, hybridization, natural selection, environmental changes, etc., with special regard to the known laws and rules that regulate such changes. The question of further mental development can only be treated with great caution. The most one can do is to establish tentative hypotheses to indicate possible developments and new stages of integration. Finally, all the results must be tested for their relevance as blueprints for a firm and deliberate shaping of man's future physical and mental development. As some tendencies which we can state with sufficient certainty are dangerous for the human future, such planning is an urgent duty of our generation.

B. *Man's future physical evolution*

The species *Homo sapiens* has developed very rapidly from early pre-human stages. This has sometimes led to the idea that our evolution is moving ceaselessly onwards and upwards towards some superman with a still larger brain. From what we have said in Chapter 5, it is clear that this is far from being the case. On the contrary, human phylogeny has now reached a more or less final stage. At least for the near future any further changes will be governed more by an increase in polymorphism than by selection of morphological or physiological characteristics.

Above all, it is unlikely that the forebrain will grow further in the next tens of millennia, or that the sense organs will improve or become more varied. Natural selection is not operating today in favour of such hereditary variants. They have neither a better chance of survival nor a higher reproductive rate. Variants could of course be selected artificially, by eugenic measures, and this could bring about alterations in mankind (cf. Chapter 6, section D), but so far there is no sign of this happening. So there is not likely to be any significant change in the psychological phenomena that correspond to the working of the brain and sense organs. The 'given' material of all human cognition – the qualities and modalities of sensation, the capability to form mental images and to associate them in multifarious manner, and also feelings and voluntary processes – will remain the same. They can at best reach some new and 'higher' stage of integration. Even if we were to develop some new organ sensitive to short waves, like X- or γ-rays, or to the magnetic field, our scientific knowledge would not be much altered, because we can already make ourselves aware of such physical processes and conditions by other means, like the fluorescent screen and the magnetic needle – using the organs that we possess now – in this case, the eyes.

On the other hand, it is safe to say that the continuous mutation of our hereditary factors and their insertion in ever-changing gene combinations will go on. This of course may lead to changes in man. But mutation is completely random and in most cases involves disturbances of some harmonious construction developed in the course of a long phylogeny. It follows, then, that the hereditary stock as a whole will deteriorate, for, whereas with animals the carriers of harmful mutants are more or less eliminated, with man they will multiply. In 1871, long before mutation was known of, Charles Darwin [39] drew attention to the danger of harmful hereditary variants often multiplying faster than better variants, because the former often produce more progeny.

The inevitable deterioration of the human hereditary stock represents a serious problem for the future, at least for all the more highly civilized peoples in whom natural selection has largely been eliminated. As in this age of air travel and international communication civilization is rapidly spreading, any people can reach a higher stage within a single generation.

Unfortunately, it is extremely difficult to assess accurately the extent of man's hereditary deterioration. So far mutation rates of harmful mutants can only be estimated in a limited number of cases. Several investigators, working with different human material, have estimated the following mutations rates per million germ cells: 10-70 mutants producing dominant achondroplasia (that is to say, disproportionate dwarfism), 43-100 producing recessive muscular dystrophy, 20-32 producing recessive haemophilia (mainly males); 5 producing microphthalmia [191, 208]. Little is known about the mutation rates for non-pathological characteristics. Moreover, since many characteristics are polygenic and depend upon the combined effects of several hereditary factors, we cannot arrive at more than a very vague assessment of the total mutation rate for man. Even taking a fairly low estimate, some 20,000 to 40,000 genes – and recent research into the basic structure of the DNA molecule makes a much larger figure probable – one can assume that about one third of all germ cells in every generation are subject to a gene mutation [261]. This means that a large number of harmful mutants could accumulate in a very few generations, because they are not being eliminated fast enough, if at all, by natural selection.

Up to now deterioration in the hereditary stock has not yet become apparent to any degree, because most harmful factors are recessive and do not show themselves frequently. They only do so when they are homozygous, a state that is more common under a system of inbreeding in small communities such as in remote villages. In future the mixing of races and peoples, the increase in urbanization (cf. Table 1, p. 123), and the 'opening up' of remote regions through improved transport will be of great value in reducing homozygosis and thereby reducing also the frequency of appearance of many hereditary defects. At the same time it must be remembered that the number of harmful genes will continue to increase, and this will make it increasingly hazardous for near relatives to intermarry.

It may be presumed that in the future there will be more intermarriage of even such distant and separate races as Negroes and whites. An innate instinct for 'releasing characteristics' inclines man towards a certain homogamy, but this instinct is not so strong that it cannot often be overlaid by other considerations. It is relatively frequent for a white girl from the lowest strata of society to marry a coloured man in some better position. And there is no general instinctive aversion to marriage with a person of mixed race, especially in the second or third generation. Indeed, such people are often particularly attractive. Equality of status for men of all races will also act in favour of miscegenation. It has on the whole been steadily increasing in the course of man's history, and there is no sign of any change in the foreseeable future. To repeat an important point here: every infusion of new blood into a population alters it permanently. Far from being lost, the foreign genes gradually spread further and further in new combinations. The wide areas of mixed race which have grown up within a few generations in several countries in South and Central America, in parts of Africa, in south-east Asia and in Hawaii show us the extent to which polymorphism can go in larger populations. European peoples, too, are a mixture of Celtic, Romanic, north Germanic, Slavic, Alpine, Turkish and other peoples.

It is very difficult to foretell what specific effects natural selection will have in the coming centuries. But it is certain that factors in the inanimate world outside will continue to have less and less influence. The climate and configuration of land and water areas are unlikely to alter markedly during this period. But the artificial world in which we live is rapidly changing in a manner that will reduce natural selection. Living conditions everywhere are becoming more hygienic. More air and light, greater cleanliness, more rational feeding, better medical care, more facilities for sport – all these are increasing the chances of survival, even for people with reduced hereditary vitality. And life in extreme climates has been made easier by artificial heating or, in the tropics, cooling systems.

Of course, all this favours many non-hereditary factors as well, which are only indirectly relevant to natural selection, but are none the less important for man. Such factors include good health, which brings the possibility of an increasing percentage of people reaching the natural span of life (70-80 years). Up to the middle of last century, the average expectation of life at birth in civilized Europe was about 30-40 years. After that date it rose rapidly. In 1900 it was 45 years for men in West Germany, 45·3 in France, 54·5 in Sweden; but in 1960 the corresponding figures were 66·7, 67·2 and 71·7 (United Nations, *Demographic Yearbook*, 1952 and 1960).

It is very probable that life in larger communities, especially in towns, has by selection increasingly raised immunity from infectious diseases. In future the same process will take place in countries where urbanization is not yet so advanced. As now, those with a weaker constitution will be more likely to die from serious illness. At the same time, diminished selection against hereditarily weak or afflicted individuals is offset to a significant and steadily increasing degree by selection through modern traffic accidents. In this sphere of selection those whose reactions are slower (possibly a hereditary feature) are possibly the most affected.

We must also consider that natural selection not only favours advantageous characteristics but also causes the maintenance of normal structures. While mutation and gene combination continue without selection, an increase in variability of many structures and functions will result. In this way, too, polymorphy will increase.

One kind of selection is likely to remain unchanged in its effects in the future: the kind that governs man's hereditary reproductive instincts, in particular their histological and physiological bases. Those who are deficient or lacking in these instincts will be less inclined to marry, and women with a feeble maternal instinct will have, on the average, fewer children. This will preserve the reproductive instincts.

We have already mentioned in Chapter 5, section B, that the 'releaser patterns' concerning the characteristics of the two sexes of human species – what we describe as 'beautiful' – will be maintained when chosing a partner for marriage. By increasing hybridization of different races the inherited releasers may become altered to a certain extent. Something 'beautiful' will always remain, however, and all kinds of anomalous characteristics (although perhaps of healthy stock) will be more or less eliminated.

As fighting instincts are correlated with sexual ones, and apparently are largely released by male sex hormones, mankind in future will still have to reckon with these potentially dangerous drives. And as natural selection operates to keep reproductive efficiency, and so the production of sex hormones, fairly constant, there is not likely to be any marked reduction in these instincts. Education, however, may control and direct them into harmless channels, though it can never eradicate them.

At present the normal effect of the reproductive instincts is a large number of children. The hereditary basis of this high birth rate was developed when *Homo sapiens* originated. At that period the loss of individuals not yet of reproductive age was very high. Even 500 years ago a high rate was necessary to keep up the population. But today, when natural selection no longer operates sufficiently to reduce it, serious difficulties have arisen. For the traditional and inherited level of increase is now at variance with today's greatly reduced need for offspring. Unless some countermeasures are taken to stabilize its numbers, the world will tend towards an intolerable degree of overpopulation [5, 50].

This danger had been realized many years ago. Commissions of the United Nations have ascertained as far as possible the number of inhabitants in every country and in the whole world. Several authors have also tried to calculate or to estimate the number of inhabitants of our planet in past decades. Their results show that the total number has steadily risen, but that this process continued rather slowly until about 1650. At the beginning of the first century the world population was probably about 250 million, in 1650 it was about 500 million (W. Staub [235]: 465 million; A. M. Carr-Saunders [27]: 545 million). In 1850 the total number had already reached 1600 million. The commissions of the United Nations were then able to publish calculations based on a more exact census: 1930, 2070 million; 1950, 2517 million; 1960, 3005 million; 1966, 3356 million. In 1970 the number was about 3477 million. These numbers show that the increase of the world population has continually accelerated since 1650. From 1900 to 1950 the world population grew annually by 0·8 per cent, in 1951-6 by 1·6 per cent, and 1960-9 by 1·9 per cent. This means

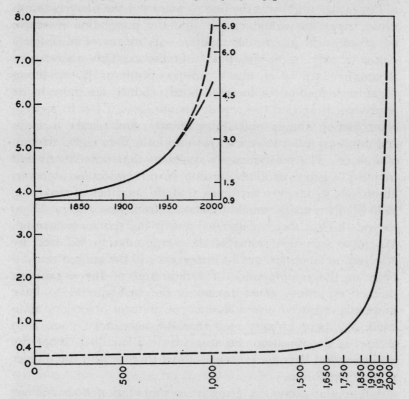

Fig. 11 Graph of world population illustrating the rate of growth up to the present day. Vertical axes give the population in thousand millions; horizontal axes give the span of years. Upper left: A.D. 1800-2000, with separate maximal and minimal assessments. (After Dorn.)

an annual increase of more than 65 million – the number of inhabitants of a large European country – and a daily increase of about 160,000 – the number of inhabitants of a large town.

The accompanying graph (Fig. 11) prepared by H. F. Dorn [49] strikingly illustrates this ominous development during the past three centuries. Should the trend continue, it is clear that the world's population in the year 2000 will touch almost 7000 million.

T. R. Malthus [144] in his much-cited *Essay on the Principles of Population* (1798) was the first to point out the dangers that a rapid expansion would entail: that the population increases by geometrical progression, whereas its means of subsistence increases only by arithmetical progression. This discrepancy is another aspect of man's unique position. Every living organism's method of increase is to produce far more of its kind than is needed to keep up its numbers. Even in asexual reproduction among unicellular animals and plants, a single cell develops into two, these two into four, then eight, sixteen, and so on. The possibility always exists that populations will increase by geometrical progression. Natural selection, however, eliminates so many individuals that the number of surviving individuals remains roughly constant from one generation to the next. Thus their subsistence and living space are assured. We have seen this principle of overpopulation followed by selection to be of paramount importance in the animal world – both in the maintenance of fitness and of the organism's further evolution. *Homo sapiens* is the first species to have markedly reduced the influence of natural selection upon itself. We have already seen that the hereditary stock is in danger of deterioration (because selection is failing to operate effectively on harmful mutants). Now there is also the danger of overpopulation.

Up to the present a general overpopulation does not yet exist. But India, China, Japan, Java, Egypt and some other countries are already so densely populated that any marked increase may lead, as it has so often in the past, to serious problems of nutrition. The root of all the difficulty is that any economic improvement, involving more intensive land cultivation and increased industrialization, always brings about an increase in the population that outstrips productivity. For instance, India is managing to improve its productivity on a large scale. But the population in 1951 was growing so rapidly that, according to the Indian Planning Commission's Report of that year, by 1956 the population would on average be worse fed than five years previously. Some parts of this vast country did in fact suffer a food crisis.

The immediate dangers are somewhat lessened by the fact that in many countries the increase results largely from a reduction of the mortality rate, which in future may be expected to remain fairly constant as medical treatment and hygienic conditions reach a normal standard.

Though many factors influence population increase, shortage of food will always be a major one. The production of food can still be considerably extended by the use of land now occupied by forests and steppes, by artificial irrigation of deserts, by the growing of suitable types of crops, by intensive campaigns against pests, by tapping additional sources of supply such as the oceans, possibly cultivating marine plants, by restricting the excess of pasture over arable land and by making available foodstuffs from leaves, by synthetic amino acids and proteins, and by a more rational balance in the choice of foodstuffs. If the present scarcity of food due to increased population is to be made good, world production must be stepped up by 2 per cent a year. So far only North America has achieved this figure [172]. If we include all the improvements at present possible (though still largely untried), the world population could be nearly doubled, to some 6000 millions [20]. We have seen, however, that this figure will be reached in a few decades. We cannot predict whether new discoveries or more rational feeding will make further increases possible.

When making these assessments, we must remember that a large percentage of the world's population is already undernourished. Estimates vary from 10 to 66 per cent [271]. Despite all the help given to the overpopulated and developing regions, the problem of overpopulation always remains primarily a national one. In the past there have always been famines. So we cannot argue that the pressure of over-population alone will suffice to curb any future increases. It is much more likely that a rise in the general level of education and instruction about reasonable family planning will stabilize the population. According to W. Fucks [58], this is linked with the degree of technological progress, and he anticipates that the figure will become stable only when it has reached about 8000 million.

Although selective pressure has ceased to operate in maintaining the production of between ten and fourteen children per family (formerly essential for survival), no clear decrease in physiological fertility can be expected during the next centuries. Reasonable thought by intelligent people about the number of children a family can afford and educate will perhaps become more powerful than instinctive reproductive drives in future. It is therefore very important to attempt a cautious forecast of the future development of population figures. Of course we cannot simply assume that the recent rates of increase will remain constant. Many factors are involved, some of them predictable, others varying incalculably. But the following factors are always of significance: (1) the number of live births, affected by the degree of urbanization, economic prosperity, ethical or religious tradition (the cult of ancestors, measures for or against birth control, political propaganda, and so on); (2) the number of deaths, affected at least by the level of civilization and by climatic conditions; and (3) the age structure of the population, dependent upon previous changes in factors listed under (1) and (2), and also indicating the trends of increase (better standards of hygiene, for instance).

If one takes these factors into account one can distinguish at least three categories here: (1) peoples with a high birth rate, a high mortality and short expectation of life; this used to include half the world's population, especially the 'under-developed' countries but also large parts of India (now rapidly moving into the second category); (2) peoples with a high birth rate and a diminishing mortality rate; these are likely to go on increasing rapidly for some time, but will soon show a slackening of the increase (for instance Central and South America); (3) balanced peoples, with a relatively low birth rate, low mortality rate and therefore a relatively long expectation of life. This includes perhaps one fourth of the world population, in particular countries of Europe and North America [cf. W. S. Thompson in R. C. Cook, 31]. More detailed research would involve adding two intermediate categories to these three.

A careful study of these probable alterations in relative population increase will enable us to assess, for the next decades at least, how much the population figures will rise in the various countries. Of course it must be a fairly rough assessment, because there is still little precise material for several countries available, and also because unforeseen political developments and complications, especially increasing birth control, may bring important modifications. In the United States the birth rate has already decreased.

A Demographic Commission of the United Nations [254] made calculations of this sort for the period up to 1980, which F. Burgdörfer [22] (using a slightly different method) has extended to the year 2000. According to these estimates the world population will be 4223 million in 1980 and about 6000 million in 2000. An annual increase by 1·8 per cent means that the population would have doubled after forty years, and an annual increase of 3 per cent – a percentage reached by some countries during the past years – would cause it to double in twenty-three years. Up to the present it seems to be absolutely impossible that the production of food can be raised in the same measure. Although the danger of overpopulation has been well known for many years, the annual increase has continued to rise at an average rate of 1·8-1·9 per cent since 1958. Hence a famine crisis will menace many countries if they do not take strong measures to reduce the birth rate.

The need for birth control was recognized in nineteenth-century England, where a league of 'Malthusians' was formed, which recommended contraceptive methods. But opposition was then too strong, and their proposals met with no success, even though some sections of the working population in England were in great want and there were almost yearly famines in parts of China and India. The breakthrough of the new ideas came only fifty years ago. In 1916 Margaret Sanger opened the first American 'Birth Control Clinic', an action that earned her a good deal of abuse as well as a prosecution. But after a world tour in 1922 to study the problems of overpopulation she succeeded in organizing the first 'International Birth Control Conference', and two years later she founded the International Planned Parenthood Federation, drawn from twenty-six national societies in different countries.

The prospects for effective birth control greatly improved when a method was discovered by which the activity of the follicle stimulating hormones in the anterior lobe of the pituitary gland, the hypophysis, and hence the maturing of the female sex cells, could be interrupted. Experiments undertaken on a large scale in Puerto Rico showed suitable pills to be reliable and apparently harmless. Cheaper mechanical means of contraception and methods to arrest the maturing of male semen have also been developed.

Meanwhile strong measures have been taken in overpopulated and underdeveloped countries to control the rapid increase. In 1960, after the population of India had risen to 415 million and threatened to double within the following thirty years, Nehru, overcoming much misgiving, advocated a drive for birth control. He also gave his sanction to voluntary free sterilization. An 'All India Planning Conference' was inaugurated, an energetic body, which has already met several times. At present, sterilization is carried out on many women who have had three children, and on men. As only the sperma-ducts or oviducts have to be cut, or the tubes of the oviduct have to be shifted, the normal sexual drives, which are controlled by hormones, are not disturbed. In Indian villages one often sees large posters now with relevant pictures and the advice 'Plan your family', 'Small family, happy family', and so on. It will take some time for any measures of success to be attained, for here as elsewhere it is a matter of breaking with ancient tradition.

Japan began issuing information and propaganda on contraception in 1948. Hundreds of consultation offices were established and midwives were given instruction. Even abortion was made legal and was carried out for a small fee in state hospitals. 1·2 million operations were performed during 1957. Of these,

500,000 were illegitimacy cases (and no doubt prevented much unhappiness for both mother and child). In 1948 the average birth rate per 1000 was 33·5, in 1960 it had sunk to 18·0. At present there is only a relatively small surplus of births. China started a movement in 1957 to limit the number of births, but this was soon halted again. However, after the population figure had risen from 667 million in 1953 to over 711 million in 1963, a new propaganda campaign was started in 1964.

But the population is rising too rapidly even in highly industrialized countries, not only because of a lowering of the mortality rate or immigration, but as a result of too many births. However voluntary limitation between 1957 and 1966 reduced the birth rate in the U.S.A. by about 25 per cent. Although members of the Roman Catholic Church and of an Orthodox group in the Protestant World Council of Churches still condemn contraception and sterilization and seek to restrict family planning to abstinence (in particular during the period of female fertility), it is astonishing that as a result of reasoned arguments it has been possible to alter such customs and ideas, thousands of years old and hallowed by tradition, so speedily. It encourages some measures of hope for the future of mankind. Of course there will be many grave difficulties ahead; but the first step in solving a problem is to see it clearly.

A point of still greater significance is the very different increase within individual peoples, which is bound up with certain profound political, historical and cultural modifications. Tables 2 and 3 show how uneven the annual rate of growth has been in the various countries concerned. If these rates should remain more or less stable for even the next 100 years, we should witness an extraordinary shifting of emphasis. In Europe the present annual rate of growth is only 0·9 per cent, while the annual increase in Central and South America is 2·8 per cent, in south Asia 2·5 per cent, and in Africa 2·3 per cent. This means that the peoples of Asia, Africa and Latin America will outgrow the European peoples. Estimates of future increase up to the year 2000 carried out by the Department of Economic and Social Affairs of the United Nations show that the population in southern Asia will multiply 2·5

TABLE 2 Population numbers in millions in 1970 and annual percentage increase from 1965 till 1970. (taken from the United Nations *Demographic Yearbook* for 1970).

	Millions	*% Increase*
World population	3632	2·0
Europe	462	0·8
Western Europe	149	0·8
Southern Europe	128	0·9
Eastern Europe	104	0·8
Northern Europe	81	0·6
U.S.S.R.	243	1·0
Asia	2056	2·3
Japan	103	1·1
Southern Asia	1126	2·8
Northern America	228	1·2
Middle and South America	283	2·9
Africa	344	2·6
Northern Africa	87	3·1
Australia and New Zealand	15	1·9
Melanesia	2·8	2·4
Polynesia and Micronesia	1·2	3·1

TABLE 3 Change of percentage increase of population in different parts of Europe from 1870 until 1960 (after W. Staub, 1951).

	1840-1870	*1930-1960*
Western Europe	11·9	0·3
Northern Europe (incl. England)	40·1	5·8
Middle Europe	20·6	7·6
Southern Europe	16·1	19·8
Eastern Europe	15·3	182·7

times during the coming three decades, in Central and South America 5·5 times, but in Europe only 0·25 times (see Table 4). It is quite probable that this unequal increase will in fact continue. It depends upon the attitude of the Catholic Church in Latin America and on the inadequate schooling among many of the Indian and African peoples. European and North American countries do their best to support African peoples by establishing schools, universities and hospitals, and by economic aid. It should be regarded as a serious omission,

TABLE 4 Minimum and maximum estimation of population increase from 1960 until 2000 and average increase, calculated on the basis of the birth and death rates, age classes and immigration. Figures in millions. *Source:* World Population Prospects of the United Nations, 1966.

Countries	1960	1980	Average	2000	Average
Sum total of all countries	2998	4147-4551	4330	5449-6994	6130
East Asia	654	966-1171	850	1118-1623	1321
South Asia	865	1379-1448	1420	1984-2444	2171
Europe	425	467- 492	479	491- 563	527
U.S.S.R.	214	269- 296	278	316- 402	353
Africa	273	434- 463	449	684- 864	764
North America	199	248- 275	262	294- 376	354
Central + South America	112	362- 383	373	532- 686	638
Australia — Polynesia	15	22- 23	23	28- 35	32
Developed countries	976	1153-1225	1194	1293-1574	1441
Developing countries	2022	1293-3306	3136	4155-5420	4688

however, that this help is not connected with intensive propaganda for birth control. We must bear in mind that the introduction of modern medical treatment and the distribution of remedies are the main causes of the population explosion in these countries.

The differential growth of such nations will at first alter social conditions and international economic relations. But it may also lead to wars of expansion. It may be sufficient to remember the earlier conquest of Manchuria by the Japanese and the Nazi slogan, 'People without space'. The alarming expansion of the coloured compared to the white population in the United States is another example of possible future conflict.

Because of the great economic and political consequences, the problem of different growth ratios in different countries can only be solved in a satisfactory manner on an international basis. Unfortunately, in view of the present world situation, there is no hope for an international treatment of these questions.

But the differential increase among various population groups in each country is also a matter of great significance for future development. The fact that some intelligent groups – for example, Hindu hermits and Roman Catholic monks, nuns and priests – have no offspring will be of particular significance in view of the small numbers of such minority groups.

It is a very disquieting fact that among most civilized peoples the higher and better educated classes produce far fewer children than do the lower strata. This is borne out by much statistical evidence. For instance, in Prussia in 1912 agricultural workers had on average 5·2 children, factory hands 4·1, apprentices and shop assistants 2·9, salaried employees 2·5, civil servants and professional people 2·0 [K. Saller, 209]. And statistical data for 1940 from the United States Bureau of the Census (published in 1945) [cf. also R. C. Cook, 31] show a very close correlation between the number of children and the level of education. The following table gives the average total number of children borne by women in the U.S.A. who in 1940 were between the ages of 45 and 49 as compared with the number of years they had spent at school or college:

1-4 years at school	4·33 children
5-6 years at school	3·74 children
7-8 years at school	2·78 children
1-3 years at college	2·37 children
4 or more years at college	1·75 children

Measured against the normal number of children necessary for the individual categories to hold their own in the total population (the replacement index), the above result shows that those in the lowest educational category increased by

97 per cent, while those with five to six years at college showed a decrease of 20 per cent. Figures based on income groups are similar. In the present century the uneducated are gradually gaining upon the educated. Every step up in the social scale amounts to a degree of sterilization. And as the differences within this scale partly derive from hereditary intellectual ability, the outlook for the future is dark indeed [31]. Moreover, as in most countries today it is possible for the gifted members of even the poorest classes to rise socially, and this is coupled with a drop in the average number of children, the danger is that in future the reserves of hereditary ability will become exhausted; reserves that had been present in the lower strata as long as its gifted members found it harder to rise in the social scale will then be lacking.

At the same time the social distinctions will become more disparate because the lower levels will mainly consist of those who are less endowed with hereditary talents. As those less gifted are as little responsible for their limited abilities as are the highly gifted for their talents, the inequality and 'injustice of nature' can only be redressed or at least diminished by social levelling, that is to say by aspiring to a more or less classless society. In order to diminish the feeling of being less gifted and to preserve social peace it will also be necessary to pay these persons inordinately well.

C. *Future intellectual and cultural evolution*

We have already noted in Chapter 4, section C, that rapid increase in population, technical progress and the advantages of centralization have led people to live more and more in towns or town-like communities. This urbanization will make rapid progress in those countries that are currently in process of industrialization. At present there are already 73 towns with more than a million inhabitants. Including the suburbs New York is inhabited by 11·4 million, Tokyo by 10·4, London by 7·9, Shanghai by 6·9, Chicago by 6·7, Moscow by 6·5, São Paolo by 5·5, Bombay by 4·8, and Calcutta by 4·7 million. Town life has various consequences with regard to the development of cultural life. The establishment of boards of management, hospitals with special departments, different types of schools, scientific institutions, large theatres and cinemas, museums, etc., makes for rational working and wide opportunities for education and amusement. Thus life becomes richer and broadly speaking more agreeable. Townsmen usually have a relatively broad basis of knowledge.

But the town-dweller lives in an artificial, non-biological milieu. His nervous system, whose hereditary structure had been adapted to life in natural conditions and in little groups, is exposed to stress by a flood of stimuli, an excess of visual and auditory irritation. Not only must he accommodate himself to sensory excitations from cars, planes, machines, telephones, radios, records, typewriters and so on, but also his attention is kept continually on the alert when driving or walking, when in the cinema or watching television.

What may be termed an 'urbanization trauma' is becoming increasingly common in centres of civilization. Its symptoms include enhanced sensitivity to noise, overexcitement, aggressiveness, and other neurotic disturbances, as well as sexual precocity [65]. The constant demands on his attention are overexciting and damaging man's sympathetic nervous system. Because this system also affects the endocrine glands, this kind of 'overstrain' leads to other harmful results. As injurious technical devices of these kinds spread to other lands, and as urbanization gains ground, we may expect the frantic pace of life to quicken still more in the immediate future.

A large part of the earth's surface has already been transformed into an artificial landscape during the past decades. Traffic by air, sea and land has increased and the road systems have been expanded. Most of the world's forests are already managed according to the rules of forestry and areas of settlement and cultivation extended. Untouched virgin lands are everywhere much reduced, and soon they will be limited to unproductive desert, tundra, coastal swamps and the higher mountains, and to a number of large nature reserves. Even these last are threatened by population pressures and some will no doubt disappear. This development seems to be inevitable because the majority of mankind will always prefer a fine park-like stretch of country laid out by man to the more varied harmony of untouched nature. Man is continually destroying original, natural scenery by introducing trees, shrubs, plants and animals from other regions either intentionally or by accident. We in northern and central Europe have already forgotten that horse chestnuts, acacias, plane trees, the evening primrose, rosebay willow herb, spurge and other plants are not indigenous to our country, and that pheasants come from Asia and Colorado beetles from America. Even in the tropics, many strange plants now rank as part of the native flora. In India and Indonesia, plants from tropical America often predominate, such as *Lantana* bushes, *Opuntia* thickets, *Mimosa pudica* by the roadside and the luxuriant water hyacinth, *Eichhornia*, in swamps and paddyfields.

But even the manmade countryside is getting further and further away from nature. In the last decades the charming farmlands of North America, no less than those in communist countries, have been replaced by the vaster and duller stretches cultivated by more efficient and profitable large scale agricultural enterprise or the collective farm. In the tropics we find vast, monotonous rubber or coffee plantations, or fields of sisal and pineapple. The men who carry out their wearisome work in a coffee plantation in Central America or on a huge Malayan rubber estate are certainly much less happy than their ancestors were, living in freedom and in tune with nature's richer profusion. In this lifeless landscape we can see the ruthless principle of selection at work: for the large-scale farms are more profitable than, and so have superseded, the smallholdings, just as chain stores and supermarkets are killing the one-man shop.

On the other hand, the rapid spread of technical devices and rational methods of working into all countries is also advantageous, since it facilitates international understanding and forces international cooperation. Modern means of communication, such as the post, telegraph and telephone, radio and television, and the aims of scientific and medical research, will link all mankind more closely together in the years to come; and so a growing number of international organizations will be required. Postal services, railways, airlines and shipping companies are already under international control. International scientific congresses and societies have developed into permanent bodies. In future the great volume of exchange in raw materials and consumer goods, and cultural planning or population projects, will mean extending a great number of new central international institutions.

The establishment of UNO and UNESCO proves that, for some years past, most countries have recognized this as an inevitable development. These two institutions are doing work of great importance for man's future well-being. They encourage the development of backward countries, the improvement of health, the spread of education and of international scientific cooperation. They organize international conferences which labour to relax political tension and smooth out conflicts. Other organizations also help in different fields: the World Health Organization, the United Nations Food and Agriculture Organization, international unions of all branches of science. The advantages are so obvious that we may expect these bodies to develop more and more into centres of management directing the future course of man's history.

How long this laudable aim can be pursued depends upon political factors, and these are of course unpredictable. But all international cooperation will be helped by long periods of peace, when events can be shaped in the interests of a common policy. The meeting and mingling of diverse peoples will promote these interests, whereas any kind of armed conflict will favour nationalistic and reactionary trends.

There is no need, however, to fear that growing international understanding will mean that smaller regions will lose their special characteristics and their cultural independence. Local differences will persist, and they are usually and quite rightly encouraged, even within the smaller states. The Hanseatic towns and Bavaria still keep their individuality within West Germany, and so do the Scots in Great Britain or the Mongol peoples in the U.S.S.R. As transport and communications have become easier, however, smaller states have tended in the past two centuries to unite into larger regional entities. This has been the case in Germany, Italy, the U.S.S.R., India and Indonesia. This tendency towards forming larger and larger blocks of states is bound to continue.

Whether the administration of these states is authoritarian (with the advantages of stricter centralization, better overall planning, and a more consistent political policy), or democratic (with greater personal freedom and the accent on private enterprise), it will tend towards a progressive levelling of the social strata. This will happen because the whole level of education will rise with the further expansion of schools, colleges, centres for adult education, radio programmes, serious periodicals and films. Of course the trend will be towards mass civilization, of which we are already seeing the beginnings. The voice and taste of the masses now decide political issues (because of individual equality in the plebiscite and the vote), as well as determining the standard of films and periodicals, the style of dress and the character of social undertakings such as 'parties' or group travel tours. Chain stores operate a kind of selection already, through their policy of profitable lines largely based on mass demand.

As democracy spreads, people will put up with this 'mass element' for the sake of the social tranquillity, which outweighs its negative aspects. Besides, fresh variants with new abilities will appear among the more diverse masses of the future. Some of these will spread rapidly, while others, like pre-adapted mutants among animals, must wait until favourable circumstances occur (free-thinking men, for instance, in Christian countries, exact philosophers in the classical sense in our unphilosophical or pseudo-philosophical age). In spite of the growing cultural uniformity, international and intersocial understanding in general will always promote cultural advance.

Because of the 'educational revolution', which has seized all countries, there will be a steady increase of scientific and technical achievements, of new findings and inventions. Work at universities and research institutes has already met with great success in countries where even three or four decades ago scientific and technical progress would have meant nothing

N

at all. The steady increase in the numbers of research centres and of students is bound to lead to greater intellectual output. However lowly the cultural level may have been a generation or two back, human brains of whatever race are capable of intellectual achievement of a high order. Technical and scientific advances will provide a material basis on which artistic talents can develop more freely. Increased polymorphism, as it continues to produce new gene combinations, will widen the chances for unique talents and achievements in science and art.

International cooperation has already created a global body of knowledge, especially in the natural sciences. There has been a movement towards a 'scientific view of things'. In industry, trade, the home, agriculture and forestry, and also in politics, the administration of justice, and even our personal life and way of thinking, we try to base our thought, actions and intentions on valid scientific facts. This trend will probably persist, and indeed grow, with an increase in experiment and calculation. Scientific methods have the great advantage that they fall in with the supra-individual realities of this world and their causal and logical laws. This kind of 'cultural empiricism' may bring a certain amount of disillusionment, but it is bound to gain ground. After all, verifiable facts are tougher than even the noblest of imponderable ideas; besides, selection is operating here as elsewhere. Yet we need not fear that aspects of life like the arts, in which emotion is of more significance than strict realism, are likely to wither away. Artistic ability has a hereditary basis and investigations into identical and non-identical twins support this view. So a fair percentage of mankind will always possess some gift for music, painting or literature and will always be able to develop this important aspect of culture.

As the great importance of science has been recognized by political authorities during the last decades, there is some danger that science may become too much guided by these authorities. This already happens in that it is those research programmes likely to yield direct economic progress that receive priority in financing. Pure research seeking only to further knowledge is put at a disadvantage in many countries. We must, however, consider that most technical and economic progress is ultimately based on discoveries of scientists who only wanted to obtain deeper insight into the laws of nature. It was not the aim of Mendel to found a basis for rational cultivation of plants, nor of Einstein, Planck and Hahn to invent an atomic power station or the atom bomb.

It will become more difficult for anyone to survey more than one limited field of research and assess its findings. Increased complexity will entail more stringent specialization. Men with a universal outlook and grasp will grow rarer, although there will be particular need of such men in the future. The sort of 'universalism' displayed by popular literature will be no substitute. Scientific world literature will give us an extremely valuable global network of knowledge, but man's brain has ceased to extend the range of what it can grasp and he can neither master nor evaluate the complicated mass as a whole.

When we now consider the development of individual branches of science, we can only predict that some recognizable tendencies will most probably persist during the next decades. Research in biology will bring us nearer to a physiochemical understanding of life processes, and indeed of life itself. Parallel with this development, medical research will discover new treatments. The stormy development of atomic physics will continue and yield further exciting results. A wider use of electronic computers will make it possible to solve complex problems in many branches of theoretical physics and mathematics. In astronomy and cosmology there are bound to be more and more discoveries of the utmost importance.

Our knowledge in the humanities, however, is not likely to extend very rapidly, although many new findings will enrich our knowledge of ancient cultures. Progress in European linguistics and history will slow down, for the essentials are already known and the field of discovery is limited.

A great deal has been said and written about the economic changes to be expected in the next decades, because the continual and often revolutionary changes in the needs of industry oblige us to consider these problems. The present

185

work, however, is concerned less with practical details than with the general consequences for mankind that will follow an alteration in the whole economic structure. It may suffice to touch on a few important points.

First and foremost, the laws of selection will continue to operate and to promote economic and technical advance (compare Chapter 4, section C). Almost everywhere industrialization will make rapid strides as more efficient appliances supplant older and less rational ones. Production that is more efficient, better and cheaper, will automatically take the place of older methods. This will often involve a beneficial measure of centralization. At the same time, new sources of materials and energy will be opened up and radically new processes of manufacture tried out. Industry will require far more basic raw materials. It was feared at one time that supplies of such natural substances as copper, tin, coal and oil might soon be exhausted or at least in short supply. However, specialists disagree on this point [4, 20, 86, 147, 260, 271]. Besides, it is to be expected that new sources of energy will supplement and partly replace traditional ones.

Above all, we may look for increasing innovations in the industrial use of the vast resources of energy released by the fission and fusion of atomic nuclei. When disintegrated, 450 g of uranium yield as much energy as do 1500 tons of coal. Known stocks of uranium and thorium are so large that they are likely to last over a millennium. If atomic fusion could be made possible astonishing new prospects for developing the world's supply of energy would be opened up. There are other sources of energy which will probably be put to much greater use in the future – for instance the sun's rays in steppeland and deserts, and the tides.

It is not possible to make any reliable forecast about new sources of nutrition. But we may assume that a much greater area of land will come under cultivation, new and valuable field produce and fruits will be grown, and more efficient agricultural methods introduced. International exchange of foodstuffs may also be further developed. Moreover, we may become able to add to our natural resources by making large-scale use of seaweed as a foodstuff (either directly or in the form of fodder), by cultivating unicellular green algae [150], by extracting edible proteins from inedible plants, by manufacturing sugar from cellulose, or by synthesizing carbohydrates, fats or proteins by other methods. However, in spite of all possible progress most authorities express the fear that mankind will increase much more rapidly than his sources of subsistence, and food crises are still a constant threat [172, 271].

Man's way of living has already been radically affected by the growing rationalization and automation of technical processes. This began with the construction of machines and is now systematically carried on. With the invention of electronic control and computers these technical methods will now expand very fast [15]. Industrial competition – itself a kind of selection – automatically promotes automation [2, 29, 53, 211, 238, 269]. Many workers become redundant, and at the same time there is a growing need for highly trained technicians, physicists and mathematicians to construct and operate these complicated machines. And this leads to fresh and often serious social problems. The more industrialized countries have been giving much consideration to these matters (see the 1955 U.S. 'Joint Committee on the Economic Report'). But every country in future will have to face the problem of increased efficiency, and in particular of automation, and instruct its young people in mathematics and physics. 'The number of white-coated workers will increase proportionate to the decrease of men in blue dungarees' [15]. And a general levelling of the social strata will continue.

This development, which is already becoming so apparent, is not merely a 'second industrial revolution'. It is the beginning of an entirely new age bearing the imprint of science, an age that will be determined by great changes in our basic raw materials, astonishing achievements by computers, marked centralization in every phase of production, and the spread of internationalism.

But all this advance is purely a matter of making better use of man's brain as it is. As we have seen (cf. p. 145), his hereditary endowment will not alter – unless indeed it deteriorates, because disadvantageous mutants are no longer subject to selection and because less gifted people multiply faster than do others. The sexual instincts, rooted in the hereditary structure of the brain and maintained by selection, will remain unchanged.

But it will profoundly affect man's cultural progress that with the greater influence of modern hygiene, medicine and surgery, the average life span will be altered during the coming decades, mainly in hitherto underdeveloped countries. In Europe too, some extension is likely. Medical skill continues to improve, eating habits are more sensible, homes are healthier, better lighted, better ventilated and air conditioned. The biological disadvantages of these 'caves' of ours are reduced. So more people than ever before will survive the natural term of life. However, this term will not be extended very much (Fig. 12). During the years 1932-4 the average expectation of life for a man of 80 was 4·84 years, in 1949-50 it was 5·26, and in 1959-60 it was 5·5 years. This represents a rise of 0·7 per cent. But during the same period the expectation of life at birth rose by 7·5 per cent (from 59·9 to 64·6 years). And in the last fifty years the chance of a woman of 80 dying within the year has declined by some 20 per cent [H. Brown, 20].

With this increase in the average span of life, man will be able to develop his abilities much more fully. Work in many scientific fields, especially, usually calls for wide experience and very extensive knowledge, which can only be acquired through the years. In future, achievements of note will more often be the work of older researchers.

The increasing tempo of scientific development will often lead to states of conflict, like the one we are experiencing today. Manners and customs, ethical and religious ideas, rarely keep pace with the changes that new knowledge and new technology bring to man's life. Ethics and religion need timeless standards and orthodox views. They are therefore essentially conservative and dogmatic. Of course, an effort is made from time to time to reconcile them with advances in scientific knowledge. This will lead to a spiritualization of the meaning and symbolic content of rites and customs. But fresh conflicts will always arise, sometimes involving a complete break with tradition and so the collapse of some ethical and religious ideas. In modernized Islamic countries there is a strong movement to have done with many ancient customs; women have ceased to

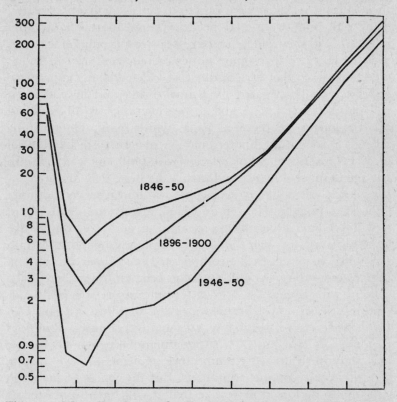

Fig. 12 Mortality figures for England for three separate periods. Vertical axis: mortality rate per 1000. Horizontal axis: age in decades. Over the years there has been a decline in mortality rates for childhood, youth and middle age; there has been less change in the rate for old age. (After Dorn.)

wear the veil and are now emancipated, and polygamy is abolished. Many communist countries have broken with religious tradition, and modern China has gone through a rapid transformation of many customs. Examples like these show what can and what will happen in other countries.

Ethical and moral ideas that do not conflict with scientific facts are the only ones that will survive.

The future development of religions will be influenced by the growing intermingling of the peoples of the world and by their getting to know each other's types of civilization better. They will both want and need to know more about other religions, and they will be more responsive to common features. The tendency to theosophy, noticeable for centuries in India, especially since the days of the wise ruler Akbar (1542-1605) and later on propagated by Ramakrishna and his followers, will possibly increase. A god to be venerated by all mankind can no longer be pictured as a 'white man'. He must be revered as something 'impersonal'. A panentheism like that of medieval mystics may link religion with philosophical views. In our age of space research and increasing biological and psychological analysis of life, many people will find it more and more difficult to imagine Heaven and Hell, angels and devils – and it will become impossible to imagine a god who thinks like human beings, for such thinking is absolutely bound to certain physiological processes in a complicated central nervous system. Hence, many humans will abandon religion altogether, or be content with Spinoza's 'deus sive mundus' or Goethe's 'God-Nature', the Hinduist Brahman, or the Buddhist Nirvana. All these processes will probably take many centuries. Religious customs, the worship of a superhuman being to whom one may pray in straitened circumstances, will be an urge in spite of rationalistic counter-arguments. But the whole of mankind will finally be forced to realize that it will have to master its fate by itself, and that it has to bear the responsibility for its future development. It does not seem probable that an increasingly Christian type of cultural development will gain ground, ending with a 'victory of God', as the English historian A. J. Toynbee [250] hopes.

The development of new ethical notions will probably proceed more quickly, for customs are to a great extent shaped by the exigencies of living and by the need for rival parties to find some workable solution. Once wars have become impossible, we may perhaps expect that the ideal image of mankind will no longer be the valiant hero in the military sense, but the fighter for the maintenance and progress of humanity. Yet at present, in a period of increasing crime rates, directly promoted by Western and thriller films and novels, such development may seem rather improbable.

In the sphere of the arts we may expect frequently changing and very diverse styles and a flow of new ideas; but compared with the sciences, there will be much less that is fundamentally new. Painting and poetry have long ago exhausted nearly all their possibilities, from the faithful reproduction of aesthetically significant natural objects and events to pure abstract work. Various arts have also been combined with others (poetry, music and visual effects in opera), or with aspects of practical life (in architecture, religious art and crafts). There will still be many successful experiments in this field, but development will follow a line of continued modification rather than of anything intrinsically new. And here, too, the styles and ideas of one nation will go on enriching and influencing others.

But besides the positive aspects of the future, certain threatening dangers must also be mentioned. A state of affairs has developed in Western countries which can only be described as a phase of decadence. Ruthless exploitation of individual liberties, the heedless pursuit of originality, as well as mercenary lack of scruple, have led to a diseased literature, unsavoury plays and films dwelling upon morbid or sensational themes or exciting the audience's or reader's sexual instincts. Painting is threatened with a descent into confusion. But by exposing our young people to all this, we are completely ignoring the fact that, in our close-knit, complex and highly organized society, the duty to give the rising generation a sound education is more pressing than ever before. At the turn of the century our youth grew up with lofty ideals. Most of our young people today start their life's work in a mood of apathy and disillusionment. A radical change in education is absolutely vital. As history teaches us, however, people always fail to see the downward curve of the decadent age they live in. Such nations are in danger of being engulfed by others still in a healthy condition.

Homo sapiens

In conclusion we must repeat that no prognostications can relate to more than the immediate future. This holds also for apparently more exact data – for instance, those worked out by eighty-two experts of the Rand Corporation in Santa Monica (California) [208]. With his 12,000 million brain cells, *Homo sapiens* is intellectually so complex, he may produce so many new combinations of abilities, that his thinking and planning may at any time lead to quite new and unpredictable results. Vital new discoveries and inventions may create new levels of integration and so change the whole direction of his scientific and cultural development. For instance, what a revolutionary invention the microscope has been! It has made an entirely new appraisal of all our life processes possible. It revealed the existence and shape of protozoa, bacteria and cell organelles and also the mysteries of fertilization and reproduction. It threw light on the functions of every organ. Modern medical skill is built upon it. And there have been other no less revolutionary inventions – printing, fire arms, the internal combustion engine. At the present day, the invention of electronic computers and spacecraft, and the discovery of atomic fission, are in the process of transforming the bases of our whole existence. As all research is now more intensive, such upheavals will become increasingly frequent. At the same time, possible future wars and political changes may also lead to unpredictable developments. These may not spring from any momentous universal economic or historical transformation; they may break out at any time because of the clash of personality between leading politicians who may be deficient in regard to culture or a sense of responsibility.

D. *Conclusions and future plans*

We may be sure, then, that the next decades will continue to develop certain tendencies. Some of these may also govern the more distant future, as selection is always operating, either biologically or culturally. It is therefore possible to draw certain conclusions applicable to any long-term planning. This is of special importance with regard to the general increase of the world population and the differing increases in individual countries. The solution of these problems needs international cooperation. This means that increased support should be given to the efforts of the international organizations such as UNO and UNESCO, and to all the other relevant international scientific unions and economic societies. Of course, conflicts between national ambitions and the necessity of reasonable international agreements will be inevitable and it will take several decades until a more or less tolerable global order can be established. Politicians and journalists of all countries have a particularly important part to play here and it will be necessary that they know and discuss these international problems and their biological basis.

At present, numerous committees and societies already exist to study future development and try to work out relevant plans in order to master the national and international problems that arise. They are especially active in the United States, the U.S.S.R., Britain, France and Germany. It is beyond the scope of this book to report in any more detail the various calculations and plans that are already published, but it is necessary to point to some of the main problems.

With regard to the threat of overpopulation, it must be recalled that above all this is a matter of individual nations. At present extensive tracts in Australia, North America, Siberia, tropical Africa, South America, New Guinea and Melanesia still remain to be 'opened up' and settled, and many other regions could absorb a much larger population than at present. Yet only a small proportion of the surplus population will be able to migrate to these regions, because only certain racial or professional groups are welcome there. Many nations will thus have to check their rate of increase, by birth control, and indeed the time may come when they will all have to do so. Although the practice runs counter to many ethical and religious traditions, these difficulties have not proved to be as insuperable as had been feared.

Enquiries in many countries have shown that most families want to have between two and four children. In the United States 90 per cent of the population consulted wanted two to four children (the average was three). In West Germany two to three children are the ideal. But even in an Islamic country like Turkey and in underdeveloped countries like Peru and Jamaica three children were considered to be the optimum number that could be brought up without economic difficulty. Hence, in order to stop overpopulation, it will only be necessary to inform the peoples of the possibilities of birth control and to distribute cheap (i.e. mechanical) preventives. Reduction of children's allowances – for instance, allowance only up to three children – and encouragement of female professional work would be additional means of diminishing the growth rate. We may thus hope that the present danger of population explosion can be banished, although famine crises still seem to be inevitable in some areas. In any case, an increase of food production, especially of the necessary proteins, which would correspond to the increase of 1·9 per cent of the world population, seems to be absolutely impossible for the time being [267, 271].

The danger that threatens mankind with continual and mostly harmful mutations presents far greater difficulties. There is only little hope that we may master these problems. Eugenic measures have to be intensified in all countries, mainly by teaching in schools and informing all classes of the population [160, 161, 236, 271]. This will be especially important with regard to those hereditary diseases – such as hereditary diabetes or haemophilia – which can be treated. Although the people in question are able to marry and may have children, they must be informed that their hereditary dispositions remain unchanged. As those who are hereditarily feebleminded cannot be approached by these means, laws governing sterilization are also a necessity. In countries with the most advanced civilizations, 2-3 per cent of the population suffer from slight feeblemindedness (debility) and one half per cent to a more severe degree (imbecility). In four-fifths of these cases the condition is hereditary [236, 259]. Since the passing of a sterilization law in Denmark (1929) the number of feebleminded births has been more than halved. It is thus quite possible to diminish this kind of deterioration in a population [110, 160, 161].

It may be still more important in future to see that those with a hereditary endowment above the average will have enough offspring. However, eugenic considerations may only achieve success if they are seen as a moral duty, as F. Galton postulated in 1905.

In order to avoid the accumulation of harmful mutants reaching a high degree – and we must expect this in future – more radical measures might be unavoidable. Even artificial insemination with spermatozoa of apparently healthy stock could eventually become necessary (at present already employed in some cases where the husband is sterile). H. J. Muller [158, 159], who drew the attention of the world at large to the danger of insufficient selection of harmful mutants, made the suggestion that 'valuable' semen might be frozen and preserved unaltered at a low temperature, and only used ten or twenty years after the donor's death. This would obviate a number of conflicts that might arise if it were used during his lifetime. However, it is practically impossible to decide whether or not the donor is of healthy stock because most harmful mutants are recessive. And the obvious moral and ethical implications scarcely need discussing. On the other hand, a favourable artificial alteration of individual gene loci would require the cultivation of human spermatozoa and a controlled alteration of individual sequences of bases in the DNA molecules. But this is a completely Utopian ideal, because we do not know the many tens of thousands of base sequences in our twenty-three chromosomes.

However, other manipulations of human characteristics and functions are discussible and they are already employed to a large extent. We use stimulating and calming drugs, we diminish pathological sexual drives by castration, and prevent dangerous overexcitement by leucotomy operations. And we may even hope that an artificial enhancement of the brain achievements by certain drugs will some day become possible.

The rapidly increasing need for technically and scientifically skilled workmen calls for a radical reform of education in many countries. Those under communist control have shown us the way in giving much more time to the natural sciences, which influence our philosophical view of the world so strongly, and which will come to have more and more practical significance. In future our 'cultured' citizens must not be allowed to leave school without any knowledge of how their own organs, their eyes, brain, liver, etc., function, what part the hormones play, how the germ tract makes for continuity from one generation to the next, how the genes ensure stability, how diseases may be inherited, how species are transformed, and how man has evolved. More especially, those who are not destined to become biologists or doctors, and so can only learn those things in the upper classes of our secondary schools, ought also to be equipped with this knowledge. Every teacher and every judge in a criminal court ought to have some idea how far a good or bad disposition may be hereditary, what a dominant influence the hormones may exert on a man's actions, and what organs and functions may be affected if the nervous system is overstrained. And the philosophy of every cultured person must include some acquaintance with how far the mystery of life has been revealed, as well as a knowledge of the phylogeny of animals and plants, of man's origins and his unique position among living organisms [cf. B. Rensch, 191].

As we shall require more and more technicians, physicists and chemists in this age of computers, atomic power and space travel, it is no less vital for us to have some knowledge of chemistry and physics, of atomic physics and astronomy, and of the mathematics essential for all exact calculations. The teaching of history should put a greater emphasis on world history. In language teaching, we should concentrate more in speaking and less on formal grammar, because the many 'exceptions' to the rules make them of little value when it comes to reading and speaking. All this shift of emphasis does not necessarily mean that much more has to be studied. The point is to select what is essential and to abandon old traditional usages in favour of what is required for the present and the future.

School reform implies some transformation in cultural ideals. The humanistic ideal of culture has yielded great achievements. However, our present culture is no longer based on the culture of the Greeks and Romans, as was the case during past centuries.

No slur is intended upon modern literature and art, but something more should be demanded of any cultured person in future than to be able to chat about a Hemingway novel, a Picasso exhibition, the latest film, or what has struck him most during a recent conducted tour to Egypt. An educated person must have some knowledge of atoms and molecules, physical and chemical laws, biological process, the history of the earth and of life – in short, he must have an adequate picture of the world.

Every kind of racial conflict must be brought to an end without delay. The era of colonialism is over, and we must now promote what has logically followed upon it – the equality of all races. As early as 1954 experts of UNESCO had formulated *Proposals on the Biological Aspects of Race* and quite recently a *Statement of Race and Racial Prejudice* [252]. We shall come to see that there is nothing behind many of our disagreements but a difference in education, tradition and various talents, and that in essence men are all rather alike.

The spread of modern means of traffic, global increase of education, global democratization and unification of cultures, a dwindling of racial conflicts and above all the necessity for international solutions of decisive problems will lead to the establishment of larger and finally global systems of administration. It is up to us to promote these tendencies continually until such ideal systems may be realized. Only then may we hope that the phase of undirected historical and cultural development will come to an end. When that happens, man will cease to be guided by the inscrutable Moira, the fate to which even the Greek gods must bow. Instead, he will direct his material and cultural advance according to a plan of his own, and to a certain extent he will also determine his future phylogenetic evolution. At the present time, any purposive line of development is still overshadowed by the danger that man may use his new weapon, atomic power, to wipe out whole nations or, in the event of a political catastrophe, even the entire species. In the past many animal species died out in consequence of the excessive phylogenetic enlargement of some organ. In this case, man's overdeveloped forebrain would have led him to his own extermination.

CHAPTER SEVEN

Sub specie aeternitatis

But what are we, after all, we humans? How did we come to be on this planet? Where is our history leading? These were the opening questions of this book. We have tried to answer them as far as present knowledge goes and at as many levels as possible. But what can we take to be the essential elements, *sub specie aeternitatis*?

It is perhaps apposite to summarize briefly the most important steps in a phylogenetic development which in the course of hundreds of millions of years has now led up to present-day man. The formation of highly complicated organic compounds, mainly protein bodies and self-reproducing polynucleotides had to take place before life emerged on the earth. Successful experiments have proved that such compounds could have originated under prebiological conditions about 4500 million years ago, after a solid covering had been formed upon the earth. Prestages of life could originate by combination of these compounds. Such prestages, which must have been similar to viruses, already possessed the most important characteristics of life: propagation, heredity and mutation by alteration of sequences of bases in the DNA molecules caused by ultraviolet and X-rays and by reaction with other chemical compounds. Self-reproduction of DNA led to the spread of these prestages. Time proportionate mutation produced reproductive variants suited in different degrees to survival in their environment. These differences led to natural selection and the beginning of continuous evolution.

After the first genuine organisms had developed – a process of which the stages can only be constructed by speculation – evolution led to growing diversity of species in consequence of continuous mutation and – after sexuality had then emerged – new gene combinations. In several lines of descent evolutionary progress took place because natural selection promoted species with more rational structures and functions.

One branch of the very ramified tree of life led to the origin of the first vertebrates about 500 million years ago. From this period onwards the line of descent leading to hominids can be reconstructed fairly clearly. Numerous fossil remains allow us to trace this line from earliest fish-like organisms (Agnatha) to true fishes – amphibians – reptiles – primitive mammals – insectivores – prosimians – monkeys and apes.

The first hominids, the Australopithecines, appeared at the end of the Tertiary period, before the beginning of the Pleistocene, about 3-4 million years ago. These upright walking prehumans still had a relatively ape-like brain, but were already capable of manufacturing most primitive stone tools. Strong selection of variants and hordes with better brain functions, greater power of generalization and planning led step by step to the genus *Homo*.

Finally, some 70,000 or 100,000 years ago, *Homo sapiens* was developed. Language and, later, writing and printing allowed traditions to be stored up and more advanced civilizations developed with increasing speed as a result of natural selection of non-inherited abilities, transmitted from generation to generation. And now civilized man has emerged, comprehending his own evolution and the laws of the universe, and growing more and more able to plan his own future.

Homo sapiens, however, represents no more than one of the many branches of the tree of life. Each individual today is simply an extremely complex product of cell reduplications in the endless succession of human germ tracts. These in turn are merely branches diverging from the common stream of all life. Yet the creature that this particular branch has produced is the highest that our earth, or indeed perhaps our solar system, has brought forth in the past 6000 million years.

It is possible to regard the whole phylogeny as a causally determined process, which began with the development of organic macromolecules and led to organisms, i.e. to highly

o

complicated self-reproducing biochemical stages of integration, and finally to *Homo sapiens*. Hence the phylogeny of organisms is very probably inextricably bound to the cosmic and geological history of our planet.

Corresponding psychic phenomena and achievements have been developed, finally leading to human thinking increasingly adapted to the causal and logical laws of the world. It is very likely that non-living matter has a proto-psychic character. The following statements and conclusions speak in favour of this assumption. (1) The hereditary substance, the DNA molecules, are capable of transmitting intellectual abilities like special talents or weakness of character. (2) The molecules or the complexes of energy of our brain neurons, the functions of which correspond to our thinking, derive from our foodstuffs. (3) It is improbable that, at some stage of the embryonic development between the fertilized germ cell and the infant at birth, something psychic, an individual soul, should arise as something fundamentally different from physiological processes, but also exhibiting characteristics of parents and ancestors. (4) The history of the solar system, our earth and its organisms was a causally determined process lasting several thousand million years. It is improbable that in the last phase of this history psychic phenomena appeared as something fundamentally different in the brains of animals and man. These phenomena cannot be regarded as further new functions of the brains because they are not causally connected with physiological brain process but run parallel to or are identical with them. And a 'free will', which would influence physiological brain processes and – in consequence – would break the law of conservation of energy, is also improbable. (5) When we analyse our sensations and thought processes in order to get an idea of what 'matter' is like, we state that colour, smell, warmth, hardness, etc., are not characteristics of matter itself. But this process of epistemological reduction does not eliminate 'awareness' as such. (6) The conceptions of matter developed by modern physics do not contradict the idea of its protopsychic character, for matter can only be regarded as a spatial and temporal system of energy. Hence a panpsychistic and identistic conception does not assume a contrast of mind and matter. It recognizes only systems of relations, which are mostly trans-subjective, but may partly enter in a stream of consciousness into our brain where they are integrated to become our psychic phenomena [more detailed representation in B. Rensch, 196, 199].

In my opinion it is possible to conceive *Homo sapiens* to be the highest and most marvellous stage of integration of 'matter', i.e. of a certain special and temporal system of relations and effects of universal causal and logical laws. During the past millennia the abilities of their brain and their growing traditions enabled human beings to understand their own essence, their phylogeny and the laws of the universe. We may hope that these abilities will also enable us to master all future problems that arise to threaten our existence. With regard to the very distant, though certain, end of the existence of our planet, it is impossible that an ultimate aim of human life should exist. The most we can do is to aspire to a reasonable social structure on our earth and an ideal way of life in a spirit of true humanism.

The knowledge that we are incorporated in a long chain of cosmic development determined by universal laws may serve as a firm basis for a noble concept of the world. Whether we accept the above-mentioned panpsychistic conception, or presume a dualism of matter and mind, or are convinced by religious doctrines, we must regard *Homo sapiens* as the product of a continuous stream of life. Every human individual is so to speak 'only' a temporary complicated stage of multiplication and differentiation of cells in the unbroken chain of germ tracts connecting the generations.

The fact that all individuals belong together because they are only links of chains of the same phylogenetic branch finds expression in all kinds of professional and cultural organizations, especially in communist countries. It was only after life in large communities became too organized because of social needs that the desire to get as much personal freedom as possible could arise. However, the present stage of unrestrained freedom in Western countries shows that this leads to weakness of character and degeneration of customs and morals. Such countries are in danger of sinking below the level of more disciplined peoples and of becoming their dependents. In the course of phylogeny all societies of higher animals have developed a hierarchical order based on inherited instincts. These orders arose independently of one another among wolves, baboons, zebras, pigeons, etc. This parallel suggests that social discipline is a physical necessity. The much narrower and more complex human societies cannot give up their system of order with impunity.

The enormous degree of complexity of our brain functions has led present-day men to feel themselves no longer creatures similar to higher animal creatures, as primitive hominids most probably did. We humans cannot imagine that our self, our individual 'soul', no longer exists after death. However, on the base of our biological, physical and epistemological knowledge, we may perhaps assume that the complex of awareness which represents an ego, a 'soul' – the *atman* of the Hindus – is a part of the universe, the Brahman, a part which will be absorbed into the all-one after death. Such a conception is in line with the interpretation of the great Indian thinker Shankara (about A.D. 800) and the still existing doctrine of *advaita*. Such a conception would also reconcile us to the idea that all life on our planet will end one day. Its primal elements will then re-enter the eternal succession determined by the basic principles of the universe which may also be equated with an impersonal god. This would also correspond to the words of St John in their original form: 'In the beginning was the logos, and the logos was with God, and God was the logos.'

References and Bibliography, Glossary, Index

References and bibliography

1 C. ARAMBOURG and R. HOFFSTETTER Découverte, en Afrique du Nord, de restes humaines du Paléolithique inférieur. *C. Rend. Hebdom. Séances Acad., Sci.*, 239 (1), 1954.

2 K. ARNOLD and L. BRANDT Grosse Rationalisierungsausstellung 1953. Arbeitsgem. f. Forsch. Nordrhein-Westfalen, Nat. wiss., H. 6, Dortmund, 1953.

3 H. AUTRUM Über Energie- und Zeitgrenzen der Sinnesempfindungen. *Naturwiss.*, 35, 1948, 361-9.

4 F. BAADE *Der Wettlauf zum Jahre 2000*. Oldenburg and Hamburg, 1960.

5 M. BATES *Prevalence of People*. New York, 1959.

6 H. BERNATZIK *Die Geister der gelben Blätter*. Gütersloh, 1961.

7 N. J. BERRILL *Man's Emerging Mind*. New York, 1955.

8 L. VON BERTALANFFY *Das biologische Weltbild*. Vol. 1. Bern, 1949.

9 —— *Theoretische Biologie*. 2nd ed. 2 vols. Bern, 1951.

10 R. BIASUTTI *Razze e populi della terra*. 3rd ed. Torino, 1959.

11 K. BIRKET-SMITH *Geschichte der Kultur*. Zürich, 1946.

12 H. F. BLUM *Time's Arrow and Evolution*. Princeton, 1955.

13 F. BRAMSTEDT Dressurversuche mit *Paramaecium caudatum* und *Stylonychia mytilus*. *Z. vergl. Physiol.*, 22, 1935, 490-516.

14 W. C. BOYD *Genetics and the Races of Man*. Boston, 1950.

15 L. BRANDT *Die 2. industrielle Revolution*. Bonn, 1956.

16 H. BRAUN Über das Unterscheidungsvermögen unbenannter Anzahlen bei Papageien. *Z. f. Tierpsychol.*, 9, 1952, 40-91.

17 H. BREITINGER Zur gegenwärtigen Kenntnis der ältesten Hominiden. *Anz. Phil.-hist K. Österr. Ak. Wiss.* (1961), No. 22, 1962.

18 H. BREUIL Le feu et l'industrie de pierre et d'os dans le gisement du 'Sinanthropus' à Choukoutien. *L'Antropologie*, 42, 1932.

19 H. BROOM and G. W. H. SCHEPERS The South African fossil apeman: the Australopithecinae. *Transvaal Mus. Mem.*, 2. Pretoria, 1946.

20 H. BROWN *The Challenge of Man's Future*. London, 1954.

21 W. VON BUDDENBROCK Über die kinetische und statische Leistung grosser und kleiner Tiere und ihre Bedeutung für den Gesamtstoffwechsel. *Naturwiss.*, 22, 1934, 675-80.

22 F. BURGDÖRFER Die Bevölkerung der Erde im Jahre 2000. *Umschau*, 58, 1958, 253-6.

23 A. BUTENANDT Biochemie der Gene und Genwirkungen. Verh. Dtsch. Naturforscher u. Ärzte, 97 Vers., 1953, 43-52.

24 M. CALVIN The origin of life on earth and elsewhere. *Persp. Biol. Med.*, 5, 1962.

25 —— Evolution of photosynthetic mechanisms. *Persp. Biol. Med.*, 5, 1962.

26 —— Communication: from molecules to Mars. *A.I.B.S. Bull.*, 1962, 29-44.

27 A. M. CARR-SAUNDERS *World Population: Past Growth and Present Trends*. 1936.

28 K. CHANG New evidence on fossil man in China. *Science*, 136, 1962, 749-60.

29 L. CHOUFFIGNAL *Denkmaschinen*. Stuttgart, 1955.

30 E. A. COLBERT *Evolution of the Vertebrates*. New York and London, 1955.

31 R. C. COOK *Human Fertility: The Modern Dilemma*. London, 1951.

32 C. ST COON Human races in relation to environment and culture. *Cold Spring Harbor Symposia Quant. Biol.*, 15, 1950, 247-58.

33 —— *The Origin of Races*. New York, 1962.

34 E. D. COPE *Progressive and Regressive Evolution among Vertebrates*. 1884.

35 M. Y. COPPENS Découverte d'un Australopithéciné dans le Villafranchien du Tschad. *C. Rend. Acad. Sci. Paris*, 1961, 3851.

36 R. A. DART The Osteodontokeratic culture of *Australopithecus prometheus*. *Transvaal Mus. Mem.*, 10. Pretoria, 1957.

37 —— Osteodontokeratic ripping tools and pulp scoops for teething and edentulous Australopithecines. *J. D.A.S.A.*, 14, 1959, 164-78.

38 —— Australopithecus, tool-user or tool-maker? *Israel Ac. Sci. Human Proc.*, Sect. Sci., No. 8. Jerusalem, 1968.

39 C. DARWIN *The Descent of Man and Selection in Relation to Sex*. London, 1871.

40 C. G. DARWIN *Die nächste Million Jahre*. Branuschweig, 1953.

41 UNITED NATIONS *Demographic Yearbook 1966*. New York, U.N. Statit. Office.

42 E. DIEBSCHLAG Psychologische Beobachtungen über die Rangordnung bei der Haustaube. *Z. f. Tierpsychol.*, 4, 1940, 173-88.

43 TH. DOBZHANSKY *The Biological Basis of Human Freedom*. New York, 1956.

44 —— *Evolution, Genetics and Man*. New York and London, 1957.

45 —— Man and natural selection. *Amer. Scientist*, 49, 1961, 285-99.

46 —— *Mankind Evolving*. New Haven and London, 1962.

46a ——*The Biology of Ultimate Concern*. New York. 1967

47 TH. DOBZHANSKY and G. ALLEN Does natural selection continue to operate in modern mankind? *Amer. Anthropologist*, 58, 1956, 591-604.

48 TH. DOBZHANSKY and M. F. A. MONTAGU Natural selection and the mental capacities of mankind. *Science*, 105, 1947, 587-90.

49 H. F. DORN World population growth: an international dilemma. *Science*, 135, 1962, 283-90.

50 G. DÜCKER Untersuchungen über geometrischoptische Täuschungen bei Wirbeltieren. *Z. f. Tierpsychol.*, 23, 1967, 452-96.

51 U. EBBECKE Angeborene Verhaltensweisen des Menschen. *Dtsch. Medizin. Wochenschr.*, 80, 1955, 854-91.

52 E. VON EICKSTEDT *Die Forschung am Menschen*. Stuttgart, 1937-64.

53 L. ERHARD and E. POTTHOFF Rationalisierung und Wirtschaft. Arbeitsgem. f. Rationalisierung Nordrhein-Westfalen, H. 5. Dortmund, 1953.

54 H. J. FLEURE and C. L. WALTON Notes on the habits of some sea anemones. *Zool. Anz.*, 31, 1907, 212-20.

55 S. W. FOX *The Origins of Prebiological Systems and their Molecular Matrices*. New York and London, 1965.

56 H. FRIEDRICH-FREKSA Die stammesgeschichtliche Stellung der Virusarten und das Problem der Urzeugung. In G. HEBERER *Evolution d. Organismen*. 2nd ed. Stuttgart, 1954.

57 C. FUHLROTT Menschliche Überreste aus einer Felsengrotte des Düsselthales. Verh. Naturhist. Ver. Preuss. Rheinlande u. Westph., 16, 1859.

58 W. FUCKS Die Naturwissenschaft, die Technik und der Mensch Arbeitsgem. f. Forschung Nordrhein-Westfalen, Nat. wiss., H. 8. Köln and Opladen, 1952.

59 F. GALTON *Hereditary Genius: An Inquiry into its Laws and Consequences*. London, 1869.

60 R. A. GARDNER and B. T. GARDNER Teaching sign language to a chimpanzee. *Science*, 165, 664-72.

Homo sapiens

61 W. GIESELER Die Fossilgeschichte des Menschen. In G. HEBERER *Evolution d. Organismen*. 2nd ed. Stuttgart, 1957. pp. 951-1109.

62 B. GLASS A biologic view of human history. *Scientific Monthly*, 73, 1951, 363-8.

63 J. GOODALL Feeding behaviour of wild chimpanzees. *Symposia Zool. Soc. London*, 10, 1963, 39-47.

64 ——— My life among wild chimpanzees. *Nat Geogr.*, 124, 1963, 272-308.

65 H. GRIMM Vergleichend-biologische Gesichtspunkte zum Urbanisierungstrauma. *Z. ärztl. Fortbildung*, 51, 1957, 945-8.

66 E. HAECKEL *Generelle Morphologie der Organismen*. Berlin, 1866.

67 ——— *Über die Entstehung und den Stammbaum des Menschengeschlechts*. Berlin, 1868.

68 J. B. S. HALDANE The rate of mutation of human genes. *Proc. 8th Internat. Congr. Genetics*, 1949.

69 ——— Natural selection. *Trans. Bose Res. Inst. Calcutta*, 22, 1955, 17-20.

70 J. L. HAMERTON Primate chromosomes. *Symposia Zool. Soc. London*, 10, 1963, 211-20.

71 H. F. HARLOW The evolution of learning. In ROE and SIMPSON *Behaviour and Evolution*. New Haven, 1958. pp. 269-90.

72 N. HARTMANN *Philosophie der Naturwissenschaften*. Berlin, 1937.

73 C. HAYES *The Ape in our House*. London, 1952.

74 K. J. HAYES and C. HAYES Picture perception in a home-raised chimpanzee. *J. Comp. Physiol. Psychol.*, 46, 1953, 470-4.

75 ——— The cultural capacity of chimpanzees. In GAVAN *The Non-human Primates and Human Evolution*. Detroit, 1955.

76 G. HEBERER Jüngere Stammesgeschichte des Menschen. In JUST *Handb. d. Erbbiol. d. Menschen*. Vol. 1. Berlin, 1940. Pp. 584-644.

77 ——— Neue Ergebnisse der menschlichen Abstammungslehre. Göttingen, 1951.

78 ——— Die Fortschritte in der Erforschung der Phylogenie der Hominoidea. *Ergebn. Anat. u. Entwicklungsgesch.*, 34, 1952, 499-637.

79 ——— Die Fossilgeschichte der Hominoidea. In HOFER, SCHULTZ and STARCK *Primatologia*. Vol. 1. Basel and New York, 1956. Pp. 379-650.

80 ——— Das Tier-Mensch-Übergangsfeld. *Studium Generale*, 11, 1958, 341-52.

81 ——— Die subhumane Abstammungsgeschichte des Menschen.

References and bibliography

In G. HEBERER *Evolution der Organismen*. 2nd ed. Stuttgart, 1959. Pp. 1110-42.

82 —— '*Zinjanthropus boisei*' und der Status der Prähomininen (Australopithecinae). *Zool. Jahrb. Abt. Syst.*, 88, 1960, 91-106.

83 —— Oldoway – das Tal des Urmenschen in der Serengeti. *Umschau*, 62, 1962, 476-79.

84 —— (ed.) *Menschliche Abstammungslehre*. Stuttgart, 1965.

85 G. HEBERER, G. KURTH and I. SCHWIDETZKY-ROESING Anthropologie. *Fischer-Lexikon*. Frankfurt a. M., 1959.

86 J. HEINRICHS Hunger und Zukunft. Kl. Vandenhoeckreihe Bd. 302-303. Göttingen, 1969.

87 G. HERDER *Ideen zur Philosophie der Geschichte der Menschheit*, Riga, 1784-91.

87a *C. J. Herrick The Evolution of Human Nature*. New York, 1956.

88 K. HERTER Weitere Dressurversuche an Fischen. *Z. vergl. Physiol.*, 11, 1930, 730-48.

89 —— Über simultanen Farbenkontrast bie Fischen. *Biol. Zentralbl.*, 69, 1950, 283-300.

90 —— *Die Fischdressuren und ihre sinnesphysiologischen Grundlagen*. Berlin, 1953.

91 S. HÖRSTADIUS Linné, die Tiere und der Mensch. Zum 250. Geburtstag Carl von Linnés am. 23 Mai 1957. *Naturwiss.*, 45, 1958, 1-4.

92 F. C. HOWELL European and Northwest African Middle Pleistocene hominids. *Current Anthropology*, 1, 1960, 195-232.

93 F. C. HOWELL and BOURLIÈRE (ed.) *African Ecology and Human Evolution*. Chicago, 1964.

94 W. W. HOWELLS *Die Ahnen der Menschheit*. (Ergänzt von G. Kurth). Zurich, 1963.

95 J. HÜRZELER *Oreopithecus bambolii* Gervais: a preliminary report. *Verh. Naturforsch. Ges. Basel*, 69, 1958, 1-48.

96 J. S. HUXLEY Biology of the Human race. In H. G. WELLS, J. S. HUXLEY and G. P. WELLS *The Science of Life*. New York, 1929.

97 —— *The Captive Shrew and other Poems of a Biologist*. New York and London, 1933.

98 —— *Evolution: The Modern Synthesis*. 2nd ed. London, 1963.

99 —— *The Uniqueness of Man*. London, 1947.

100 —— *Man in the Modern World*. London, 1947.

101 —— *Essays of a Humanist*. London, 1964.

102 T. HUXLEY *Evidence as to Man's Place in Nature*. London and Edinburgh, 1863.

103 JOINT COMMITTEE ON THE ECONOMIC REPORT *Automation and Technological Change*. Hearings before the Subcommittee on the Economic Report Congress of the United States. 48 Congr., 1st Sess., Sec. 5(a) of Public Law 304. Washington, 1955.

104 J. KÄLIN Die ältesten Menschenreste und ihre stammesgeschichtliche Deuting. In KERN *Historia Mundi*. Vol. 1. Bern and Munich, 1952. Pp. 33-98, 525-9.

105 I. KANT Rezension von Moscatis Schrift: Von dem körperlichen wesentlichen Unterschiede zwischen der Struktur der Tiere und Menschen. 1771. In E. CASSIRER *Immanuel Kants Werke*. Vol. II. Berlin, 1922. Pp. 437-42.

106 —— Idee zu einer allgemeinen Geschichte in weltbürgerlicher Absicht. Berliner Monatsschr. 1784, 386-410. In E. CASSIRER *Immanuel Kants Werke*. Vol. 4. Berlin, 1922.

107 T. KAPUNE Untersuchungen zur Bildung eines 'Wertbegriffs' bei niederen Primaten. $\mathcal{Z}.f.$ *Tierpsychol.*, 23, 1966, 324-63.

108 M. KAWAI Newly acquired precultural behavior of the natural troop of Japanese monkeys on Koshima Island. *Primates*, 6, 1965, 1-10.

109 S. KAWAMURA The process of subcultural behavior among Japanese macaques. In C. H. SOUTHWICK (ed.) *Primate Social Behavior*. New York, 1963. Pp. 82-90.

110 T. KEMP Genetic-hygienic experience in Denmark in recent years. *Eugen. Rev.*, 49, 1957.

111 J. KEOSIAN *The Origin of Life*. New York and London, 1964.

112 F. KLUGE and A. GÖTZE Etymologisches Wörterbuch der deutschen Sprache. Berlin and Leipzig, 1934.

113 H. KLÜVER *Behavior Mechanisms in Monkeys*. Chicago, 1933.

114 O. KOEHLER Vom Erlernen unbenannter Anzahlen bei Vögeln. *Naturwiss.*, 29, 1941, 201-18.

115 —— 'Zähl'-Versuche an einem Kolkraben und Vergleichsversuche an Menschen. $\mathcal{Z}.f.$ *Tierpsychol.*, 5, 1943, 575-712.

116 —— 'Zählende' Vögel und vorsprachliches Denken. *Verh. Dtsch. Zool. Ges.*, 1949, 219-38.

117 W. KÖHLER *Intelligenzprüfungen an Menschenaffen*. 2nd ed. Berlin, 1921.

117a——*The Mentality of Apes*. 3rd ed. New York, 1948.

118 G. R. H. VON KOENIGSWALD Die Phylogenie des Menschen. *Naturwiss.*, 40, 1953, 128-37.

119 —— *Begegnungen mit dem Vormenschen*. Düsseldorf, 1955.

120 —— Das Alter der Hominiden. *Anthropol. Anz.*, 29, 1965, 163-70.

121 —— *Die Geschichte des Menschen*. 2nd ed. Berlin, 1968.

References and bibliography

122 A. KORTLANDT Handgebrauch bei freilebenden Schimpansen. In B. RENSCH (ed.) *Handgebrauch u. Verständigung bei Affen u. Frühmenschen.* Bern and Stuttgart, 1968. Pp. 59-102.

123 A. KORTLANDT and M. KOOIJ Protohominid behaviour in primates. *Symposium Zool. Soc. London,* 10, 1963, 61-88.

124 A. KÜHN Nachweis des simultanen Farbenkontrastes bei Insekten. *Naturwiss.,* 1921.

125 G. KURTH Überlegungen zu den zoogeographischen Klimaregeln. *Forsch. u. Fortschr.,* 30, 1956, 293-7.

126 —— (ed.) *Evolution und Hominisation.* Stuttgart, 1961.

127 —— Australopithecinen in der Sahara. *Naturwiss. Rundschau,* 1962, 68-9.

128 W. LA BARRE *The Human Animal.* Chicago, 1954.

129 J. VAN LAWICK-GOODALL New discoveries among Africa's chimpanzees. *Nat. Geogr.,* 128, 1965, 802-31.

130 L. S. B. LEAKEY A new fossil skull from Olduvai. *Nature,* 184, 1959, 491-3.

131 —— New finds of Olduvai Gorge. *Nature,* 189, 1961, 649-50.

132 —— The juvenile mandible from Olduvai. *Nature,* 191, 1961, 417-18.

133 L. S. B. LEAKEY *et al. Olduvai Gorge 1951-1961.* New York and Cambridge, 1965.

134 L. S. B. LEAKEY and M. D. LEAKEY Recent discoveries of fossil hominids in Tanganyika: at Olduvai and near Lake Natron. *Nature,* 202, 1964, 5-7.

135 L. S. B. LEAKEY, P. V. TOBIAS and J. R. NAPIER A new species of the genus *Homo* from Olduvai Gorge. *Nature,* 202, 1964, 7-9.

136 W. E. LE GROS CLARK *History of the Primates.* 4th ed. London, Nat. Hist. Museum, 1954.

137 —— *The Fossil Evidence for Human Evolution.* Chicago, 1955.

138 —— *The Antecedents of Man.* Edinburgh, 1959.

139 J. C. LILLY *The Mind of the Dolphin,* 1967.

140 R. LINTON *The Tree of Culture.* New York, 1955.

141 P. LÖGLER Versuche zur Frage des 'Zähl'-Vermögens an einem Graupapagei und Vergleichversuche am Menschen. *Z. f. Tierpsychol.,* 16, 1959, 179-217.

142 K. LORENZ Die angeborenen Formen möglicher Erfahrung. *Z. f. Tierpsychol.,* 5, 1943, 235-409.

143 ——Über angeborene Instinktformeln beim Menschen. *Dtsch. Medizin. Wochenschr.* 77, 1953, 1566-9, 1604-6. *Z. menschl. Vererb. u. Konstit. forsch.,* 32, 1954, 385-9.

144 T. R. MALTHUS *An Essay on the Principle of Population as it affects the Future Improvement of Society.* London, 1798.

145 E. MAROLD Versuche an Wellensittichen zur Frage des 'Zähl'-Vermögens. *Z. f. Tierpsychol.*, 3, 1939, 170-223.

146 E. MAYR *Animal Species and Evolution*. Cambridge, Mass., 1963.

147 G. MCGHEE Natürliche Hilfsquellen der Welt: Die Situation heute und in der Zukunft. Arbeitsgem. f. Forsch. Nordrhein-Westfalen, Nat. Wiss. H. 136. Köln and Opladen, 1964.

148 P. B. MEDAWAR *The Future of Man*. London, 1959.

149 A. MEESTERS Über die Organisation des Gesichtsfeldes der Fische. *Z. f. Tierpsychol.*, 4, 1940, 84-149.

150 M. MEFFERT Grosskultur von Grünalgen: Eine neue Nahrungs-quelle? *Umschau*, 55, 1955, 388-90.

151 S. L. MILLER A production of aminoacids under possible primitive earth conditions. *Science*, 117, 1953.

152 D. MIYADI On some new habits and their propagation in Japan-ese monkey bands. *Proc. 12 Internat. Congress Zool. London (1958)*, 1959, 857-60.

153 M. F. A. MONTAGU (ed.) *Culture and Evolution of Man*. New York, 1962.

154 D. MORRIS *The Biology of Art*. London, 1962.

155 H. L. MULLER Genetic principles in human population. *Amer. J. Psychiat.*, 113, 1956, 481-91.

156 —— An estimate of the mutational damage in man from data on consanguineous marriages. *Proc. Nat. Acad. Sci.*, 42, 1956, 855-63.

157 —— Further studies bearing on the load of mutations in man. *Acta Genet. Statist. Medica*, 6, 1956, 157-68.

158 —— The guidance of human evolution. In D. J. INGLE and S. O. WAIFE *Perspectives in Biology and Medicine*. Univ. Chicago Press, III (1), 1959, 1-43.

159 —— Human evolution by voluntary choice of germ plasm. *Science*, 134, 1961, 643-9.

160 H. NACHTSHEIM Unsere Pflicht zur praktischen Eugenik. *Bundesgesundheitsblatt*, 18, 1963, 277-86.

161 —— Die qualitative Bevölkerungsbewegung: Erbgesund-heitspflege-Notwendigkeiten und Möglichkeiten einer Planung. Universitätstage, 1965. Wissenschaft und Planung, 158-74. Berlin, 1965.

162 M. T. NEWMAN The application of ecological rules to the racial anthropology of the aboriginal New World. *Amer. Anthropologist*, 55, 1953, 311-27.

163 O.E.C.D. *New Thinking in School Biology*. Report on the O.E.C.D. Seminar on the Reform of Biology Teaching. La Tour de Peilz, 1962.

164 K. P. OAKLEY *Man the Tool-Maker.* 4th ed. London, Natural History Museum, 1958.
165 —— *Frameworks for Dating Fossil Man.* London, 1964.
166 A. J. OPARIN *Die Entstehung des Lebens auf der Erde.* Berlin and Leipzig, 1947 (Moscow and Leningrad, 1936).
167 —— The Origin of Life. 3rd ed. London and New York, 1957.
168 —— Das Leben. Seine Natur, Herkunft und Entwicklung. 1963.
169 —— *The Origin of Life on Earth.* Reports on the International Symposium of August 1957 in Moscow. 1959.
170 L. PASTEUR Die in der Atmosphäre vorhandenen organisierten Körperchen. Prüfung der Lehre von der Urzeugung. *Ostwalds Klassiker d. Naturwiss,* 39, Leipzig (originally in *Annales de Chimie et de Physique,* 3rd ser., 64, 1862).
171 A. PEIPER Menschenkind und Affenjunges. *Experientia,* 17, 1961, 529-38.
172 N. W. PIRIE Future sources of food supply: scientific problems. In ROYAL STATISTICAL SOCIETY *Food Supplies and Population Growth.* Edinburgh and London, 1963. Pp. 34-52.
173 M. E. D. POORE *Botany Ecology and Natural Resources.* Inaugural Lecture, University of Malaya, 1963.
174 A. PORTMANN *Vom Ursprung des Menschen.* Basel, 1944.
175 —— *Biologische Fragmente zu einer Lehre vom Menschen.* Basel, 1944.
176 W. PREYER *Die Seele des Kindes.* 7th ed. Leipzig, 1908.
177 A. REMANE Die Geschichte der Menschenaffen. In G. HEBERER *Menschl. Abstammungslehre. Fortschr. d. Anthropogenie 1963-1964.* 1965. Pp. 249-309.
178 —— Die Geschichte der Tiere. In G. HEBERER *Die Evolution der Organismen.* 3rd ed. Stuttgart, 1967. Pp. 588-677.
179 B. RENSCH Umwelt und Rassenbildung bei warmblütigen Wirbeltieren. *Arch. f. Anthropol.,* N.F., 23, 1935, 326-33.
180 —— Studien über klimatische Parallelität der Merkmalsausprägung bei Vögeln und Säugern. *Arch. f. Naturgesch.,* N.F. 5, 1936, 317-63.
181 —— Neuere Probleme der Abstammungslehre. *Die transspezifische Evolution.* Stuttgart, 1947. 2nd. ed. 1954 (*Evolution above the Species Level:* London, 1959, New York, 1960).
182 —— *Psychische Komponenten der Sinnesorgane: Eine psychophysische Hypothese.* Stuttgart, 1952.
183 —— Ästhetische Faktoren bei Farb- und Formbevorzugungen von Affen. *Z. f. Tierpsychol.,* 14, 1957, 71-99.
184 —— Die Abhängigkeit der Struktur und der Leistungen tierischer Gehirne von ihrer Grösse. *Naturwiss.,* 45, 1958 145-54.

Homo sapiens

185 B. RENSCH Die Wirksamkeit ästhetischer Faktoren bie Wirbeltieren. *Z. f. Tierpsychol.*, 15, 1958, 447-61.
186 —— The laws of evolution. In S. TAX *Evolution after Darwin.* Vol. 1. Chicago, 1959. Pp. 95-116.
187 —— Evolution als Eigenschaft des Lebendigen. *Studium Generale*, 12, 1959, 153-9.
188 —— Malversuche mit Affen. *Z. f. Tierpsychol.*, 18, 1961. 347-64.
189 —— Die Evolutionsgesetze der Organismen in naturphilosophischer Sicht. *Philosophia Naturalis*, 6, 1961, 288-326.
190 —— Gedächtnis, Abstraktion und Generalisation bei Tieren. Arbeitsgem. f. Forsch. Nordrhein-Westfalen, Nat. Wiss., H. 144. Köln and Opladen, 1962.
191 —— Notwendigkeit einer Reform des Biologie-Unterrichts in Europa. *Praxis d. Naturwiss. B. Biol.*, 11, 1962, 182-7.
192 —— Versuche über menschliche 'Auslöser-Merkmale' beider Geschlechter. *Z. Morphol. u. Anthropol.*, 53, 1963, 139-64.
193 —— Probleme der Willensfreiheit in biologischer und philosophischer Sicht. *Hippokrates*, 33, 1963, 1019-32.
194 —— Über ästhetische Faktoren im Erleben höherer Tiere. *Naturwiss. u. Medizin* (n + m), 2, 43-57 (Boehringer). Mannheim, 1965.
195 —— The evolution of brain achievements. In DOBZHANSKY, HECHT and STEERE *Evolutionary Biology*, 1. New York, 1967. Pp. 26-68.
196 —— Biophilosophie auf erkenntnistheoretischer Grundlage (*Panpsychistischer Identismus*). Stuttgart, 1968. (*Biophilosopy*, New York, 1971).
197 —— (ed.) *Handgebrauch und Verständigung bei Affen und Frühmenschen.* Bern and Stuttgart, 1968.
198 —— Ästhetische Grundprinzipien bei Tier und Mensch. In G. ALTNER (ed.) *Kreatur Mensch.* Munich, 1969. Pp. 134-44.
199 —— Die fünffache Wurzel des panpsychistischen Identismus. *Philos. naturalis*, 11, 1969, 129-50.
200 B. RENSCH and J. DÖHL Wahlen zwischen zwei überschaubaren Labyrinthwegen durch einen Schimpansen. *Z. f. Tierpsychol.*, 25, 1968, 216-31.
201 B. RENSCH and G. DÜCKER Versuche über visuelle Abstraktion bei einer Schleichkatze. *Z. f. Tierpsychol.*, 16, 1959, 671-92.
202 D. F. ROBERTS Body weight, race and climate. *Amer. J. Phys. Anthropol.*, n.s., 11, 1953, 533-58.
203 J. T. ROBINSON *Meganthropus*, Australopithecines and Hominids. *Amer. J. Phys. Anthropol.*, n.s., 11, 1953, 1-38.
204 —— '*Homo habilis*' and the Australopithecines. *Nature*, 205, 1965, 121-4.

204a A. ROE and G. G. SIMPSON (eds.) *Behavior and Evolution.* New Haven, 1958.

205 A. S. ROMER *Man and the Vertebrates.* 2nd ed. Chicago, 1941.

206 J. ROSLANSKY (ed.) *The Uniqueness of Man.* Amsterdam, 1969.

207 B. ROTHBLATT (ed.) *Changing Perspectives on Man.* Chicago and London, 1968.

208 H. ROTTA and R. SCHMID Der mögliche Entwicklungstrend der Menschheit. Eine Vorschau auf die Jahrundertwende. *Naturwiss. Rundschau*, 20, 1967, 278-83.

209 K. SALLER *Angewandte Anthropologie.* Stuttgart, 1951.

210 A. SAXENA Lernkapazität, Gedächtnis und Transpositionsvermögen bei Forellen. *Zool. Jahrb., Abt. Allg. Zool.*, 69, 1960, 63-94.

211 B. SCHELSKY Der Mensch in der wissenschaftlichen Zivilisation. Arbeitsgem. f. Forsch. Nordrhein-Westfalen, Geisteswiss., H. 96. Köln and Opladen, 1961.

211a I. I. SCHMALHAUSEN *Factors of Evolution.* New York, 1953.

212 H. SCHMIDT *Geschichte der Entwicklungslehre.* Leipzig, 1918.

213 A. SCHOPENHAUER *Die Welt als Wille und Vorstellung.* 1859.

214 G. SCHRAMM Biochemische Grundlagen des Lebens. *Naturwiss. Rundschau*, 16, 1963, 98-96.

215 E. SCHREIDER Regulation thermique et évolution humaine. *Actes IV Congr. Internat. Soc. Anthrop. Ethnol.*, 1, 92-7. Vienna, 1954.

216 A. H. SCHULTZ The specializations of man and his place among the Catarrhine primates. *Cold Spring Harbor Symposia on Quant. Biol.*, 15, 1950, 37-53.

217 —— Einige Beobachtungen und Masse am Skelett von *Oreopithecus* im Vergleich mit anderen catarrhinen Primaten. *Z. Morph. Anthropol.*, 50, 1960, 136-49.

218 —— Die rezenten Hominoidea. In G. HEBERER *Menschl. Abstammungslehre. Fortschr. d. Anthropogenie 1963-1964.* Stuttgart, 1965.

219 —— Form und Funktion der Primatenhände. In B. RENSCH Handgebrauch und Verständigung bei Affen u. Frühmenschen. Bern, 1968. Pp. 9-30.

220 M. SCHULZE-SCHENCKING Untersuchungen zur visuellen Lerngeschwindigkeit und Lernkapazität bei Bienen, Hummeln und Ameisen. *Z. f. Tierpsychol.*, 27, 1970, 513-52.

221 I. SCHWIDETSKY *Das Menschenbild der Biologie.* Stuttgart, 1959.

222 —— *Die neue Rassenkunde.* Stuttgart, 1962.

223 C. SHERRINGTON *Man on his Nature.* 2nd ed. Cambridge, 1953.

224 H. SICK *Tukani.* Berlin and Hamburg, 1957.

225 E. L. SIMONS The early relatives of man. *Scient. American*, 211, 1964, 50-62.

P

226 E. L. SIMONS On the mandible of *Ramapithecus*. *Proc. Nat. Acad. Sci.*, 51, 1964, 528-35.

227 —— New fossil apes from Egypt and the initial differentation of Hominoidea. *Nature*, 205, 1965, 135.

228 G. G. SIMPSON The principle of classification and a classification of mammals. *Bull. Amer. Mus. Nat. Hist.*, 85, 1945.

229 —— *The Meaning of Evolution*. New Haven, 1949.

230 —— *Tempo and Mode in Evolution*. New York, 1944.

230a *This View of Life*. New York, 1964.

231 K. DE SNOO *Das Problem der Menschwerdung im Lichte der vergleichenden Geburtshilfe*. Jena, 1942.

232 H. SPATZ Menschwerdung und Gehirnentwicklung. *Nachr. Giessener Hochschulgesellsch.*, 20, 1950, 32-55.

233 O. SPENGLER *Der Untergang des Abendlandes*. 2 vols. 1918-22.

234 D. STARCK Die Neencephalisation. In G. HEBERER *Menschliche Abstammungslehre*. Stuttgart, 1965. Pp. 103-44.

235 W. STAUB *Allgemeine Wirtschafts- und Handelsgeographie*. Munich and Basel, 1951.

236 C. STERN *Principles of Human Genetics*. 2nd ed. London, 1960.

237 C. P. STONE *Comparative Psychology*. 3rd ed. New York, 1911.

238 R. STREHL *Die Roboter sind unter uns*. Oldenburg, 1952.

239 J. M. STYCOS The outlook for world population. *Science*, 146, 1964, 1435-40.

240 H. SUZUKI A palaeanthropic man from Amud Cave, Israel. *Commun. VII Internat. Congr. Anthrop. and Ethnol. Sciences*. Moscow, 1964.

241 M. TELLIER Reconnaissance par le toucher d'objets connus par la vue chez le macaque. *Bull. Soc. Roy. Sci. Liège*, 5, 1932, 114-17.

242 P. TEILHARD DE CHARDIN *Le Phénomène Humain*. Paris, 1955.

243 W. H. THORPE *Science, Man and Morals*. Ithaca, New York, 1966.

244 W. H. THORPE and D. DAVENPORT Learning and associated phenomena in invertebrates. *Animal Behaviour*, Suppl. 1. London, 1964.

245 R. THURNWALD *Die menschliche Gesellschaft*. Vol. 2. Berlin and Leipzig, 1932.

246 M. TIGGES Muster- und Farbbevorzugung bei Fischen und Vögeln. *Z. f. Tierpsychol.*, 20, 1963, 129-42.

247 F. TILNEY *The Brain from Ape to Man*. 2 vols. New York, 1927.

248 N. TINBERGEN *The Study of Instinct*. London, 1950.

249 P. V. TOBIAS The Olduvai Bed I Hominine with special reference to its cranial capacity. *Nature*, 202, 1964, 3-4.

250 A. J. TOYNBEE *A Study of History*. Vols I-IV. 1934-9.

251 E. TYSON *Anatomy of a Pygmy Compared with that of a Monkey, an Ape and a Man*. London, 1751.

252 UNESCO *Four Statements on the Race Question*. Paris, 1969.

253 UNITED NATIONS *Demographic Yearbooks*, 1952, 1960, 1966, 1970. New York.

254 UNITED NATIONS *World Population Prospects as Assessed in 1963*. U.N. Population Studies No. 41. New York, 1966.

255 UNITED STATES BUREAU OF THE CENSUS *16th Census of the United States, 1940; Population: Differential Fertility of 1940 and 1910, women by number of children ever born*. Washington, 1945.

256 F. VOGEL A preliminary estimate of the number of human genes. *Nature*, 201, 1964, 847.

257 K. VOGT *Vorlesungen über dem Menschen, seine Stellung in der Schöpfung und in der Geschichte der Erde*. 1863.

258 H. VOLK Schöpfungsgeschichte und Entwicklung. Schrift. Ges. Förder. Westf. Wilhelms Univ. Münster (Westf.), 1955.

259 O. VON VERSCHUER *Genetik des Menschen*. Munich and Berlin, 1959.

260 P. WALDEN Naturwissenschaftliche Alternativen für Weiterentwicklung der materiellen Kultur. *Naturwiss.*, 42, 1955, 497-9.

261 H. WALTER Die Häufigkeit spontaner Mutationen beim Menschen. *Umschau*, 60, 1960, 200-9.

262 S. L. WASHBURN The analysis of primate evolution with particular reference to the origin of man. *Cold Spring Harbor Symposia Quant. Biol.*, 15, 1950, 67-78.

263 —— Tools and human evolution. *Sci. American*, 203, 1960, 63-75.

264 —— (ed.) *Classification and Human Evolution*. Chicago, 1963.

265 F. WEIDENREICH The brain and its role in the phylogenetic transformation of the human skull. *Trans. Amer. Philos. Soc.*, 5, 1941, 31.

266 H. WEINERT *Stammesentwicklung der Menschheit. Die Wissenschaft.* Vol. 104. Braunschweig, 1951.

267 PANEL OF THE WORLD FOOD SUPPLY *Report on the World Food Problem*. Washington, 1967.

268 R. WICHTERMANN *The Biology of Paramaecium*. New York, 1953.

269 N. WIENER *The Human Use of Human Beings*. 1951.

270 L. WINTER *Der Begabungsschwund in Europa*. Pähl (Obb.), 1962.

271 G. WOLSTENHOLME *Man and his Future*. Ciba Symposium. London, 1963.

272 J. WOOD JONES *Man's Place among the Mammals*. London, 1929.

273 —— The premaxilla and the ancestry of man. *Nature*, 159, 1947.

274 J. B. WOLFE Effectiveness of token-rewards for chimpanzees. *Com p.Psychol. Monogr.*, 12 (5), 1936.

275 A. WÜNSCHMANN Quantitative vergleichende Untersuchungen zum Neugierverhalten höherer Tiere. *Z.f. Tierpsychol.*, 20, 1963, 80-109.

276 R. M. YERKES *Chimpanzees: A Laboratory Colony.* New Haven, 1943.

277 R. M. YERKES and A. W. YERKES *The Great Apes: A study of Anthropoid Life.* New Haven, 1929.

278 J. Z. YOUNG Learning and discrimination in the Octopus. *Biol. Rev.*, 36, 1961, 32-96.

279 F. E. ZEUNER *Dating the Past.* 2nd ed. London, 1950.

280 T. ZIEHEN *Erkenntnistheorie auf psychophysiologischer und physikalischer Grundlage.* Jena, 1913.

281 —— *Die Grundlagen der Psychologie.* 2 vols. Leipzig and Berlin, 1915.

282 —— *Erkenntnistheorie.* Vol. 1, Jena, 1934; Vol. 2, 1939.

Short glossary of technical terms

Achondroplasia (= Chondrodystrophy): Disproportionate dwarfism, a hereditary condition involving the abnormal ossification of skeletal cartilage. In this condition the long bones of the limbs remain stocky, and the proportions of other parts, notably the pelvis, may also be affected.

Acrania: A group of invertebrates containing a few species which are most closely related, in development and structure, to the vertebrates. They share the following features with primitive fish: a fore-gut with gill slits, a spinal cord, a notochord (see below), a similar arrangement of blood vessels and of musculature, and a similarity of structure in the larva.

Agnatha: A group of primitive fishes which includes the lamprey. Their most primitive features are the fully developed notochord (see below), the absence of jaws, the presence of unpaired fins and a single nasal opening, and a labyrinth with only two semicircular canals. The larva resembles that of the Acrania.

Alleles: Genes occupying the same relative position (locus) on homologous chromosomes (chromosomes derived from the father's and mother's sides). They may represent different hereditary states of the same locus.

Appetitive behaviour: A behaviour pattern usually evoked by some 'mood' or 'state' (e.g. hunger, the drive to reproduce), which normally induces an animal to move or lurk until it comes into contact with whatever will satisfy the instinct in question (e.g. food, a mating partner).

Branchial pharynx: A type of fore-gut with branchial clefts, typical of vertebrates and of those invertebrates nearest to them. All land animals 'up' to man still possess these in embryonic stages (as branchial pockets).

Catarrhine monkeys: Monkeys with a narrow nasal septum. They are only found in Africa and in south and east Asia, not in South America.

Homo sapiens

Chondrodystrophy: see *Achondroplasia*

Chromosomes: Thread-like structures which carry the inherited characteristics. They are usually observable only during the process of cell division, when they contract spirally (cf. *Deoxyribonucleic acids* and *Genes*).

Convergence: The development of similarity between two formerly different groups as a result of similar conditions of selection.

Cope's rule: A rule stating that there is frequently a progressive increase in body size in a line of descent (particularly frequent among mammals).

Crossopterygii (lobe-finned fish): A group of fish dating from the Devonian, ancestors of the amphibians and thus also of the land vertebrates.

Deoxyribonucleic acids (DNA): Molecules carrying inherited characteristics within the cell nucleus. They consist of polynucleotid chains, double helices of alternate phosphate and sugar (deoxyribose) groups, held together by two different pairs of bases (in the case of animals adenine and thymine, cytosine and guanine). The different sequence of these pairs determines the genetic information transmitted by individual parts of the DNA molecules.

Devonian: see *Geological eras*.

Diploid: A chromosome set is diploid when, as a result of fertilization, it contains a homologous pair of each individual type of chromosome (except the Y chromosome and sometimes the X chromosome). Mature germ cells, with one set of chromosomes, are said to be *haploid*.

Dominant: A hereditary factor (gene) is said to be dominant if within the diploid chromosome set it produces the same characteristic in single (heterozygous) or double (homozygous) dose. In this case it effectively dominates the expression of its corresponding partner (i.e. its homologous allele), when that partner differs from it as a result of mutation. Hereditary factors dominated by another allele are said to be *recessive* to it.

Eocene: see *Geological eras*.

Ganglionic cells: Neurons = nerve cells.

Gene drift: Variation, with time, in the frequency of hereditary factors within a population (reproductive community). Such genetic changes are often more frequent in smaller populations because beneficial mutants can reach a high percentage more quickly, whereas harmful ones are more likely to disappear entirely (= *Sewall Wright effect*).

Gene flow: The spread of hereditary characteristics through a ductive community or species.

Genes: Hereditary characteristics presumed to be present in the chromosomes, in the plastids (e.g. chloroplasts) and in some of the other organelles of the cytoplasm (in mitochondria and possibly in ribosomes). Those that lie on the chromosomes are segments of DNA molecules. They normally belong to structurally differentiated units (Operons).

Geological eras: The following eras have been distinguished in accordance with geological and palaeontological findings: 1 Pre-Cambrian (Proterozoic). 2 Palaeozoic: Cambrian, Ordovician, Silurian, Devonian, Carboniferous, Permian. 3 Mesozoic: Triassic, Jurassic, Cretaceous. 4 Cainozoic: Tertiary (Palaeocene, Eocene, Oligocene, Miocene, Pliocene), Quarternary (Pleistocene, Holocene).

Haploid: see *Diploid*.

Heterosis: The superiority of hybrids over the two parental types, e.g. in size or vitality.

Heterozygous: Offspring of hybridization are heterozygous if the parents differ in one or more homologous hereditary factors (alleles). If all or certain of the factors are alike in both, the offspring are said to be fully or partly (i.e. for those particular factors) homozygous.

Homozygous: see *Heterozygous*.

Hormones: 'Chemical messengers' – secretions formed in certain endocrine glands (e.g. thyroid, adrenal, pituitary, gonad), or in other tissues. They are carried in the blood stream and regulate metabolism, development, sexual functions and several instinctive processes.

Identism: Philosophical doctrine according to which mind and matter are ultimately the same.

Interspecific selection: Selection as a result of competition or conflict between members of different species.

Intraspecific selection: Selection among the members of a species.

Life cycle: The individual's course from the ovum (or bud or dividing cell) through the embryonic and adolescent stages to maturity and then to death.

Mammillae: Nipples.

Microphthalmia: A hereditary eye condition with various grades of deformity (splitting of the lens, iris or chorioid membrane; there may also be opacities in the lens).

Homo sapiens

Miocene: see *Geological eras*.

Mood: (1) In the psychological sense, a mental condition in which emotions, by a process of diffusion, become involved in several distinct sequences of mental images. (2) In regard to behaviour, a physiological condition that sets up a specific pattern of appetitive behaviour (see above) and leads on to a continuance of instinctive processes.

Motor nerves: Nerves carrying impulses to the muscles and other effector organs.

Mutations: Random alterations in the hereditary characteristics owing to changes within single genes, to rearrangement or loss of chromosome sections, or by changes in the number of chromosomes.

Neurons: Nerve cells; ganglion cells.

Neurosis: Over-excitation induced by nervous or psychological situations of conflict characteristically expressed in heightened irritability, violence of certain reactions, and often aggressiveness.

Notochord: Skeletal rod made up of cells of connective tissue, which supports the longitudinal axis of the body in tunicates, lancelets, and the most primitive fish (the Agnatha, in which there is also a cartilaginous spinal column). In more advanced vertebrates with a well developed bony vertebral column, the notochord remains embryonic.

Palaeocene: see *Geological eras*.

Panentheism: A philosophical doctrine according to which God is an essence immanent in all things.

Panpsychism: Conception that all things are psychic (or 'protopsychic') in the most general sense.

Phototaxis: Reflex adjustment or movement in relation to the direction of light.

Pleistocene: see *Geological eras*.

Pliocene: see *Geological eras*.

Polymorphism: Multiplicity of hereditary varieties within a species or race.

Pongidae: The family of anthropoid apes.

Population: Group of animals forming a reproductive community.

Pyramidal tract: A nerve tract in higher mammals leading directly from the cortex of the forebrain through other parts of the brain to the spinal cord.

Recessive: see *Dominant*.

Recombinant: An individual whose array of genetic characteristics is the result of the reassortment (or recombination) of parental genes.

Releaser: A feature in the environment of an animal (such as the obvious characteristics of a mating partner or of an enemy), which releases instinctive action (mating, or flight) by means of an inherited nervous mechanism.

Sensory nerves: Nerves which convey sensory impulses from the sense organ to the brain.

Theosophy: A philosophy that considers what different religions have in common, with the object of moulding them into a religion of unity.

Theriodontidae: An extinct group of reptiles intermediate between reptiles and mammals.

Triassic: see *Geological eras*.

Vestigial structure: A more or less functionless structure, resulting, in the course of evolution, from a degeneration of an earlier functional structure.

Index

Index

Index